AF361340

Winning Our Wonder

Winning Our Wonder

Rhetorical Re/Constructions of American Civil War Women on the Web

Patty Wilde

THE UNIVERSITY OF SOUTH CAROLINA PRESS

Published by the University of South Carolina Press
Columbia, South Carolina 29208

uscpress.com

Printed in the United States of America

Library of Congress Cataloging-in-Publication Data
can be found at http://catalog.loc.gov/.

ISBN: 978-1-64336-598-5 (hardcover
ISBN: 978-1-64336-599-2 (paperback)
ISBN: 978-1-64336-600-5 (ebook)

This book will be made open access within three years of publication thanks to Path to Open, a program developed in partnership between JSTOR, the American Council of Learned Societies (ACLS), University of Michigan Press, and The University of North Carolina Press to bring about equitable access and impact for the entire scholarly community, including authors, researchers, libraries, and university presses around the world. Learn more at https://about.jstor.org/path-to-open/.

For Genevieve and Elizabeth

Contents

List of Illustrations

Introduction

Remembering "Women Worthies"

So it is by some natural instinct that we admire, not the small streams, clear and useful as they are, but the Nile, the Danube, the Rhine, and above all the Ocean . . . that what is useful or necessary is easily obtained by man; it is always the unusual which wins our wonder.

 —Longinus, *On the Sublime*

In the days following 25 May 2020, the world watched and rewatched video footage of a white police officer murdering George Floyd, an unarmed Black man, on the streets of Minneapolis, Minnesota. Though there is a long legacy of racialized violence in the United States, Floyd's documented death publicly laid bare these realities, galvanizing thousands of Americans to protest the systemic racism that continues to haunt the nation. Rendering perceptible how political and social power and pressure can reconfigure the commemorative landscape, more than 150 Confederate statues, plaques, and other markers of memory were removed or otherwise changed during this time (Southern Poverty Law Center).

As exemplified by the response to Floyd's death as well as the massacre at Emanuel African Methodist Episcopal Church in Charleston, South Carolina in 2015 and the car attack in Charlottesville, Virginia in 2017, calls to eliminate Confederate iconography often intensify in the wake of racist acts of terrorism. Still, appeals to eradicate these symbols have been met with considerable resistance. Proponents claim that these markers are neutral reminders of historical events and that their removal is an attempt to sanitize history. Such a position, however, fails to consider the constitutive power of symbols that give rise to public memory, generally defined as visions of the past that are used for purposes of the present. In contrast to official history, which, in the words of David Blight, "asserts the authority of academic training and canons of evidence" ("If

You Don't"), public memory is an affect-laden, socially negotiated phenomena that both reflects and reproduces the values and priorities of a particular group.

Instantiations of Lost Cause ideology, a movement that arose shortly after the Civil War but lingers to this day, Confederate monuments help perpetuate the romanticized view that the South engaged in a heroic fight in pursuit of freedom, culture, and states' rights, but undergirding this vision of the war was a desire to maintain white supremacy and the racialized hierarchies that subjugated and oppressed people of color. As Confederate monuments proliferated, often during periods marked by struggles for racial equality, so too did the Lost Cause mythos and the racist views that it promoted. In a statement released in response to the violent events in Charlottesville, the American Historical Society explains that "The bulk of the monument building took place not in the immediate aftermath of the Civil War but from the close of the nineteenth century into the second decade of the twentieth. Commemorating not just the Confederacy but also the 'Redemption' of the South after Reconstruction, this enterprise was part and parcel of the initiation of legally mandated segregation and widespread disenfranchisement across the South. Memorials to the Confederacy were intended, in part, to obscure the terrorism required to overthrow Reconstruction, and to intimidate African Americans politically and isolate them from the mainstream of public life." Given this history, the removal of these Confederate symbols can help advance racial equality. Far from shallow gestures, their elimination strikes at the heart of latent and explicit racist ideologies.

But because "the battle still rages over whether this is fundamentally a white nation or a multiracial democracy," as Steve Phillips argues, how the war is remembered continues to be fought (8). While much of this debate has rightly centered on Confederate monuments, questions of how race and slavery are taken up in recollections of this nation-defining event persist. Reflecting a growing interest in diversity, equity, and inclusion, there has been a notable push to attend more fully to the roles that women played in the war, resulting in new commemorative layers that add dimension to established views of the past. But to study these ways of remembering and their constitutive effects, we have to look beyond the monuments and memorials that feature, "more often than not, a white heterosexual cisgendered male," as Tasha Dubriwny and Kristen Poirot rightly observe, and toward the mnemonic enterprises where recollections of women are produced and diffused (199).

Turning to the World Wide Web, a powerful and influential source of public memory, I explore in this book how Civil War women are narrativized in digital spaces, focusing my analysis on those most commonly discussed on the web: Rose O'Neal Greenhow, Belle Boyd, Harriet Tubman, Sarah Emma Edmonds, Loreta Janeta Velazquez, and Susie King Taylor. Serving as spies, soldiers, and nurses, they "win our wonder," to borrow the phrasing of Longinus, standing out from their contemporaries who aided the war efforts in more conventional but essential ways. Contributing to their notable online presence, these women documented their extraordinary labors in books published during and shortly after the war. Serving as wellsprings of memory, their narratives exemplify the power of print to preserve the past. But though these accounts inform how Greenhow, Boyd, Tubman, Edmonds, Velazquez, and Taylor are remembered, their war stories inevitably take a different shape as they are retold on the web. Inspired by theories of intersectional feminism, I draw on rhetorical circulation studies to chart these changes, focusing specifically on how discussions of race and gender shift as they move from the original print sources to digital spaces. As the case studies that comprise this book suggest, online reconstructions of these women foreground their exceptional contributions to the war while minimizing or eliding entirely the documented views of race and slavery that are recorded in originary materials. These rearticulations of the past inform how the public remembers the war, an event that continues to haunt contemporary social, political, and cultural contexts, but because the stories we tell more broadly reflect and shape how we see the world and our place in it, these narratives inevitably contribute to normative notions of race and gender specifically as they relate to notions of citizenship and belonging.

The Ideological Functions of Public Memory

While memories of political and social events tend to lose their affective force with passing generations, the American Civil War continues to occupy a significant place in the national imagination. But despite its far-reaching influence, as Alice Fahs asserts, it is often remembered "as a white masculinist conflict, rather than a cataclysmic event that rent and remade the fabric of life for all Americans" ("The Feminized Civil War" 1493). Illustrative of Fah's observation, women have been largely excluded from many physical sites that propagate public memory, confirming Marianne Hirsch and Valerie Smith's assertion that "What a culture remembers and what it chooses to forget are intricately bound up with issues of power and hegemony," and thus race and gender (6). Contributing to a growing body of scholarship that examines the rhetorical dimensions of public memory, *Winning Our Wonder* specifically attends to the ways in which these intersecting axes of identity are constructed in commemorations of Civil War women and the social, cultural, and political impact of the recollections that they generate.

From a contemporary neuroscientific perspective, individual memories are formed by an active process of absorbing, encoding, storing, and recalling previous experiences, but as French sociologist Maurice Halbwachs asserts, "it is in society that people normally acquire their memories" (38). Influenced by the work of Henri Bergson and Émile Durkheim, Halbwachs believed that memories are evoked through "frameworks" that "reconstruct an image of the past which is in accord, in each epoch, with the predominant thoughts of the society" (40). These ever-evolving social structures function as a mobius strip that conjure visions of the past imbued with a given community's priorities that are then, in turn, rearticulated back into that framework. Suggestive of different disciplinary priorities, these communal acts of remembering have been called "collective memory," "popular memory," "cultural memory," and "social memory,"[1] but in this project, I purposefully employ the term "public memory," defined by Greg Dickinson, Carole Blair, and Brain Ott as the "beliefs about the past [that] are shared among members of a group, whether a local community or the citizens of a nation-state" (6). In addition to reflecting most accurately the outward-facing memories of the Civil War women that I examine, this term also "best encapsulates memory work's potential within composition and rhetoric, a discipline that is fundamentally concerned with public discourse and democratic action," as noted by Jane Greer and Laurie Grobman (5).

One of the canons of rhetoric, memory has a long-established relationship with the persuasive arts. Though *memoria* has historically focused on strategies for memorizing speeches, this connection has been reimagined through the lens of public memory studies. Following the lead of Ekaterina Haskins, I conceptualize public memory in this project as a kind of epideictic rhetoric (*Popular Memories* 9). From the Greek meaning "for expedition or show," the epideictic branch was traditionally employed at events such as funerals, festivals, births, and marriages. In contrast with its judicial and deliberative counterparts, epideictic rhetoric commends or condemns its subjects, and in doing so, as Jeffery Walker explains, "cultivates the basic codes of value and belief by which a society or culture lives; it shapes the ideologies and imageries with which, and by which, the individual members of a community identify themselves; and perhaps, most significantly, it shapes the fundamental grounds, the 'deep' commitments and presuppositions, that will underlie and ultimately determine decision and debate in particular pragmatic forums" (9). Understanding public memory as an instantiation of the epideictic brings more clearly into focus how visions of the past participate in the construction and propagation of normative sociocultural codes. Reinforcing the defining beliefs of a given group, mechanisms of memory contribute to the formation of what Benedict Anderson calls the "imagined community." "It is *imagined*," Anderson explains, "because the members . . . will never know most of their fellow-members, meet them, or even hear of them, yet in the minds of each lives the image of their communion" (15). While Anderson writes specifically about the formation of the nation-state, his theory is broadly applicable to a diverse range of contexts. Though individuals possess distinct recollections of the past shaped by their experiences with different communities, memory fortifies intragroup relations through the shared knowledge and beliefs conveyed through particular visions. What we remember and their attendant ways of seeing, knowing, and being function as a shibboleth of identity that marks one group as distinct from another. In this way, as Barbie Zelizer posits, "Remembering becomes implicated in a range of other activities having as much to do with identity formation, power and authority, cultural norms, and social interaction as with the simple act of recall. Its full understanding thus requires an appropriation of memory as social, cultural, and political action at its broadest level" ("Reading the Past" 214).

Highly influential, public memory contributes to the construction of given communities, however they might be defined or imagined. But while some recollections are vivid, others are more faint or obscured entirely. This imbalance is indicative of the ways in which power informs memory. What we remember is largely determined by the creation of "sources . . . archives . . . narratives . . . and history" as Michel-Rolph Trouillot asserts (26). But the "presences and absences" that necessarily emerge during these moments of production "are neither natural or neutral," he maintains (48). Manufactured by "official" and "vernacular" sources, to use the terminology of John Bodnar, memory is created by both dominant cultural leaders and "ordinary people" (13–14). But mirroring the power allocated to these groups, visions of the past are afforded differing degrees of persuasive influence, circulating concurrently in a range of shapes, sizes, and forms that collectively constitute an evolving stratum of memory.

Fashioned from stone and steel, monuments and memorials tend to endure for long periods of time. Though their influence is typically limited to their immediate geographic context, these sites continue to "speak for their sponsors long after their voices are silent" as Carol Mattingly observes ("Women's Temple" 147). Because the dominant culture generally controls public space, the mechanisms of memory featured in these places tend to reflect their ideological priorities. In the United States, these sites have most commonly mirrored white masculine culture, confirming G. Mitchell Reyes's observation that "whiteness" functions "as the invisible hand of official memory" (2). From Lincoln to Lee, memories of the Civil War have traditionally centered the experiences of white men, an observation that is corroborated by the estimated 4,000 to 6,000 extant Confederate and Union markers (Magness; "Ten Facts").[2] As exemplified by the 2021 National Monument Audit, this trend aligns with more general patterns of remembrance. Of the 48,000 monuments[3] surveyed in this study, the majority feature white men; among the top fifty most commonly commemorated individuals, there are only five people of color, three women, and no "US-born Latinx, Asian, Pacific Islander, or self-identified LGBTQ+ people" (Monument Lab 17).

Mirroring dominant culture in the United States, the commemorative markers made in the image of white men can be counted among the many signs and symbols that give rise to the phenomenon of whiteness, understood in this project as the construction of the white race and the privileges afforded to it. Race, broadly conceived, acquires its shape through everyday rhetorical acts that subtly teach us how to categorize humans through "the marking of *bodies*," in the words of Ramon Grosfoguel (11; emphasis in original). While these taxonomies lack definitive essence, the power afforded to them has significant consequences, as "[s]ome bodies are racialized as superior and other bodies are racialized as inferior" (Grosfoguel 11). Positioned at the top of the hierarchy, white racial identity is the hegemonic force that undergirds US society, setting its social, cultural, political, economic, legal, linguistic, and educational standards. Though it intersects with other markers of identity, such as gender, class, sexuality, and gender expression, whiteness informs the varying degrees of privilege and marginalization an individual may experience, the white phenotype has long signified power.

Because it "reside[s] in its already defined position as everything" as Thomas K. Nakayama and Robert L. Krizek assert, whiteness can be difficult to perceive, especially for those who identify as white (293). But as George Lipsitz asserts, it is against this "unmarked category" of whiteness that "difference is constructed" (369). Born out of the myth of modernity and the imperial and colonial projects that it rationalized, modern conceptions of racial difference emerged with the rise of European colonialism. As Anibal Quijano contends, the development of "'race' . . . was placed as one of the basic criteria to classify the population in the power structure of the new society, associated with the nature of roles and places in the division of labor and in control of the resources of production" (216). Though this view of racial stratification has a long history, it continues to impact the contemporary moment, assigning power and authority to those deemed white while subjugating bodies taxonomized as Black and brown. While these divisions are made to seem natural, as sociologists Michael Omi and Howard Winant make clear, "Human bodies are visually read, understood, and narrated by means of symbolic meanings and associations. . . . Not because of any biologically based or essential difference among human beings . . . but because such sociohistorical practices as conquest and enslavement classified human bodies for the purposes of domination" (13). Reinforcing racial difference and the power afforded to these constructions, racialization relies on rhetorical symbols, including sites of memory, to codify these hierarchies. Just as representations of white men help fortify normative notions of dominant white culture, the relative absence of people of color from these sites likewise has significant consequences. Marginalized by omission, their general exclusion from public places of memory contributes to the sociocultural scripts that rationalize oppressive systems and participate in their subjugation.

It is significant, however, that the whiteness associated with these particular sources of public memory is distinctly androcentric, suggestive of how the construction of race is inextricably tied to gender. As Cindy Griffin and Karma Chávez observe, "there never are situations in which one woman's whiteness and another woman's Blackness or brownness do not profoundly affect or inform what it means to be a woman" (7). Generally defined as the roles, behaviors, and expectations ascribed to differently sexed bodies, gender, Judith Butler teaches us, is performative: "There is no gender identity behind the expressions of gender; that identity is performatively constituted by the very 'expressions' that are said to be its results" (34). Though gender is fluid, it has historically been dichotomized through everyday acts that define "woman" in opposition to "man," reifying these categories of identity. A series of repeated acts that participate in the construction of identity, expectations of sex and gender are naturalized through various rhetorical forces that are then reproduced in our everyday actions and behaviors. In this way, as K. J. Rawson reminds us, "woman" is a "complex identity *production* and performance" ("Queering" 41; emphasis in original).

While sex and gender are socially negotiated phenomena, there are real material consequences of being a woman, understood in this project as anyone who identifies as such. Gender inequalities continue to endure in matters of pay, distribution of various labors, healthcare needs, reproductive rights, legal entitlements, and political representation—just to cite a few examples. The degree of impact apportioned to women differs according to how they are raced, classed, and otherwise identified, illustrating how power is shaped "by many axes that work together and influence each other," as Patricia Hill Collins and Sirma Bilge maintain (31). Embedded in US social structure, these interlocking taxonomies and the authority afforded to them, are rendered visible through sites of memory. As the National Monument Audit confirms, women are far less frequently featured in these sites of memory than their male counterparts. Reflecting and reproducing social hierarchies, women's absence from these public places subtly suggests that they and the roles traditionally assigned to them are inferior and insignificant. Though relatively few women are commemorated in US monuments and memorials, those who are featured in these places of public memory tend to be white. While there are notable exceptions, such as Harriet Tubman and Sacajawea, by comparison, women of color are commemorated far less frequently and in much more limited capacities, suggestive of the diminished power and agency generally afforded to them.

Ways of Remembering the American Civil War

Reproducing established hierarchies of power, mechanisms of memory contribute in significant and subtle ways to the formation of identity, culture, and community, including normative notions of race and gender. But these constructions take on additional meaning in the context of the American Civil War. Described by Robert Penn Warren as "the great single event of our history" (3), the war is a potent cultural touchstone that shapes contemporary conceptions of the nation, citizenship, and belonging. Part of the nation's origin story, the Civil War and its history and myths inform how we think about who counts as citizen and who does not. What we remember in the context of this event is, then, indicative of who we think we are as a country and who we strive to be. Though this omission notably impacts women of color to greater degree, the historical omission of women from Civil War memories is broadly suggestive of their inferior political and social status. Women's considerable absence, then, from public sites of Civil War memory is telling. Investigating this erasure, what Alice Johnston Myatt describes as a process that "hides, discredits, marginalizes, or eliminates the history of an individual, leading to a loss of public memory, regardless of when such loss occurs" (58), I review in this section the history of Civil War memory in broad strokes, tracing how women's war experiences have been forgotten.

In the years immediately following General Robert E. Lee's surrender at Appomattox, Confederate supporters did not have the resources to expend on war commemorations. For this reason, Union monuments and memorials were some of the first to emerge on the stage of public memory, honoring the sacrifices made by white soldiers who helped protect and preserve the country. As Robert Cook explains, these sites of remembrance focused on how the Union "had saved the United States as a nation with a unique democratic mission in the world" (5). Though women also worked in myriad ways in support of this cause, their contributions were largely neglected in these early signifiers of memory. Commenting on this absence, Frank Moore writes in *Women of the War,* published in 1866, that women "do not figure in the official reports; they are not gazetted for deeds as gallant as were ever done; the names of thousands are unknown beyond the neighborhood where they live, or the hospitals where they loved to labor" (v–vi).[4] Yet, as Moore documents in his lengthy tome, many women took up the mantle of the Union, meeting the needs of the moment to help keep the country intact. Prevalent through the Reconstruction period, the Unionist view gradually faded as other ways of remembering took hold; but suggestive of the cumulative nature of memory, the general elision of Union women from recollections of this momentous event had a lasting impact, contributing to present-day visions that often fail to consider their contributions and experiences.

Unionist memories sometimes nodded to the pursuit of racial justice, what Blight calls the "emancipationist vision" of the war (*Race and Reunion* 2). Emphasizing the role that Black Americans played in the struggle against slavery, these memories aligned with changing social and political realities of the years immediately following the war. Although they faced considerable obstacles during Reconstruction, many legislative initiatives passed during this time expanded racial equality, including the Civil War Rights Act of 1866 as well as the ratification of the Fourteenth and Fifteenth Amendments, which granted citizenship to all people born in the United States and gave African American men the right to vote. Focusing on the fight for freedom, the emancipationist tradition largely centered Black men and their military contributions. Their intervention proved essential during a pivotal moment of the war, but their service also marked an important step in their ongoing march toward citizenship. Until the Emancipation Proclamation was issued in 1863, Black men were prohibited from enlisting in the Union Army. Commemorating their service, then, was another way of asserting and affirming their place as equal citizens.

Propagating this vision through localized vernacular contexts, including anniversaries, marches, parades, and other celebrations, these countermemories of the war nuanced more homogeneous visions of the past. But indicative of intersectional inequities, Black women and their service have been far less frequently acknowledged, though as Thavolia Glymph asserts, they played essential roles in this historic event: "Black women sympathized with the Union, fought, prayed, sacrificed, and died for it and fought for their freedom. They were soldiers' wives and refugees who labored on plantations run or leased by the Federal government; they were cooks and field hands, mothers and daughters. The vast majority remained enslaved for the duration of the war, but they made Confederate-occupied plantations, farms, towns, cities, factories, and hospitals sites of resistance" (88). Omitted from the production of memory, Black women's war contributions are documented in few extant sources and sites, limiting public recollections of their role in this consequential event.

In stark contrast, Lost Cause memories continue to circulate widely, informing latent and explicit white supremacist ideologies. Minimizing the role that slavery played in the war, this vision of the past sought to preserve and perpetuate established racial hierarchies. Edward Alb Pollard explained the position in *The Lost Cause: A New Southern History of the War of the Confederates* (1867): "the war properly decided only what was put in issue: the restoration of the Union and the excision of slavery; and to these two conditions the South submits. But the war did not decide negro equality. . . . And these things which the war did not decide, the Southern people will still cling to, still claim, and still assert in them their rights and views" (752). Such sentiments gained more traction as Reconstruction came to a close with the Compromise of 1877, an agreement that awarded Northern Republican Rutherford B. Hayes the presidency after a highly contentious election. In return, Southern Democrats called for an end to Reconstruction and the various protections it provided the newly emancipated, including a military presence in the South that helped deter violent attacks. Capturing the failure of the moment, W. E. B. Du Bois writes, "The slave went free; stood a brief moment in the sun; then moved back again toward slavery," as the Jim Crow era was ushered in (30). Lost Cause visions of the war and the ideologies that they promoted overtook much of the South, made apparent through the considerable number of Confederate monuments and memorials produced during the turn of the twentieth century. Suggestive of how women contributed to the construction of the Lost Cause ideology, local chapters of the United Daughters of the Confederacy held various events to fund the constructions of these monuments (Mills xviii). Recognizing these efforts and, more generally, their place in Southern society, war veterans later honored Confederate women in monuments and memorials that "showed the idealized figure of woman as queen of the domestic sphere . . . [or] as a mother who read the story of the war to the next generation, training her sons to fight the next battle for southern honor" (Mills xxv).

With the end of the Reconstruction, there was increased pressure for the North and South to make amends and repair the deep chasm that fractured the country, contributing to the "reconciliationist vision" of the war (Blight, *Race and Reunion* 2). Circulating concurrently with the Lost Cause's more explicit expressions of white supremacy, this particular view attends to the shared military experiences of white Union and Confederate soldiers, emphasizing their valor and courage. Reflecting the social and political realities of the period, the overlapping ways of remembering the war exhibit the formidable challenge of reconciling a fragmented country. Blight explains that despite the high tensions, "many Americans increasingly realized that remembering the war, even the hatreds and deaths on a hundred battlefields . . . became, with time, easier than struggling over the enduring ideas from which those battles had been fought" (*Race and Reunion* 31). But reconciliationist memories came at the expense of African Americans and progress toward racial parity. In centering white unity, Black service and sacrifice were neglected. These articulations and silences were codified in "[t]he creation of the first national military parks, popular magazines, plays, and even political campaigns," as Caroline Janney asserts, which "encouraged northerners and southerners to embrace their former foes in the spirit of brotherly love and American progress" (161).

White-centered Lost Cause and reconciliationist trends continued to dominate the national landscape until the 1960s when advances made by the Civil Rights movement and second-wave feminists prompted a more critical look at traditional ways of remembering the war, particularly during its centennial anniversary. Responding to calls for more diverse and inclusive perspectives, there was a notable push to nuance how we remember this influential event. Efforts to diversify memories of the Civil War were renewed and expanded during the sesquicentennial anniversary of the conflict, as demonstrated by a growing number of commemorative enterprises featuring women. Speaking to the importance of women's experiences, Stephanie McCurry reminds us that "Women don't usually tell war stories. Almost everything we know about war comes from men. But women's perspective transforms our vision of war because they live through that history differently. They see things that men do not" (10). But while discernable efforts have been made to shed light on women's experiences of the war, the sources that evoke these memories are neither equally distributed nor carry the same persuasive weight as their white male counterparts.

Remembering Those Who Win Our Wonder

Though websites typically don't have the longevity and gravitas afforded to physical monuments and memorials, they contribute to the stratum of memory, serving as cultural building blocks that inform how we see and understand the world around us. Because humans are profoundly shaped by what we intake through our senses, we are in subtle and overt ways affected by what we experience on the web. In recognition of this constitutive power, we have recently witnessed politically motivated efforts to reshape and control what is made available online to the general public. This is particularly true of social media platforms, which I do not address in this project, that use algorithms to offer emotionally charged, polarizing, and sensational material to keep users engaged for a maximum amount of time. But algorithms, of course, also inform our search results, as Safiya Noble asserts: "information monopolies such as Google have the ability to prioritize web search results on the basis of a variety of topics," determining what sites emerge and in what order (24).

A simple Google search for the words "women and the American Civil War" yields a multitude of sites, though mentioned with particular regularity are the women I discuss in this book: Rose O'Neal Greenhow, Belle Boyd, Harriet Tubman, Sarah Emma Edmonds, Loreta Janeta Velazquez, and Susie King Taylor. The frequency with which their names are broached in the context of the Civil War begs the question, as posed by Dickinson, Blair, and Ott, "What renders messages—memories or other kinds of contents—believable, persuasive, or even compelling to particular audiences at particular time in particular circumstances?" (14). Creating their own sources of memory, these women wrote themselves into history, affirming Pierre Nora's observation that "Modern memory is, above all, archival. It relies entirely on the materiality of the trace, the immediacy of the recording, the visibility of the image" (13). Life-writing genres, as Sidonie Smith and Julia Watson maintain, "are not merely transparent 'accounts' of some past experiences, or exact records of historical events in people's lives or the life of the nation" (6). But they do act as "a monument of a kind," in the words of Samuel Hynes, that help "refute and subvert the collective story" (220). While many women kept personal journals and diaries documenting their lives during the war, over one hundred published narratives of their experiences; though illustrative of how sources of memory are shaped by extant power dynamics, the majority of these books were composed by white women. These published personal narratives document the diverse experiences of women during the American Civil War, though almost half focus on their labors as hospital workers. While these accounts can reshape contemporary recollections of the war, the most sensational of these narratives circulate with greatest regularity on the web. Greenhow and Boyd describe their experiences as Confederate spies. Tubman's biographies detail her service to the Union as a nurse, scout, and spy. Edmonds's and Velazquez's books document their experiences dressing as men so they could fight on behalf of the Union and Confederacy respectively. And Taylor documents her service to the 33rd United States Colored Troops as a nurse, cook, and laundress in one of the few published autobiographical accounts of the war published by a Black woman. Standing out from their many contemporaries who contributed to the war efforts in conventional but essential ways, the women I discuss in the case studies offered herein are generally considered to be "exceptional."

As feminist scholars have long observed, extraordinary women, often "queens, warriors, and other female 'worthies,'" are usually the first to appear in historical narratives otherwise populated with powerful white men (Chernock 116). Because the exceptional emerges in opposition to what is considered "normal" in a given context, their stories are particularly memorable. As explained in *Rhetorica ad Herennium,* "When we see in everyday life things that are petty, ordinary, and banal, we generally fail to remember them, because the mind is not being stirred by anything novel or marvelous. But if we see or hear something exceptionally base, dishonorable, extraordinary, great, unbelievable, or laughable, that we are likely to remember a long time" (xxi). Although this instruction was meant to help orators improve their individual recall, the point more broadly extends to public memory. Capturing the audience's attention, the unusual dwells in individual and collective consciousnesses in powerful ways. Resisting conventional standards of womanhood, these figures can inspire a deep sense of affiliation in audiences, what Dickinson, Blair, and Ott identify as "the principal affective modality" of public memory (16). Exemplifying what women can do, they blaze a trail a possibility for those who follow them.

But while sensational stories of women are captivating, even inspiring, they largely replicate dominant cultural standards built on white, Western, cishet, patriarchal epistemologies. Defying socially constructed notions of womanhood, exceptional women perform male-coded labors and activities from which they have historically been denied, even forbidden. When Laurel

Thatcher Ulrich wrote that "[w]ell-behaved women seldom make history," she was not celebrating extraordinary women, but was rather lamenting the fact that the achievements of everyday women often ignored (20). Though "women worthies . . . d[o] not tell us much about those activities in which most women engaged, nor d[o] . . . [they] tell us about the significance of women's activities to society as a whole," as Gerda Lerner cautions, they often receive considerable attention, while the contributions of everyday women are relegated to the dustbin of history (5). In feminist rhetorical studies, this matter is perhaps most famously taken up in Barbara Biesecker's critique of Karlyn Kohrs Campbell's work on nineteenth-century female orators and activists. Although the notable rhetors Campbell recovers interrupt the male-dominated rhetorical canon, as Biesecker argues, these efforts fail "to challenge the underlying logic of canon formation and the uses to which it has been put that have written the rhetorical contributions of collective women into oblivion" ("Coming to Terms" 144). Though she was specifically addressing rhetorical histories, Biesecker's point can be readily transposed to public memory: as epideictic acts, recollections of exceptional women reproduce the perspective that "[w]omen don't really exist unless we 'make something of ourselves' in the public world" (McIntosh 8).

Although feminist scholars have long acknowledged the problems of what Adrienne Rich calls "female tokenism," shallow attempts to diversify public memory persist, as demonstrated by common retellings of Greenhow, Boyd, Tubman, Edmonds, Velazquez, and Taylor ("What Does a Woman Need to Know?" 5). Though they ostensibly make attractive additions to male-dominated accounts of the war, their stories demonstrate the problems of an additive approach to diversity, equity, inclusion, and access. While their exceptional labors as women are amplified in common digital retellings of their lives, the more complex race-related issues documented in their published accounts are minimized or elided entirely, illustrating how whiteness informs these reconstructions. Perpetuating established memorialization patterns associated with the war, retellings of exceptional white Southern women uncritically lionize their contributions to the Confederacy, while narratives of white Union women typically fail to acknowledge or critique their own questionable discussions and depictions of race. Race is only visible in the context of the Black "other," but even then, considerations of slavery are often highly curated, limiting what is conveyed about this cruel institution and its lasting impact. In foregrounding discussions of gender while downplaying race, digital accounts flatten difference, evoking decidedly idealized memories that fail to acknowledge slavery and the racialized hierarchies that justified its existence.

Reconstructions of Civil War Women on the Web

To arrive at the conclusions offered in this book, I draw on rhetorical circulation studies and feminist theory, following the lead of scholars such as Jessica Enoch, Danielle Griffin, and Karen Nelson who "track, how, why, and for what purpose women and their rhetorics have moved; to explore the ways these rhetorics have been taken up, recast, and mobilized in various rhetorical situations and for particular ends" (6). Broadly attending to the ways rhetoric travels beyond the original sites of delivery, I map how the personal narratives of Greenhow, Boyd, Tubman, Edmonds, Velazquez, and Taylor have been retold on the web, a highly influential source of public memory. In undertaking this project, I take inspiration from Vicki Tolar Burton's theory of "rhetorical accretion," which examines "the process of layering additional texts over and around the original text" (547).[5] To this end, I first examine what Burton calls "core texts," in this case, the published personal accounts that document the lives of these six women (548). Though inevitably bearing the imprint of the writer's positionality, these narratives serve as essential sources of memory that continue to feed contemporary recollections of these Civil War women. Now available in critical editions, facsimile copies, and on a variety of digital platforms, these books function as a blueprint that enables us to see how their stories have changed as they are retold in new contexts. Because, as Laurie Gries observes, "material artifacts generate traceable consequences in their wake, which contribute to their ongoing rhetoricity" (*Still Life With Rhetoric* xiv), I specifically examine how the print texts of Greenhow, Boyd, Tubman, Edmonds, Velazquez, and Taylor are restoried through "remediation" what Jay David Bolter and Richard Grusin describe as the "refashion[ing]" of old media into new products (15). This pursuit, explain Joanne Garde-Hansen, Andrew Hoskins, and Anna Reading, invites "us to think about digital media not as a radical break but as a process of reformulating, reformatting, recycling, returning and even remembering other media" (14). While digital biographies perform the traditional work of describing a life, their form and content is notably different, shaped by the distinct context of the World Wide Web and the needs of those who use it. Easily retrieved with a few strokes of the keyboard, these biographies reflect a need for quick digestible bites of information, suggestive of how medium informs genre. Though all life writing is necessarily skewed, magnifying certain details while eliding and diminishing others, this inevitability is particularly acute in the digital forms examined in these case studies discussed herein. Necessarily shorter in length, digital biographies sometimes consist of only a few hundred words. Although compressing a life in such a way predictably limits what can be communicated, additional meaning is gained in ways specific to the web, including hyperlinks, multimedia productions, and other digital paratextual features. In examining the biographies of Greenhow, Boyd, Tubman, Edmonds, Velazquez, and Taylor, I chart what is included, excluded, added, and otherwise altered in these retellings, staying attuned to what Jacqueline Jones Royster and Gesa Kirsch describe as the "ebbs and flows within ever-changing, often broadening circles of interaction [that] enables us to see how the past can reach into the present and how the close at hand might reach toward the distant and further away" (101).

Contributing to the amalgam of memory, digital biographies offer site users visions of the past that inform the present. In ways similar to traditional physical sites of memory, these snapshots play a formative role in our contemporary society. "Whether we are conscious of it or not," Kristin Sorensen affirms, "our sense of ourselves, our nation, and our history is entwined with the images and words offered to us through our media" (163). Although stories of Civil War women are largely absent from commissioned sites of memorialization, they live on through popular media, aligning with Marita Sturken's observation that mechanisms of memory "are increasingly visual technologies of mass and mediated forms—photographs, films, television shows and digital images" ("Memory, Consumerism, and Media" 75). Probing these connections, scholars from a range of disciplines have explored the ways in which various types of media help shape public memory of historical events. In his work on popular memory, the war, and film, Gary Gallagher contends that "More people have formed perceptions about the Civil War from watching *Gone with the Wind* than from reading all the books written by historians since Selznick's blockbuster debuted in 1939. Even moderately successful movies attract a far larger audience than the most widely read nonfiction books dealing with the conflict" (9–10). While the film industry has contributed to how we remember the war, *Winning Our Wonder* examines a potentially even more powerful source of remembrance: the World Wide Web, a powerful source of public memory that, as Garde-Hansen, Hoskins, and Reading contend, "provid[es] unprecedented global accessibility—and participation in the creation of memories" (1). With its "promise of representational diversity, collective authorship, and interactivity," the web as a source of public memory is "in need of exploration and critique," a call that is even more urgent in the age of generative artificial intelligence technologies that replicate dominant ways of thinking as recorded on the web (Haskins, *Popular Memory* 49). Though the web features millions of pages and sites that reflect a diversity of perspectives and experiences, as studies like Catherine Knight Steele's *Digital Black Feminism* confirm, whiteness and androcentricity continue to haunt many online spaces, particularly those associated with official sources of memory. Illustrative of the cumulative nature of memory, many official and participatory sites that contribute to memories of the war still bear traces of Lost Cause and reconciliationist visions, shaping contemporary conceptions of race, gender, and citizenship.

Recognizing that my positionality affects my analysis, I want to acknowledge my "politics of location," in the words of Adrienne Rich, to demonstrate how the "thinking and speaking" represented in this book are connected with "the body of *this* particular living human individual, a woman" ("Notes on a Politics" 213, emphasis added). Though I have tried to approach this project both reflectively and reflexively, I recognize that my experiences as a white, heterosexual, cisgendered, and able-bodied woman of relative means and privilege inevitably inform and limit my thinking on this topic. As Rich aptly observes, "Marginalized though we have been as women, as white and Western makers of theory, we also marginalize others because our lived experience is thoughtlessly white, because even our 'women's cultures' are rooted in some Western tradition" ("Notes on a Politics" 219). By acknowledging my own complicity in this tradition, I aim to confront the myth of researcher neutrality that hides white, Western, epistemic power, but I also invite dialogue about the topics discussed in this book with the hope of advancing richer, more nuanced storytelling practices, particularly on the web.

A project that has been over a decade in the making, the research that I share in this book began around 2010 after I watched Ken Burns et al.'s *The Civil War*. When it originally aired in 1990, 13.9 million viewers tuned in, breaking the record for most watched educational series on PBS (Toplin xv). Since then, millions more have previewed the documentary, contributing to how one of the most contentious events in the history of the United States is remembered. While it won many accolades, Burns was roundly censured for centering the experiences of white male politicians and soldiers in his film. As historian Catherine Clinton observes, "women were all but invisible" in the eleven-hour film ("Noble Women as Well" 67–68). Of the more notable exceptions to this general exclusion, however, is the brief discussion of Greenhow, Boyd, and a Black woman named Mary Elizabeth Bowser (a.k.a. Mary Jane Richards and

Mary Jane Richardson). Appearing in episode seven, "Most Hallowed Ground," Greenhow, Boyd and Bowser were introduced in the segment of the film that discusses Civil War spies. In his distinct voice, David McCullough regaled audiences with stories about how Greenhow "ran a Confederate spy ring just a few blocks from the White House," while Boyd "coax[ed] secrets out of Union officers" (Burns et al.). And perhaps most remarkable: "One Northern agent, a black servant by the name of Mary Elizabeth Bowser, even worked inside the Confederate White House" (Burns et al.). Although the segment is only a few minutes in length, the stories of Boyd, Greenhow, and Bowser made a deep impression on me. Since then, I have sought to better understand these women, and others like them, exploring what makes their memories stick and linger.

My initial research started with Bowser, but traces of her life and labors proved difficult to locate, suggestive of the limitations of material sources of memory, specifically as they concern Black women; consequently, I did not include Bowser in this study. Gravitating toward the published accounts of Civil War women, I read the memoirs of Greenhow and Boyd, taking particular note of how they talked about slavery, but as I read their own accounts against the war stories that circulated online, I noticed that their proslavery rhetoric was often omitted from these retellings. Sanitizing their experiences, common digital biographies highlighted their sensational experiences as female spies, while their documented white supremacist views were ignored. As my research moved outward and I examined other personal accounts of Civil War women's experiences, similar kinds of patterns surfaced, hinting at the sociocultural proclivities and biases that inform narratives of the war and the women involved with it more specifically. But of import, these commemorative patterns can be observed in an array of sites that give rise to memories of women, calling attention to the importance of establishing more socially just ways of recalling the past. Collectively, we are what we remember.

Overview of Chapters

To account for the inequities associated with the production of memory and the sources that engender it, particularly as they concern published personal narratives, I have chosen to cover Tubman and Taylor in separate chapters, allowing me to deepen my analysis of their war stories and the artifacts that advance their memory. In contrast, I conjoin my discussion of Greenhow and Boyd and Edmonds and Velazquez in the chapters that follow. While some details are lost in linking their stories, such an approach enabled me to point to prevailing commemorative trends that haunt our memories of the Civil War and contemporary understandings of identity and belonging.

Commencing the case studies offered in *Winning Our Wonder,* I take up the war stories of Confederate spies Rose O'Neal Greenhow and Belle Boyd as circulated by the American Battlefield Trust (ABT), a well-known and respected source of Civil War information on the web. As is typical of digital retellings of these Confederate women, the ABT focuses on Greenhow's and Boyd's experiences as spies and prisoners. But in an act of rhetorical selection informed by whiteness, the site omits the troubling views of slavery that are captured in their autobiographical accounts. Published first in England and then in the United States, both Greenhow's *My Imprisonment, and the First Year of Abolition Rule at Washington* (1863) and Boyd's *Belle Boyd in Camp and Prison* (1865) defend white supremacist racialized hierarchies that justify slavery as a "positive good." In redacting these views, their biographies ultimately echo Lost Cause visions of the war that minimize the role that slavery played in this consequential historical event and its lasting social, political, and economic impact.

In chapter 2, I examine the layers of memory that comprise public recollections of Harriet Tubman and her service to the Union, particularly as it concerns the Combahee River Raid, a mission that she helped plan and execute that liberated hundreds of enslaved people. These experiences were documented in varying degrees in two biographies authored by Sarah Hopkins Bradford: *Scenes in the Life of Harriet Tubman* (1869) and *Harriet, The Moses of Her People* (1886). Extending Sara C. VanderHaagen's scholarship on the memorializing potential of biographical genres, I first examine how these books contributed to dominant memories of Tubman. Though there are some notable differences in the composition of these two texts, particularly in how Tubman's war experiences are conveyed, her work with the Underground Railroad is very much centered in Bradford's biographies. Yet reflecting reconciliationist traditions that prioritize white reunion, these labors have historically been minimized in subsequent commemorative projects. But nuancing these common memories, the National Park Service (NPS) linked a detailed account of her Civil War experiences and her role in the Combahee River Raid that was published in the summer of 2020. Though a recent addition to the NPS site, this reinscription of Tubman's war labors is suggestive of how digital layering practices can "texture" fossilized recollections of the past.

Building on the concepts of rhetorical selectivity and layering, in chapter 3 I examine the popular memories of women warriors of the American Civil War, focusing specifically on how Civil War spies and soldiers Sarah Emma Edmonds and Loreta Janeta Velazquez are depicted in Wikipedia entries. In contrast to official sources of memory shaped by dominant power groups, participatory sites invite broader publics to contribute to narratives of the past; generally considered to be more inclusive and democratic, such approaches to memory, it is often assumed, better reflect the views and values of everyday people, but as I demonstrate through my study of these Wikipedia entries, whiteness, too, haunts the pages of this widely referenced source of information. In theory, the immediacy of Wikipedia edits and its overall collaborative nature make it a potentially productive place for engaging with complicated entanglements of the past, because different editors bring different perspectives to a given entry that gradually grow in depth and in substance, but Wikipedia editors are a relatively homogenous group, which is reflected in the evolution of how Edmonds and Velazquez are depicted. In their earliest iterations, Wikipedia pages featuring Edmonds and Velazquez were structured around the most extraordinary elements recorded in their published personal narratives, echoing patterns of rhetorical selection discussed in chapter 1. But composing trends suggest that site editors have increasingly wrestled with the veracity of Edmonds's and Velazquez's claims. While such tendencies are not necessarily surprising, they do prompt questions about the priorities of the editors and how they inform the construction of Wikipedia narratives, especially as these entries neglect how Edmonds and Velazquez discuss race and slavery in their books. Though Edmonds was committed to emancipatory principles, her book is indicative of the ways that white superiority was more subtly maintained through the amplification of racial difference. A Cuban-born Confederate, Velazquez was a proponent of slavery, even enslaving a man named Bob who accompanied her on the battlefield. Eclipsing these more controversial details is indicative of another way that gender as a singled axis of identity is foregrounded and discussions of white supremacy and slavery are sidelined.

The final case study is an examination of how Susie King Taylor's *Reminiscences of My Life in Camp with the 33rd United States Colored Troops, Late First S.C. Volunteers* (1902) has been retold into an Ersi StoryMap featured on the Library of Congress (LOC) website. A formerly enslaved woman, she worked as a nurse, cook, laundress, and teacher for an African American regiment, experiences which she documented in her book. Drawing from her account, the StoryMap is highly visual multimedia production that reimagines her war experiences, utilizing images from the massive collection of photographs and other images from the LOC. But including only a handful of representations of Black women, it struggles to advance what Sarah Lewis calls "representational justice," visuals of the past that advance racial equity. This gap, I maintain, is suggestive of the limitations of the material archival artifacts, particularly as they concern multiply marginalized individuals.

In addition to exploring how published accounts have been rescripted in online spaces, thereby evoking and shaping public memories of the Civil War, I discuss in the conclusion the evolution of memory and how allies can help spur this commemorative process along while better attending to interlocking oppressions of race and gender. As rhetoric and composition scholars, we are keenly aware that the quest for a definitive past is futile. "All of historical work," as Robert Connors reminds us, "is provisional, partial" (21). But in these postmodern realities of public memory there exist great possibilities. Memories are not inert; ever-changing, they both shape and are shaped by the beliefs and values of a respective community. Showcasing some strategies for altering such legacies, this last chapter calls readers to move from analysis to action through challenging overly simplistic depictions of women while also expanding who is taken up in these conversations of the war and to what ends.

CHAPTER 1

Selective Memories

Rhetorical Re/Constructions of Rose O'Neal Greenhow and Belle Boyd

Perhaps more than any other people, Americans have been locked in a deadly struggle with time, with history. We've fled the past and trained ourselves to suppress, if not forget, troublesome details of the national memory, and a great part of our optimism, like our progress, has been bought at the cost of ignoring the processes through which we've arrived at any given moment in our national existence.

    —Ralph Ellison, "The Blues"

In the wake of the murder of George Floyd, protesters in Richmond, Virginia gathered around the Jefferson Davis Memorial on Monument Avenue on 10 June 2020, and toppled the statue of the Confederate president. Originally erected in 1907, the Davis Memorial was financed by funds raised by the United Daughters of the Confederacy, a group that "played a critical role in sustaining a potent remembrance of southern suffering and heroism that helped not only to bolster their own social status but also to sustain racial segregation into the second half of the twentieth century," Robert J. Cook explains (5). The Davis Monument helped advance such Lost Cause goals, serving as an epideictic enterprise that shaped the perspectives of the local community. When the statue fell, demonstrators celebrated its collapse, gathering jubilantly around the tarnished hulk of bronze that lie in the street. But on a 60-foot granite column above the empty pedestal where Davis once stood remained the Vindicatrix—a sculpture of a white woman whose right finger pointed up to the sky while her left hand held a Confederate shield. Otherwise known as "Miss Confederacy," this remnant of the memorial highlighted the role that women played in the Confederacy, signifying the distinct place that they occupied in Lost Cause mythology, a spurious interpretation of the war that suggests that the South fought, not over slavery, but against the tyranny of its Northern oppressors. Historian Karen Cox explains that "The North had accepted the Lost Cause narrative as fact, which was an essential element of reunion" (151). But, she continues, "That narrative . . . was, at its core, about preserving white supremacy. Reconciliation had allowed white southerners to return to the American fold as patriots, not traitors. . . . For African Americans, however, the results of this reunion would add decades onto their journey for freedom" (151). Although the Vindicatrix was eventually removed by the city in July 2020, its lingering presence speaks to the insidious ways that Lost Cause ideology is embedded in the memories of Confederate women that emerge from the symbolic layers from the past. While statues of Confederate men continue to fall, stories of brave and devoted Confederate women endure, often without question or critique.

A study of any number of Confederate women could potentially illustrate this phenomenon, but in this chapter, I focus on Rose O'Neal Greenhow and Belle Boyd. The stories of these Confederate spies are widely retold in popular narratives of the war, especially those that seek to diversify perspectives of this contentious cultural event. Contributing to their lasting legacies are their published personal accounts, respectively titled *My Imprisonment and the First Year of Abolition Rule at Washington* (1863) and *Belle Boyd in Camp and Prison* (1865). While these narratives capture Greenhow's and Boyd's astonishing experiences as Confederate spies and Union prisoners, they also function as a kind of Confederate apologia, defending the South as they disparage the Union. Originally published in England, their books attempt to sway British public opinion of the war. In pursuant of this objective, both Greenhow and Boyd attempt to alter their readers' perceptions of slavery, advancing commonly proffered arguments that sought to justify human bondage. Despite Greenhow's and Boyd's documented views on slavery, these facets of their narratives are rarely addressed in the contemporary retellings, illustrating the power of rhetorical selection to shape meaning and memory.

Informed by Kenneth Burke's theories of terminisitic screens, I examine acts of reflection and deflection as stories are retold in different contexts, focusing on what features of a given account are repeated (or not), how, and in what ways. Describing the production of the past, Michel-Rolph Trouillot explains, "Something is always left out while something else is recorded . . . whatever becomes fact does so with its own inborn absences" (49). Concentrating specifically on narratives of Greenhow and Boyd, I trace how their books inform the brief digital biographies that circulate on the web. Though their stories do the important work of diversifying androcentric narratives of the Civil War, they also exemplify some of the problems with shallow attempts to build more inclusive historical narratives. Never neutral, rhetorical selection is necessarily influenced by the priorities of those rescripting the past. Bearing traces of whiteness, the resulting narratives foreground their exceptional experiences as female spies while minimizing or eliding entirely slavery and the role that they played in its preservation. Echoing Lost Cause visions of the war, these accounts subsequently shroud these Confederate women in "heroism immunized from motive," underscoring their bravery while neglecting to acknowledge what motivated them to act in the first place (Blight, *Race and Reunion* 96). Illustrative of the prevalence of this reframing, I write about a similar phenomenon in "(Re)telling the Times," concentrating specifically on how these Confederate women are exhibited in the *New York Times* "Disunion" series, a site that was created in commemoration of the sesquicentennial anniversary of the Civil War.

Building from this scholarly endeavor, in this chapter I focus on how these Confederate women are depicted by the American Battlefield Trust (ABT), a nonprofit organization that helps conserve battlefields from the Civil War and other national conflicts. Functioning as what John Bodnar calls an "official" source of memory, what he defines as "a nationalistic, patriotic culture that mediates an assortment of vernacular interests" (14), the ABT is primarily charged with "preserv[ing] America's hallowed battlegrounds and educat[ing] the public about what happened there and why it matters" ("Our Work: About the American Battlefield Trust"). Their elaborate and extensive website was created in service of this mission. Attracting millions of viewers annually, this site is an influential source of Civil War memory that warrants greater attention ("Civil War Trust"). Similar to other (web)sites featuring these Confederate women, the ABT's accounts amplify Greenhow's and Boyd's incredible experiences as female spies and prisoners, failing to address their documented views of slavery.

Rhetorical Reflection/Deflection

Memory is always "partial," asserts Barbie Zelizer: "No single memory contains all that we know, or could know, about any given event, personality, or issue" ("Reading the Past" 221). Reflective of the rhetorical mechanisms that propagate memory, some facets of the past are annunciated as others are necessarily silenced in the memory production. Burke's discussion of terministic screens proves particularly useful here for understanding this dialectic: "Even if any given terminology is a *reflection* of reality," he explains, "by its very nature as a terminology it must be a *selection* of reality; and to this extent it must function also as a *deflection* of reality" (45, emphasis in original). To illustrate his point,

Burke recalls looking at photographs taken of the same subject using different colored filters: "Here something so 'factual' as a photograph revealed notable distinctions in texture, and even in form, depending upon which color filter was used for the documentary description of the event being recorded" (45). Even when the same subject is symbolically represented, what elements are reflected and refracted in a rhetorical event affect the meaning that emerges. But examined in an isolated instance, the slant of memory can be difficult to see; perspective is needed to gauge the impact of rhetorical selection, as Burke's example makes clear: it is through viewing the same photograph through different lenses that its construction is made perceptible. Taking inspiration from this approach, I examine how Greenhow and Boyd have been remembered, beginning with their influential published personal accounts. Though these narratives, too, are acts of rhetorical selection, they offer a meaningful starting point from which subsequent retellings can be compared. While their memoirs focus on their experiences as spies and prisoners, they also function as pro-Confederate propaganda that attempted to allay their British readers' concerns with slavery, as I argue in this section. But in an act of rhetorical deflection informed by whiteness, these facets of their recorded experiences are rarely taken up in digital biographies that circulate online, influencing how audiences perceive these women.

Widely available today in print and digital form, the published accounts of Greenhow and Boyd aided recent efforts to broaden contemporary memories of the Civil War. Subverting expectations of gender, their spy stories make seemingly attractive additions to popular remembrances that have long centered the experiences of white soldiers and politicians. As historian Stephanie McCurry observes, "the Union's military experience with women in the path of their armies was an entirely unexpected and deeply unsettling element of the war. It subverted longstanding assumptions about women's political identity and status, and provoked a profound reassessment of the protections accorded to noncombatants" (17). While Confederate women interfered with Union efforts in a variety of ways, they were particularly "dangerous because of their role in conveying military intelligence. They were caught running rebel spy networks all over the district, including inside Union refugee camps" (McCurry 37). Providing first-hand accounts of such espionage experiences, Greenhow's and Boyd's books describe these transgressive labors in captivating detail.

Although Queen Victoria and Prime Minister Palmerston declared England to be officially neutral during the war, many Confederate supporters believed that Great Britain would come to their aid in their fight against the Union. Not only did Britain depend on the cheap cotton the South produced, but explains historian Amanda Foreman, "Twice in four years Britain and the North were on the brink of war" (xxiv).[1] Capitalizing on these precarious political circumstances, Greenhow recalibrated her support of the Confederacy after she was released from prison. Ann Blackman, Greenhow's biographer, reports that Confederate President Jefferson Davis chose Greenhow to be "his personal emissary to Europe, hoping in vain to persuade the British and French to recognize the Confederate government" (x). While abroad, Greenhow met with high-ranking officials and nobility, including Prime Minister Palmerston and Napoleon III, attempting to secure support for the Confederacy. Recognizing the power of the pen to engage in battle, Greenhow also made connections with James Spence and Henry Hotze, founders of the pro-Confederate publication in England, *The Index* (Ross 229). In 1863, she published her *My Imprisonment* in London, which offers her own account of the war and the role she played in it. But likely "backed by Confederate funds," her book was also "used to whip up sentiment for the South," as Ishbel Ross asserts (223). Censuring the Union soldiers, politicians, and policies, her memoir functioned as propaganda designed to influence British perception of the contentious event.

Boyd's memoir was also published in London, though shortly after General Robert E. Lee surrendered to General Ulysses S. Grant. Still, in ways similar to Greenhow, Boyd used her narrative to tarnish the reputation of the Union in the eyes of her British readers. While her dedication to the Confederacy can be clearly observed in her memoir, she also attempted to use her book as leverage for the release of her imprisoned husband, S. Wylde Hardinge, a Union naval officer who helped Boyd flee to England. After marrying Boyd abroad, Hardinge returned to the States where he was arrested for aiding the enemy. She wrote a letter to President Lincoln directly on 24 January 1865, noting that "My Book was not originally intended to be more than a personal narrative, but since my husband's unjust arrest I had intended making it political, & had introduced many atrocious circumstances respecting your government with which I am so well acquainted and which would open the eyes of Europe to many things of which the world on this side of the water little dreams" ("Letter to Abraham Lincoln").[2] Lincoln never responded to Boyd's request, and working with George Augusta Sala, a popular British writer and an ardent supporter of the Confederacy, she published her memoir in May 1865 (Kennedy-Noelle 4).

Because Greenhow and Boyd were both aware that many British citizens would be deterred from supporting the Confederacy because of its connection to slavery, an enterprise they found repugnant, both writers offer proslavery arguments in their books in an attempt to make the practice more tolerable to their readers. Contrasting Kimberly Harrison's observation that a number of Confederate women "directly expressed doubts about slavery" in their private diaries, Greenhow and Boyd publicly endeavored to make slavery as palatable as possible (136). To help advance this goal, they both attack the ethos of the Union, calling into question its alliance with the abolition movement. As they similarly articulate, the Union strategically partnered with abolitionists to expand and fortify their base—not because they necessarily believed in the moral obligation to emancipate enslaved peoples. As Boyd writes in her book, "I will not attempt to defend the institution of slavery, the very name of which is abhorred in England; but it will be admitted that the emancipation of the negro was not the object of Northern ambition; that is, the faction which grasps exclusive power in contempt of general rights" (73). Making a comparable argument, Greenhow makes the following statement in her memoir: "slavery, although the occasion, was not the producing cause of the dissolution. The contest on the part of the North was for supreme control, especially in relation to the *fiscal action* of the Government. This object could not be fully attained by a mere *numerical majority.* To secure *this majority,* and thus complete the *political ascendency* of the North, the policy of '*no more Slave States* was formally set forth'" (167, emphasis in original). In situating the war as an act of "Northern aggression," Greenhow and Boyd attempt to position the Union's support of abolitionist goals as political posturing. Both published after the Emancipation Proclamation was enacted, which did not manumit enslaved people living in border states, their books renewed questions about the North's true commitment to liberation.

Exploiting this kernel of doubt, Greenhow and Boyd also question the ways in which slavery was depicted in popular books and magazines. Because slavery had long been abolished in England and most of its colonies, "Few Britons had ever seen how slaves really lived," as Foreman explains (27).[3] Abolitionist-oriented literature helped cement British aversion to the "peculiar institution," a formidable obstacle that Greenhow and Boyd addressed in their own accounts. Though slavery was characterized as inhumane in a range of popular publications that widely circulated at the time, Greenhow and Boyd suggest that these narratives were inaccurate, composed for political purposes. Critiquing the abolitionist writers and preachers who galvanized audiences against slavery, Greenhow asserts that these narratives were mere hyperbole: "The best talent was employed to decry the institution of slavery. Romance writers exercised their inventive genius to draw thrilling pictures of its horrors. The pulpit lent its powerful aid, and fulminated the thunders of the Church in terms of burning eloquence, until a feeling of fanaticism was aroused rarely equaled in fury, and men rose to power only as they favoured the madness of the hour" (94–95).[4] Taking a similar approach in her book, Boyd maintains that the representations of slavery specifically found in Harriet Beecher Stowe's *Uncle Tom's Cabin* (1852) and Henry Wadsworth Longfellow's *Poems on Slavery* (1842) were imagined, intentionally crafted to demonize slavery and the South: "Is the ghost of Uncle Tom laid? Has the slave dreamed his last dream? Will Mrs. H. B. Stowe and Mr. Longfellow admit that in either instance the hero owes his reputation for martyrdom to a creative genius and to an exquisite fancy? or will they still contend that the negro slave of the Confederate States is, physically and morally, a real object of commiseration?" (74). As captured in their books, both Greenhow and Boyd condemn common depictions of slavery that paint the practice as cruel and brutal, asserting that such characterizations were socially and politically motivated. While these passages invite British readers to reconsider what they know about slavery and how they acquired such perceptions, these rhetorical maneuverings also give Greenhow and Boyd the opportunity to share perspectives that attempt to quell their audience's moral concerns.

Countering harsh depictions of slavery, Greenhow and Boyd both suggest that the dynamic between enslaver and enslaved was symbiotic, imbued with a genuine and mutual affection that was typically occluded from popular literature. Failing to understand these attachments, many people "were ignorant, save theoretically, of that institution [of slavery], and of the benign and paternal manner in which it was conducted in the South," Greenhow asserts (10). As a result, Greenhow later writes, "Nowhere on earth, not even in happy England, does there exist between the various classes of society such harmony, such sympathy, as the South" (182). Giving this particular point more attention, Boyd leans on the "loyal slave" trope commonly observed in Lost Cause narratives as she discusses her "negro maid" (78). Although Boyd never identifies her "maid," Sharon Kennedy-Noelle suggests that her name is Eliza Corsey, a "runaway from the Deep South [who] found refuge with the Boyds as their slave" (36). Exemplifying Corsey's love and devotion, Boyd recounts how Corsey incurred great risk to protect her from potential harm. Boyd explains, for example, that when Union troops "broke into our house . . . for the purpose of hunting for 'rebel flags . . . without my orders, my negro maid promptly rushed up-stairs, tore down the obnoxious emblem, and before our enemies could get possession of it, burned it" (82). And when Boyd was arrested, Corsey "clasped her arms around my knees, and passionately implored permission to attend me" (121). If slavery was as inhumane as it was portrayed in popular sources, Boyd insinuates through her narrative, surely her own maid would be eager to flee, yet Corsey remained devoted to her. Written in an effort to mitigate harsh views of slavery, especially those espoused by popular sources, such anecdotes attempt to persuade Boyd's audience that Corsey loved her and supported the Confederacy.

Exemplifying the kinds of narratives commonly proffered to justify slavery, Boyd's discussion of Corsey reifies the "positive good" view of human bondage. Attributed to John C. Calhoun, this defense of the institution maintained that slavery was not evil, but rather a mutually beneficial arrangement that helped "civiliz[e] and improv[e]" the Black race "not only physically, but morally and intellectually" while "sustaining the supremacy of the white race." To varying degrees, both Greenhow and Boyd reflect and perpetuate the "positive good" perspective. As previously noted, Boyd stated that those with Black skin "prefer[ed] servitude to freedom" (73), a position that she reinforces through her narratives of Corsey. Greenhow, however, is more candid about her white supremacist views:

> If the question were simply whether it would not be better for the South to have four millions of intelligent, industrious, and valiant freemen in the place of four millions of African slaves, it would be neither so delicate nor difficult of solution. But the question which taxes the practical statesmanship and philanthropy of the Southern people is of a far graver character. It is this. Two races—one civilized, the other barbarous—being locally intermingled, what does the good of society require—the freedom or servitude of the barbarous race? The South believe that the freedom of the blacks, under such circumstances, would result certainly in their final extermination, and that servitude is best adapted to their intellectual and moral condition. (181)

Race, Greenhow ultimately concludes, "is as fixed and immutable as any other law of nature," and the white race is "the superior race" (181).

Woven throughout their sensational spy stories, Greenhow's and Boyd's proslavery positions attempt to normalize human bondage to their British readers in an effort to gain support for the Confederacy. Accusing the Union of political manipulation, they maintain that the North sought to control the South, capitalizing on abolitionist sentiment to help achieve this goal. Though slavery had been portrayed in popular media as cruel and violent, they maintain that such depictions were exaggerations. Countering these narratives, Greenhow and Boyd offer their own distinct "positive good" view of slavery. Describing her relationship with her "maid," Boyd attempts to advance the notion that people of color preferred slavery to liberation. More explicit, Greenhow openly acknowledges her beliefs in white superiority/Black inferiority, maintaining that this racialized hierarchy necessitates white dominion. But though these proslavery positions are clearly documented in their books, they are often deflected from common retellings that circulate online. Suggestive of the whiteness that informs these retellings, this act of rhetorical selection radically changes how Greenhow and Boyd are publicly received.

Though the personal narratives of Greenhow and Boyd are themselves rhetorically selective, they are written records of the past from which subsequent mechanisms of memory are born but also measured. As their war stories are retold and remediated into digital biographies that circulate online, some facets of their narratives are reiterated and augmented while others are necessarily omitted. In her discussion of rhetorical histories, Jacqueline Jones Royster describes this process as a kind of landscaping: "We select, focus, and develop, bringing more clearly and vibrantly into view particular features that we frame and foreground, while simultaneously disregarding or minimizing other features and dimensions that we might have selected, developed, and showcased instead" (148). Never objective, rhetorical selection is informed by the priorities of those who restory the past. Exposing the ways that whiteness haunts dominant memories of the war, typical retellings of Greenhow and Boyd center their transgressions as women, forgoing discussion of their white supremacist views of race and human bondage, a rhetorical move distances white women from slavery and the role that they played in its preservation. Though similar kinds of landscaping trends can be observed in other case studies offered in this book, in notable contrast, the retellings of Harriet Tubman and Susie King Taylor, two Black women whom I discuss at length in later chapters, typically address their experiences as enslaved women, though the more troubling details are still often omitted. These rhetorical trends contribute to the belief that slavery is a problem only for people of color, not the white men and women who supported this oppressive institution. While Greenhow and Boyd subverted expectations of white womanhood during the war, they did so in order to preserve slavery. Divorcing motive from action, when their documented proslavery positions are excised from common retellings, they are portrayed as valiant, even commendable women.

While such patterns of rhetorical selection are discernable in the many websites that take up Greenhow and Boyd, in this case study, I specifically examine how the ABT depicts these Confederate spies on their widely consulted website. The ABT occupies competitive real estate on the web as a popular source of Civil War history, sharing information with millions of site visitors. While the organization has a strong web presence, the origins of the ABT can be traced back to 1987 when four National Park Service (NPS) historians partnered with a Civil War scholar and two Civil War enthusiasts to seek out privately held resources to preserve targeted Civil War battlefields (Zeller 43–44). Originally called the Association for the Preservation of Civil War Sites (APCWS), the group aimed to fill the conservation gaps not covered by the NPS and local state parks. Zoning laws and the limitations of these publicly funded sources prevented them from acquiring "the vast majority of battlefield acreage on which young American men by the thousands had fought and died for the causes in which they believed" ("Three Decades in the Trenches"). Righting this wrong, the APCWS set out to save battlefields that were otherwise being turned into parking lots and shopping centers. Highly successful, by 1990 the APCWS had successfully preserved over "660 acres at eight different battlefields" ("Three Decades in the Trenches"). In 1999, the APCWS merged with the American Battlefield Protection Foundation, a private foundation that similarly sought to "attract corporate donations" (Hadar). This fusion eventually resulted in an expansion in scope of the battlefields recovered, which now includes land linked with the Revolutionary War and the War of 1812, and a subsequent change in nomenclature to reflect this expanded purview: the American Battlefield Trust.[5]

As professed in their mission statement, the ABT is committed to preserving battlefields and educating the public about them, relying largely on private donations to support these endeavors. This objective is made particularly perceptible by the red "Donate" and "Join" buttons located on the header featured at the top of all its web pages. Although the ABT was "[a]lready the premier online resource for Civil War history," the site underwent a considerable overhaul in 2017 to strengthen its digital arm, consolidating materials that were housed on different sites ("Redesigned"). Now centrally located at battlefields. org, the ABT site offers users general information about America's wars at home, including free curricula for educators, panoramic views of battlefields, maps, photographs, articles, and close to 500 short biographies of noteworthy players in American military history. Exemplifying the dynamic nature of the web, these materials are in constant flux, undergoing additions, updates, and revisions. But at present, and in alignment with established historical trends, the majority of these biographies tell the stories of white men; only about 30 entries discuss Civil War women, eight of whom are women of color. While this asymmetrical coverage generally contributes to white, androcentric memories of the war, the ABT's accounts of Greenhow and Boyd further reveals how these retellings are shaped by whiteness. Though the ABT pledges to "represent our nation's complex story with accuracy, objectivity and integrity," its biographies of Greenhow and Boyd fail to acknowledge their proslavery positions ("Our Mission"). In ways typical of common retellings of their war stories, the ABT magnifies their extraordinary experiences as spies and prisoners, deflecting how they sought to normalize human bondage. As a result, Greenhow and Boyd are painted as admirable figures, though illustrative of how selection manifests differently according to context, their contributions are rarely acknowledged in the dominant memories of the war.

Rose O'Neal Greenhow

An internet search for "Rose O'Neal Greenhow" yields thousands of results, including general reference sites such as Brittanca.com and Wikipedia; popular historical sources like History.com and warhistoryonline.com; gender-centric pages, including the dangerouswomenproject.org, womenshistory.org, and womenhistoryblog.com; and the digital archival collections at Duke University and the National Archives that hold Greenhow's papers and letters. Neither neutral nor objective, the ever-evolving Google algorithm typically positions the ABT's biography of Greenhow near the top of the search list, increasing the likelihood that site users will click on the link to learn more about this Confederate spy (Noble 3). For those already on the ABT site, Greenhow's digital biography can be accessed through the "Women in War" link located at the top of the homepage, providing interested parties with another point of access to the page.

A common convention of digital biographies, Greenhow's photograph (fig. 1) marks the opening of this 1,300-word account of her life. Putting a face to her name, this oval-shaped black and white image hints at her elevated socioeconomic status: she wears a fashionable black dress, and her hair is neatly pulled back. She looks stern as she gazes into the distance. One of the few extant photos of Greenhow, this image circulates widely online in many retellings. Digitally available without restriction through the Brady-Handy Collection in the Library of Congress Prints and Photographs Online Catalog, it is a *carte de visite,* a type of photograph that was popular during the Civil War because it was faster and less expensive to produce. The war marked a period in which the "medium of photography matured and flourished," as hundreds of thousands of images documented life in new and consequential ways (Rosenheim 1). But as Daniel C. Blight astutely observes, "photography has always played an integral role in the maintenance of the political and social hegemony of whiteness. . . . The technology of the camera is not innocent, nor are the images it produces or the people who make them" (xx). As I discuss in greater detail in my analysis of the Susie King Taylor StoryMap, photographs of the war tend to depict white men, contributing to contemporary public perceptions of the Civil War as a white event. While images such as the ones of Greenhow and Boyd are consistent with this visual trend, they also call attention to the roles that white middle- and upper-class women played during the conflict. Though largely ignored in conventional histories, "The War caused many southern women to move beyond the traditional feminine sphere and to take responsibilities usually reserved for men," Harrison asserts (243). Exemplifying Harrison's point, Greenhow worked as a Confederate spy, capitalizing on conventional expectations of gender to acquire and share information. But without the digital biography to contextualize the image, site users do not know what they are looking at; the image loses its meaning. Helping them understand what they see, the accompanying alphabetic text inevitably influences how the photograph is understood.

Discursively, Greenhow is framed as a Confederate heroine in the ABT's digital biography, an angle that is woven throughout the narrative. "Unfortunately for the Federal government," as the opening paragraph reads, she "was a 'Southern woman' and a Confederate spy" who was vehemently committed to her cause. Though ambiguous in meaning, this descriptor—used here and later in the brief overview of her life—implies a commitment to slavery ("Rose O'Neal Greenhow"). Though excluded from the ABT's discussion of Greenhow, she was born into a slave-owning family around 1813 or 1814 in Montgomery County, Maryland. An iteration of the ABT's account claimed that Greenhow was "thirteen or fourteen, her *mother* died suddenly,"[6] though it was Greenhow's father, John O'Neal, who passed when she was young ("Rose O'Neal Greenhow," emphasis added). "Unable to take care of Rose and her sister," the passage read, "her *father* sent them to live with relatives in Washington, D.C." ("Rose O'Neal Greenhow," emphasis added). Exemplifying the ease with which websites can be amended, this error has since been corrected, but there is no record or acknowledgment of this change. Because these biographies inform subsequent retellings, such mistakes potentially ripple outward into new sites

FIGURE 1. *Mrs. Rose Green-how,* taken between 1855 and 1865. Circulating widely online, the photograph is featured in the ABT's digital biography of Greenhow. Credit: Library of Congress, Brady-Handy Collection, Prints & Photographs Division, LC-BH82- 4513.

of memory. Though it has since been amended on the ABT site, this particular inaccuracy has noteworthy rhetorical consequences. While Greenhow does not discuss the circumstance of her father's death in her book, secondary sources have dug more deeply into this facet of her early life. According to Greenhow's biographer Ann Blackman, O'Neal fell from his horse when he was drunk, causing significant head injuries. Jacob, a man enslaved by Greenhow's father, found O'Neal "past recovery" and "gave him one blow in a moment of intoxication occasioned by the imprudence of [O'Neal] in furnishing him with a large quantity of whiskey" (63). While the doctor was unable to determine which injury led to O'Neal's death, Jacob was ultimately blamed for the incident and sentenced to death by hanging (Blackman 60–63). Though this incident is seldom addressed in common biographies, when it is taken up, Jacob is often reported to have "murdered" O'Neal.[7] Such a framing, particularly when cleaved from the broader context of slavery, paints her father as a victim, inviting the audience to sympathize with Greenhow and her early losses.

Although explicit discussion of Greenhow's mother and father is scrubbed from the most recent version of the ABT's digital biography, the current retelling similarly primes site users to identify with Greenhow, noting that she was "born into obscurity" and that she was "mocked for her low birth" ("Rose O'Neal Greenhow"). While her marriage to Dr. Robert Greenhow helped elevate her "socialite" status, he died in a tragic accident before the start of the Civil War. After her husband's passing, Greenhow further worked to establish herself in the city, using a government pension to buy "a house four blocks north of the White House," as noted in the ABT's retelling. To illustrate the reach of her influence, the ABT mentions some of her most famous acquaintances, including Dolley Madison, General P. G. T. Beauregard, William Seward, and Jefferson Davis. This powerful but politically diverse assemblage of figures helps substantiate the claim that Greenhow "maintained political alliance with Southern Democrats and Northern Republican," but when the Civil War broke out, she firmly aligned herself with the Confederacy," prompting her to become a spy ("Rose O'Neal Greenhow").

The leader of an espionage ring that "spanned several states and included 48 women and two men," Greenhow is portrayed as a bold and defiant woman fiercely dedicated to the cause ("Rose O'Neal Greenhow"). In holding this position, she bucked traditional expectations of gender, but because these violations were committed in service of the Confederacy, they were deemed acceptable by many Southern stakeholders who otherwise followed upheld conventional constructions of gender. Although the ABT notes that Greenhow undertook several different espionage missions, its account of her contributions to the First Battle of Manassas is particularly detailed. Echoing Greenhow's own account of the event, the ABT reports that she learned that the Union intended to "consolidat[e] their forces and . . . advance on Manassas" ("Rose O'Neal Greenhow"). While she doesn't explain in her book how she acquired this information, the retelling asserts that it came from Henry Wilson, a senator from Massachusetts who actively opposed slavery, as explained on the site. Though not articulated explicitly, there is an underlying sense that she charmed him into sharing this intelligence, a point that is substantiated in other sources, including digital documents on the National Archives website, which reports that Wilson had professed his love for Greenhow. The ABT explains that Greenhow enlisted the aid of a fellow female spy to deliver these plans to Confederate officials. In her book, she does not reveal the name of her accomplice, but adding a sense of authenticity to the narrative, the ABT identifies her co-conspirator as Bettie Duvall. Offering intriguing details about their venture, the ABT reports that "Rose wrote a cipher and hid the note in Duvall's hair. Duvall then snuck out of Washington dressed as a lowly farmer woman and made her way to . . . Virginia" to deliver the information to Confederate forces ("Rose O'Neal Greenhow"). Greenhow's plan worked: "the Confederate Army was able to consolidate their forces and prepare for the Federal attack." Suggestive of a connection between Greenhow's efforts and the outcome of the event, the ABT then reports that the Confederates won "the First Battle of Manassas," also known by Unionists as the First Battle of Bull Run ("Rose O'Neal Greenhow"). As framed in this retelling, Greenhow was a key player in this event, helping to secure an important Confederate victory.

But exemplifying how women's experiences are excluded from more predominant military histories of the war, Greenhow's labors don't travel much outside of her biography on the ABT website, a point that is made particularly visible through the biography's hyperlinks. As is common, there are links embedded into the ABT's narrative of Greenhow, which take site users to other internal pages associated with relevant historical actors and events. While hyperlinks "facilitat[e] interconnectedness among different sources," they are also an act of rhetorical selection: determining what words and phrases are chosen and then linked to what sites informs the meaning of the text (Haskins, "Between Archive and Participation" 405). Adding layers to Greenhow's biography, the hyperlinks alter the memory born from digital sites. Shaping how site users understand Greenhow's narrative, her biography links to the ABT page "Bull Run: First Manassas," which describes the "first full-scale battle of the Civil War." But undermining its discussion of Greenhow's contributions, "Bull Run: First Manassas" neither mentions the intelligence that she and Duvall shared with Beauregard nor reciprocally links to her biography. Participating in white androcentric visions of the war, the ABT's account of this battle focuses primarily on Union General Irvin McDowell and Confederate General P. G. T. Beauregard and the soldiers who fought and died under their leadership. Although Greenhow's contributions are extraordinary when considered individually, they are rendered less significant, and even hyperbolic, in more status quo narratives. In this way, "Bull Run: First Manassas" is considered "history" proper, while Greenhow's experiences exist on the periphery as "women's history."

While details of such incredible acts are entertaining, they problematically elevate memories of Greenhow. Failing to address what motivated her to defy convention, this retelling echoes Lost Cause visions of the war that ignore the role that slavery played in this much-disputed event. Such acts of reflection/ deflection can also be observed in the ABT's retelling of Greenhow's prison experiences. As explained in the biography, "Rose, while brilliant at collecting information, was careless about storing information. She kept copies of messages sent to Beauregard in coded and decoded form, maps of the Union fortifications, and other incriminating documentation in her home" ("Rose O'Neal

FIGURE 2. *Greenhow, Mrs. & Daughter (Imprisoned in Old Capitol Prison in Washington D.C.) Confederate Spy,* taken prior to 1864. This photograph is also included in the ABT's brief biography of Greenhow. Credit: Library of Congress, Brady-Handy Collection, Prints & Photographs Division, LC-BH832- 2492.

Greenhow"). Her cover was blown when Detective Allen Pinkerton confirmed that she was responsible for leaking intelligence to the Confederacy and placed her under house arrest in August 1861. Paralleling her own account, the ABT reports that Greenhow consistently defied these orders, speaking to her determination and loyalty to the cause. Depicted as a paragon of female strength and devotion, Greenhow actively defied Union authority. Referencing key scenes from her memoir, the ABT describes Greenhow's continued attempts to run the espionage ring while under house arrest, explaining that she "was able to communicate with members of her network via different colored handkerchiefs that she waved through the window and notes that were smuggled in and out of her house" ("Rose O'Neal Greenhow"). Because of these antics, she was transferred to the Old Capitol Prison in Washington, DC.

Visually complementing this experience is an image featuring Greenhow and her young daughter Rose (fig. 2). Contextualizing the photograph, the caption explains that the picture was taken in 1862 at the Old Capitol Prison where the mother and daughter were held after Greenhow's arrest. But further testifying to her commitment to the Confederacy, even this imprisonment "did not stop Rose from being a nuisance." As the ABT describes it, she "smuggle[d] in a

Confederate flag to her prison cell and wave it from the prison window" ("Rose O'Neal Greenhow"). Although Greenhow resisted the Union at every turn, this image advances another story, one intended to elicit sympathy from its viewers. Documenting her plight as a mother in prison, it captures Greenhow sitting in a chair outside the prison; she appears solemn as she clutches "Little Rose" around the waist and holds her close. Casting Greenhow in a sympathetic light, the image captures her plight as a mother in prison and, more broadly, the sacrifices she made on behalf of the Confederacy during the war. As Jacqueline Glass Campbell observes, Confederate women "saw their roles as vital to the preservation of both the southern family and the southern nation, linking their personal survival to the larger goal of southern independence" (104). Greenhow's loyalty and sacrifice are made visible in this photograph of her and her daughter, a point that is augmented by the closing textual sections of the ABT biography.

Greenhow's espionage work and time in prison made her a Confederate "hero," in the language of the ABT, but further extricating gendered acts from Confederate objectives, the organization also describes how, though the Union banished her to the South, she took the daring step of violating these orders to travel to Great Britain and France on a "diplomatic mission . . . to garner support and funds" ("Rose O'Neal Greenhow"). While in England, she wrote her memoir *My Imprisonment and the First Year of Abolition Rule at Washington.* Financially lucrative, her book yielded "'two thousand dollars' worth of gold,' which Greenhow purportedly planned to donate to the Confederacy" ("Rose O'Neal Greenhow"). But before she could follow through with this transaction, she died unexpectedly, making her a martyr for the Confederate cause. A passenger aboard a British blockage runner headed for the United States, Greenhow drowned with her pockets full of gold when the captain ran the boat aground after it was observed by Union ships. As articulated by the ABT, "Her body was found several days later and was buried with full military honors by the Confederacy. After her death, she became a revered symbol for the Confederate Cause and left a legacy of Confederate espionage" ("Rose O'Neal Greenhow").

Today, the canonization of Greenhow continues through the many digital biographies that amplify her exceptional experiences as a female spy and prisoner, including those produced by the ABT, an established source of Civil War memory. While her book inspires these sensational retellings, it also documents her explicit white supremacist beliefs, but as retold in popular media, this facet of her war story is expurgated from memory. A narrative repercussion of this omission, she is depicted as a decidedly modern, even admirable, woman. Severing purpose from action, these retellings focus on white heroism, ignoring the role that race and slavery played in this contentious event.

Belle Boyd

Hyperlinked from the ABT page on Greenhow, the digital biography of "Maria 'Belle' Boyd" is recommended as a companion read, the first entry on the list. Sharing many commonalities, Greenhow and Boyd were both Confederate spies who were eventually caught and imprisoned by the Union, and subsequently, fled to England where they wrote books about their war experiences. Though more dramatic, even apocryphal at moments, *Belle Boyd in Camp and Prison* was written to damage the Union legacy in the eyes of Boyd's British readers, who generally opposed slavery. Attempting to shatter the beliefs that the Union was motivated by moral disapproval of human bondage, Boyd asserts that the North strategically capitalized on abolitionist sentiment to secure greater support for the Union. While this argument persists in some contemporary conversations of the war, Boyd wields it here to promote the "positive good" view of slavery. While her proslavery position certainly informed her commitment to the Confederacy, this view is commonly expurgated from the many retellings of her story that circulate online.

Most typically, biographies frame Boyd as a daring and duplicitous woman devoted to the Confederacy. Found on thousands of sites across the web, these retellings further exemplify how discursive acts of rhetorical selection can contribute to a whitewashed perspective of the war. Following suit, the ABT's biography of Boyd focuses on her experiences as a spy and prisoner while censoring any discussion of slavery. Although many of the biographies hosted on the ABT site are anonymously composed, the nearly 900-word entry on "Maria 'Belle' Boyd" is attributed to Mary Lou Groh. There is no additional context provided about the author or explanation as to why she was assigned to write this piece, but the site does include a list of the sources that she consulted. Further confirming the commemorative power of memoir, Groh draws considerably from *Belle Boyd in Camp and Prison* in her rendition of Boyd's life. Though Groh concedes that the book is "exaggerated" in parts, she nonetheless excerpts some of its most incredible scenes, many of which depict Boyd resisting conventional scripts of gender but also manipulating them for her benefit. While this retelling reveals how Confederate women like Boyd threatened the Union, absent of her proslavery commitments, it generally casts Boyd in a positive, though melodramatic, light.

FIGURE 3. *Belle Boyd,* taken between 1855 and 1865. The photograph of the Confederate spy is featured in her ABT biography. Credit: Library of Congress, Brady-Handy Collection, Prints & Photographs Division, LC-BH82- 4864 A.

Aligning with the generic conventions of biographies, the ABT's entry on Boyd commences with a visual of its subject (fig. 3). Unlike many of the women discussed in these case studies whose images are captured in only one or two photographs, many extant pictures of Boyd are in circulation. After the war, as Groh explains, Boyd performed dramatic reenactments of her experiences as a Confederate spy, "bill[ing] her show as 'The Perils of a Spy' and herself as 'Cleopatra of the Secession.'" To help publicize these endeavors, Boyd was the subject of many photographs, including the one repurposed in the ABT entry. Taken around 1870, this *carte de visite* is also part of the Brady-Handy Photograph Collection located in the Prints and Photographs Online Catalog at the Library of Congress. Depicting Boyd standing next to a chair with her arm draped over the top of it, the image captures her dramatically gazing downward. Commenting on the dress's "hanging sleeves and elaborate bodice," Kennedy-Nolle surmises that the gown was likely "a costume for one of her theater roles. Her hair is pulled into a fashionable 'waterfall'—a departure from the modest, smooth styles worn during the war years" (12). Though it helps diversify male-oriented visions of the war, the image has a histrionic quality to it that is brought more clearly into focus with Groh's retelling of Boyd.

As is typical of many biographical accounts, the ABT begins its narrative of Boyd by discussing her early family life, but following rhetorical patterns also observed in the ABT's account of Greenhow, this retelling does not acknowledge that she "was the daughter of a locally prominent slave owning family" (Faust 215). Instead, as Groh euphemistically phrases it, Boyd was born into a "prosperous family with strong Southern ties" in Martinsburg, Virginia (now West Virginia). But her father's position as an enslaver is not acknowledged in the ABT account, even as Groh notes that he "was a soldier in the Stonewall Brigade" and "at least three other members of her family were convicted of being Confederate spies." Groh also neglects to mention Boyd's slave, Eliza Corsey, whom Boyd discusses at length in her book. As previously noted, Boyd uses Corsey to animate the "positive good" view of slavery, including several passages in her book that document the devotion of her "maid," who chose to stay with Boyd, even when she had a chance to escape. Far from extraneous, such details offer site users essential context for understanding what motivated Boyd and her family to pursue such drastic measures in their support of the Confederacy.

Although Boyd worked as a nurse at the start of the war, an experience that she briefly discusses in her book, the ABT biography begins with the story of her deadly encounter with a Union soldier, a narrative that is repeated in many biographical accounts of her life. Reflecting the extraordinary dimensions of *Belle Boyd in Camp and Prison,* Groh writes that Boyd "shot and killed a drunken Union soldier." To contextualize this dramatic and violent scene, Groh draws from Boyd's memoir to explain that the soldier had insulted Boyd and her mother. As Boyd describes the situation, "I could stand it no longer . . . we ladies were obliged to go armed in order to protect ourselves as best we might from insult and outrage'" (quoted in Groh). Drawing from Boyd's book again, Groh reports that Boyd's actions were vindicated, because it was determined that Boyd had committed no wrongdoing: "the commanding officer . . . inquired into all the circumstances with strict impartiality, and finally said I had 'done perfectly right'" (quoted in Groh). Documenting this kind of harassment does the important work of illustrating for contemporary readers the violent circumstances that some Confederate women faced. As historian Crystal N. Feimster asserts in an important though controversial article, "many southern women feared sexual assault," and hundreds, perhaps thousands of women suffered rape, though, such narratives were also used as propaganda during the war to slander the Union (127). Although there is no clear consensus on the legitmacy of Boyd's reported experiences, this story is often presented as fact in many retellings. Reflective of sensational narrative priorities, this tension goes unexplored. Instead, Boyd is uncritically depicted as a fearless woman who bravely stands up to her Union oppressor by shooting him dead in his tracks.

While Boyd's encounter with the Union soldier has been replayed repeatedly in her biographies, her spy experiences feature even more prominently in common retellings. Groh's account is no exception in this regard, but notably, her rendition highlights the ire that Boyd provoked in Union media, suggestive of the disruption that she and other Confederate woman caused during the war. As McCurry asserts, "The damage to the distinction—the disruption of the pairing of women and innocence and the related erosion of civilian immunity— had roots in the struggle of the Union Army with the enemy women" (54). Indicative of this break, Groh explains that the Union press nicknamed Boyd "'La Belle Rebelle' . . . 'the Rebel Joan of Arc,' and 'Amazon of Secessia.'" When employed in their earliest context, these monikers were meant to slight Boyd, drawing readers' attention to a new enemy. To similar effect, Groh includes a passage from a *New York Tribune* article that comments on Boyd's dramatic dress. Reviewing the Confederate iconography that Boyd incorporated into her attire, the passage reports that Boyd wore "a gold palmetto tree [pin] beneath her beautiful chin, a Rebel soldier's belt around her waist, and a velvet band across her forehead with the seven stars of the Confederacy shedding their pale light therefrom." The intricate details offered in this passage sharpen the violent punch line that follows: "the only additional ornament she required to render herself perfectly beautiful was a Yankee halter [noose] encircling her neck." As these excerpts illustrate, Northern media attacked Confederate women like Boyd through misogynistic rhetoric that sought to scorn and scare them into submission, alluding to the very real threat that Boyd and other Confederate women like her posed to the Union.

Building on this impression, Groh shares several stories about Boyd's espionage efforts, directly excerpting some of the more enthralling passages in *Belle Boyd in Camp and Prison*. Focusing specifically on her inventions during the battle of Front Royal, one of her most notable accomplishments, Groh recounts how Boyd discovered Union Major General Nathaniel Banks's plans to retreat, compelling her to ride fifteen miles to share intelligence with Confederate Major General Thomas J. 'Stonewall' Jackson. Retelling the exciting and thrilling story, Groh explains how Boyd ran on the battlefield at Front Royal to share valuable logistical information with Jackson. In Boyd's words, as repeated on the ABT site, "the Federal pickets . . . immediately fired upon me . . . my escape was most providential . . . rifle-balls flew thick and fast about me . . . so near my feet as to throw dust in my eyes . . . numerous bullets whistled by my ears, several actually pierced different parts of my clothing" (quoted in Groh). Rhetorically selective, this fast-moving scene calls attention to the extraordinary lengths to which Boyd went in service of the Confederacy. Indicative of the significance of her efforts, the Confederacy won this battle, and citing Boyd's memoir, Groh reports that Jackson "acknowledged her contribution and her bravery in a personal note." Though Groh goes to great lengths to demonstrate the contributions that Boyd made to the Confederacy, illustrative of how women's labors are frequently segregated from male-centric scripts, Boyd's purported role in this victory is not mentioned elsewhere on the ABT site, including the biographies of Banks and Jackson that are hyperlinked in this section of Boyd's page.

But while Boyd's story is excluded from dominant narratives of the war, typical retellings of her life do not acknowledge her white supremacist beliefs, exemplifying the ways rhetorical selection shapes public memory. Instead, common retellings of Boyd focus on the ways that she used traditional expectations of gender to her advantage. Focusing the more deceitful elements of her espionage work, Groh excerpts a passage that describes how Boyd used her feminine wiles to elicit Union secrets from unsuspecting Federal soldiers, further exemplifying how gendered notions of the civilian radically shifted during the war. As Groh reports, "On one occasion [Boyd] wooed a Northern soldier to whom she wrote, 'I am indebted for some very remarkable effusions, some withered flowers, and last, but not least, for a great deal of very important information . . . I must avow the flowers and the poetry were comparatively valueless in my eyes.' Boyd continued, 'I allowed but one thought to keep possession of my mind—the thought that I was doing all a woman could do for her country's cause.'" In feigning interest in the Union soldier, Boyd was able to elicit key Union secrets, throwing into doubt the role that women generally played during times of war. Although such acts of deception potentially push the bounds of Boyd's respectability, Groh reiterates that Boyd was driven to such extremes by an overwhelming sense of loyalty to the Confederacy. As Boyd asserts in a passage recirculated by Groh, "I was doing all a woman could do for her country's cause."

It is worth noting that while discussions of how Boyd used her sexuality to her advantage are prevalent in digital retellings, so too are remarks about her appearance, bringing into greater relief how deviation from conventional gendered scripts can be quickly and severely punished. Citing a source "contemporary" to Boyd, Groh reports that "'without being beautiful, [Boyd] is very attractive . . . quite tall . . . a superb figure . . . and dressed with much taste.'"

Other digital accounts of Boyd, however, are much harsher. The *Encyclopedia Virginia*, for example, references historian John Bakeless who reported that Boyd "wasn't really an especially pretty girl. Surviving portraits show that she looked rather like one of those horses she rode so perfectly—a long face, a very long nose, and prominent teeth" (quoted in DeMarco). The instinct to address Boyd's appearance affirms the observation made by Rosie White: when "women spies cross the boundaries of femininity . . . [they] are shepherded back to it by visual codes of beauty, whiteness and heterosexuality" (4). Pervading popular depictions of women, historical or otherwise, discussions of Boyd's physical appearance make clear how slippery such retellings can be. Foregrounding the exceptional, these narratives nimbly move from celebrating Boyd to degrading her, suggestive of the fine line between admiration and disgust in public memories of sensational women.

Similar to narratives of Greenhow, common retellings also discuss Boyd's experiences as a Union prisoner, signifying to site users Boyd's willingness to sacrifice even her freedom for the Confederacy. Although she was arrested several times for her work as a spy, Boyd "managed to avoid incarceration until 29 July 1862, when she was finally imprisoned in Old Capitol Prison in Washington, D.C.," as Groh explains. But like Greenhow, Boyd was a defiant prisoner: "She waved Confederate flags from her window, she sang Dixie, and devised a unique method of communicating with supporters outside. Her contact would shoot a rubber ball into her cell with a bow and arrow and Boyd would sew messages inside the ball" (Boyd quoted in Groh). Through these narratives of defiance, Groh helps perpetuate Lost Cause visions of Confederate women who, unwavering in their support of the Confederacy, endure great personal sacrifice for the greater good of the cause.

In the closing sections of the ABT biography, Goh turns the audience's attention to Boyd's domestic affairs, adding to the drama of the retelling. After Boyd was released from prison in December 1863, she was banished to the South, but like Greenhow, she fled to England instead. Though subsequently arrested, she met Union naval officer Samuel Wylde Hardinge, who, as Groh explains, helped Boyd escape to Canada before meeting her in England where the two wedded on 25 August 1864. Though Groh notes that the couple lived in England for two years, she withholds discussion of Hardinge's arrest and Boyd's letter to President Lincoln that asked for her husband's release in return for suppressing the publication of *Belle Boyd in Camp and Prison*. After Hardinge died a few years later, Boyd returned to the United States, as Groh reports, but spotlighting the sensational, the ABT narrative reveals that Boyd married two more times: first, in 1869, she wed John Swainston Hammond, an Englishman who fought on behalf of the Union; they were married for sixteen years and had four children together. But as Groh continues to explain, Boyd divorced Hammond in 1884 and married Nathaniel High Jr. two months later, noting that High was seventeen years her junior. While such intimate details can make for exciting stories, they also diminish Boyd's ethos, calling into question her loyalties and moral code. But discussion of Boyd's postwar relationships makes the absence of her proslavery statements all the more conspicuous. While Groh deems these marriages worthy of narrative space, Boyd's proslavery positions that animate her commitment to the Confederacy are not.

As is typical of biographical genres, the ABT page closes with information about Boyd's death. As Groh reports, Boyd "died, in poverty, of a heart attack at age 56 on 11 June 1900 while on tour in Kilbourn (now Wisconsin Dells), Wisconsin. She is buried there, in Spring Grove Cemetery." While the circumstances of her death are tragic, her legacy as a Civil War spy continues to live on in service of Lost Cause visions of the past. As memorized in both physical and digital sites, Boyd was a dedicated and courageous women who subverted rigid standards of gender to support a cause in which she so vehemently believed. What motivates that commitment, however, goes unspoken, illustrating the power of rhetorical selection informed by whiteness to shape narratives of the past that continue to haunt the present.

Selective Memories and Lingering Visions of the Lost Cause

Though seemingly benign, the Vindicatrix bears traces of Lost Cause ideologies that maintain that the Confederacy fought a just and moral war over freedom and state's rights. A symbol of white supremacy, the statue pays homage to Southern women and their love for and devotion to the Confederacy. But in this act of rhetorical selection, white women's connection to slavery is ignored, burying the distinct ways they supported and benefited from human bondage. Like the Vindicatrix, common retellings of Greenhow and Boyd advance white supremacist notions of a righteous South, failing to reckon with the legacy of slavery. While they take different commemorative shapes—each with distinct mnemonic limitations and affordances—common biographies of Greenhow and Boyd similarly uncouple their gender-defying endeavors from the racist ideologies that inspired them. Though my analysis focuses on only two examples of how they are reconstructed in one official site of Civil War memory, they are generally representative of how whiteness shapes the ways their stories are retold in the digital sphere: while their transgressive experiences as women are magnified to advance liberatory visions, their white supremacist views are omitted or abated. Exemplifying the power of rhetorical selection to seemly disaggregate issues of gender from race, Greenhow and Boyd are thus depicted as valiant women. Though my analysis focuses on how they are represented by the American Battlefield Trust, this rhetorical trend is generally representative of how whiteness shapes the ways their stories are generally retold in the digital sphere.

Because the "Past is never dead. It's not even past," as William Faulkner poetically reminds us, these retellings have sociocultural consequences. Participating in the epideictic tradition, such accounts give rise to public memories that shape views of the past for purposes of the present. In magnifying their exceptional experiences while severing their connection to slavery, biographical retellings, including those hosted by the ABT, depoliticize their very political stories. Exemplifying the power of rhetorical selection, Greenhow and Boyd are thus depicted as valiant women, while more generally, the war is disconnected from human bondage. These sanitized depictions quietly work to buoy Lost Cause ideology that helps sustain current iterations of white supremacy through a pretense of supposed neutrality. Without acknowledging the role that white women played in the institution of human bondage, past injustices and their lasting effects can never be righted, as I argue in this chapter and throughout the book.

But of significance, mechanisms of memory are malleable. On 8 July 2020, the Vindicatrix statue that was perched on a 60-foot column above Jefferson Davis was finally removed after its long tenure in the former Confederate capitol. Elevated in a boom lift, workers pried the copper statue loose; then, after it was secured with straps, they attached the figure to a crane and lowered it to the ground where it was loaded onto a truck and carted off to an unknown location. Many hands participated in this laborious endeavor, as scores of people looked on, watching history in the making. Requiring significantly less effort and no heavy equipment, online biographies can be amended to offer a fuller view of the war. Though memory is inescapably incomplete, what is reflected and deflected in common retellings can be refocused to acknowledge slavery and the role that it played in Greenhow's and Boyd's experiences of the war. Adding new layers to the monolith of memory, such nuanced retellings hold them accountable for efforts to preserve human bondage while doing the necessary work of disrupting white romanticized visions of the past.

CHAPTER 2

Layers of the Past

Ways of Remembering Harriet Tubman

[M]emory is the product of a multitude of impulses, drawn together in the
form of a collage, or approximation of a past event.

 —Jay Winter, *Remembering War*

While most Confederate statues were removed from Richmond, Virginia's
Monument Avenue in the months following the murder of George Floyd, the
figure of Robert E. Lee on his horse remained in the former Confederate capitol
until September 2021. Though then-Governor Ralph Northam pledged to take
down the monument, a symbol that was erected in the Jim Crow era to promote racial segregation, several injunctions were filed against the state to keep
the 21-foot bronze statue temporarily in place. But suggestive of how public
memories are "'overwritten' by new stories that speak more directly to latter-
day concerns and are more relevant to latter-day identity formations," citizens
took matters into their own hands, painting the monument and its plinth with
statements like "Black Lives Matter" and "Stop White Supremacy" (Erll and
Rigney 2). In a similar attempt to "reappropriat[e] the symbolic value of . . . [the
Confederate] statue in favor of Black history," multimedia artists Dustin Klein
and Alex Criqui used a light projector to superimpose images of well-known
Black figures—including Floyd himself—onto the statue, adding another coat
of memory to the Confederate monument (Sanchez and Moore).[1] While these
various commemorative efforts prompt questions about who is memorialized,
why, how, and by what forces, they are also broadly instructive, illustrating in a
visual way how public memory emerges from layers of material and discursive
sources that generally reflect the particular time, location, and sociocultural
context in which they were developed.

Surveying the rhetorical dimensions of memory's layers, I examine in this
chapter pieces of the ever-changing commemorative whole that have helped

propagate public recollections of Harriet Tubman, one of the many notable Black leaders that Klein and Criqui projected onto the Lee monument. Inviting reflection on how Black women in particular are remembered in the context of the American Civil War, Tubman's image serves as a reminder that, despite concerted efforts to diversify perspectives of the war, women of color are taken up far less frequently in the commemorative enterprises that give rise to memories of this influential event. As historian Thavolia Glymph confirms, "The story of black women's fight, the war they waged for Union and freedom and to be accorded even the small rights white women claimed, continues to exist on the margins of the Civil War historiography. Their politics and their wartime struggles remain largely invisible" (10). Although Tubman is one of the most widely recognized Black figures in the United States, Glymph's observation generally holds true for this notable figure as well. While she is the subject of many sites of memory, including a growing number of monuments, two national parks, two US postage stamps, and an award-winning biopic film, these sources most commonly center Tubman's experiences with the Underground Railroad. Though her work on this front is worthy of celebration, it has historically been the primary focus of her legacy, overshadowing other ways that she advanced racial equality. In addition to her work as a Union nurse, spy, and scout, Tubman also contributed to the planning and execution of the Combahee River Raid, considered "the largest and most successful slave rebellion in the US history": 756 enslaved people were liberated during the mission (Fields-Black xxiii). Despite the historic significance of her service, this dimension of Tubman's life has been given short shrift in common commemorative enterprises.

Peeling back the layers that contributed to this dominant vision of Tubman, I first analyze the biographies of Tubman written by Sarah Hopkins Bradford. Commemorative cornerstones, Bradford's books "infected for good or ill, almost all subsequent biographical portraits" of Tubman, as Milton C. Sernett attests (4). Suggestive of how sites of memory are infused with a carbonlike residue, these accounts capture the evolving social views of the war espoused by the dominant white culture. Published in 1869 "while many Northerners were still in a triumphal mood," *Scenes in the Life of Harriet Tubman* offers a more complex version of Tubman's service to the Union (Sernett 340). In addition to sharing details of her militaristic contributions, *Scenes* also documents her experiences with racism in both Northern and Southern states. But supplanting this commemorative layer, Bradford released *Harriet, the Moses of*

Her People in 1886. Though there is considerable overlap between these books, Bradford's description of Tubman's war experiences in *Moses* bear traces of the "reconciliationist vision" of the war, which foregrounded white reunion while minimizing Black contributions and experiences. Exemplifying how new layers can erode established memories, *Moses* has had a lasting impact on how Tubman has been remembered, circulating widely as "the reprint of choice" (Larson 269). Though memory and the sites from which it arises are in constant flux, certain ways of seeing the past can ossify, becoming "so habitual as to be taken for granted," in the words of Kendall Phillips ("The Failure of Memory" 218). As this particular vision of Tubman has been retold and repeated over time, her association with the Underground Railroad has become more entrenched in American public memory.

But demonstrating the web's potential to crack open fossilized views of the past, a growing number of digital sites have taken up Tubman's service to the Union, promoting a more inclusive vision of the war that incorporates Black women's experiences. Probing this trend, I focus specifically on how she is represented online by the National Park Service (NPS), a federal agency charged with "preserv[ing] unimpaired the natural and cultural resources and values of the National Park System for the enjoyment, education, and inspiration of this and future generations" ("About Us"). Though the NPS oversees many physical properties, it has a considerable web presence that provides information on its parks and historic sites while also serving as an instructional resource. In service of this mission, the NPS hosts hundreds of digital pages featuring famous historical figures, including Tubman. In its biographical account of Tubman, the NPS does discuss her Civil War labors, though in limited ways. But illuminating the commemorative possibility of digital media, the article "Harriet Tubman and the 54th Massachusetts" was created in August 2020. Detailing Tubman's fight against the Confederacy during the Civil War, this piece adds a critical layer that contours how Tubman is remembered in the public sphere. Deepening awareness of her service to the Union, this article offers key details about Tubman's war experiences, particularly as they concern the Combahee River Raid. Such an addition demonstrates that, in contrast to physical monuments and memorials, online biographies can be amended with relative ease to accommodate new historical perspectives as well as evolving social mores. As I discuss throughout this chapter, the power to readily add, edit, and erase information can be both advantageous and detrimental to diversifying public memory. While the NPS exemplifies how websites can make meaningful contributions to ways of seeing the past, these advances can just as easily be revised or reframed for less than noble purposes.

The Medium Is the Memory

Though memory is generated in the mind of an individual, it is "crystallized" and "finds refuge" in what Pierre Nora calls *lieux de mémoire,* or sites of memory that are rhetorically crafted to prompt particular visions of the past (7). Motivated by a desire to remember, these sources inform present perspectives that reflect the commemorative needs and desires of discrete communities. The rhetorical mechanisms used to communicate that memory vary widely, collectively constituting what Nathan R. Johnson terms "memory's infrastructure," the many "pieces of a past . . . [that] anchor, shape, and compose remembering and forgetting" (15). Shaping how we understand the days of yore, the apparatuses that give rise to public memory are vast, each possessing distinct affordances and limitations. Exemplifying how the medium shapes the memory, the creation and maintenance of monuments and memorials, for example, require time, political power, coordination, and funding; as such, they are limited in production and thus rhetorically elevated as signifiers of memory. But what amplifies the suasive impact of these sites also restricts them: the relative temporal, spatial, and material fixity of these entities constrains their capacity to respond to changing social and cultural beliefs. But memory, as we know, is not inert. While the forms that memory take are created to "stop time, to inhibit forgetting, to fix a state of things, to immortalize death, and to materialize the immaterial," as Nora observes, "it is also clear that *lieux de mémoire* thrive only because of their capacity for change, their ability to resurrect old meanings and generate new ones along with new and unforeseeable connections (this is what makes them exciting)" (15). But as exemplified by Klein and Criqui's overlay of Tubman onto Lee and the later removal of the statue, memory and the structures that produce it can change in response to the milieu in which they are created, adding dimension to visions of the past, though the impression made by the original manifestation often still lingers.

Textual sources also contribute to the commemorative landscape that constitutes public memory. As Samuel Hynes maintains, if we "take *memorial* to be the general term for a class of collective gestures of public commemoration . . . then we must surely say that . . . written recollections . . . must also be memorials" (205, emphasis in original). Bradford's biographies of Tubman are suggestive of the memorializing potential of this genre. Commonly understood as the story of a life, biographies offer a material record that shapes how a person is remembered, making "an individual life story legible beyond that individual life," as Sara C. VanderHaagen asserts, "and, in doing so, emphasize the 'public relevance of private life,' as Michael Warner put it" (10). Exemplifying Warner's claim echoed by VanderHaagen, Bradford's *Scenes* and *Moses* serve as essential commemorative devices, significantly influencing Tubman's legacy. Though biographies are nonfiction genres, they are not neutral; rather, as demonstrated by Bradford and her books, these narratives are very much shaped by the writer, their positionality, and the social circumstances that afforded them access to publication, but also the exigency that motivates writers to tell a particular story about a given subject.

In ways similar to archives, personal accounts can be incredibly influential sources of memory that beget new ways of seeing and understanding the past. While these stories can be remediated into a range of forms, web pages have distinct commemorative features. Because they can be created and updated relatively easily, they can be implemented and revised quickly, exemplifying Aaron Hess's point that "In cyberspace, architecture and material existence are not as concrete as in physical or offline memorials" (819). Responding to evolving sociocultural priorities, web pages will necessarily undergo updates and changes, but because these alterations are not publicly documented and shared, how new evidence, insights, and shifting values shape this space is not rendered legible. While there are some notable exceptions—including Wikipedia, which I discuss in chapter 3, and the Internet Archive's Wayback Machine that has been capturing web content since 1996, to name just two examples— many digital amendments do not leave traces that can be easily accessed and observed, obscuring the ways that web sites shift and layer memory over time.

Exemplifying the consequence of failing to documented web changes, when the second Trump administration came into power and ordered a "digital content refresh" (Parnell) that would purge all government websites of diversity, equity, and inclusion language, they significantly altered the NPS's page on the Underground Railroad, which is described as "one of the most significant expressions of the American civil rights movement during its evolution over more than three centuries" (Betts). Instead of leading with Tubman's quote about being a conductor on the Underground Railroad, the heading of the page featured a series of postage stamps that read "Black/White Cooperation" (Betts). After receiving significant pushback, the page was again updated, but thanks to the Wayback Machine, these iterations have been preserved. Erasing the history of memory, this example serves as an important reminder of the ephemerality and malleability of web content: what is present in one moment may change in the next; what was absent in one viewing may later appear. But when there are no records of these revisions, it becomes more difficult to track the movement of memory and the motivations and forces driving how we see and understand ourselves and each other. While this example received a lot press, alerting the public to the change in content, web revisions are often quieter. If a mistake is made and not publicly acknowledged, the error can potentially live on in subsequent re-circulations.

With each accretion, omission, and alteration, a new layer of memory is added to a bricolage of remembrance that collectively shape contemporary perspectives. "Layering thus becomes—at once—representation in space and recursive movement throughout time," in the words of Daniel Anderson and Jentery Sayers (82). Examining layers of memory reveals that, though recollections are ever evolving, when particular manifestations are repeated over time and in different contexts, they form distinct impressions of the past that contribute to views of the present. This kind of ossification can be observed in prevailing memories of Tubman. Historically, Tubman has been most commonly associated with the Underground Railroad. Leading dozens of enslaved people to freedom in Canada after she fled human bondage, she is rightfully characterized as a selfless and fearless leader. Because this version of Tubman's story was repeated in various sites, it calcified, "uphold[ing] timeless and uncontested understandings of history" (Adams 391). But while Tubman's bold and courageous endeavors are worthy of celebration, her commitment to abolition was much more capacious. Indefatigably working to lift up the newly freed while fighting to end slavery, Tubman also served the Union as a nurse, spy, and scout. But aligning with reconciliationist visions that traditionally downplayed Black experiences of the war, these contributions have been less frequently acknowledged in common sites of public memory.

Biographies as Base Layers of Memory

While murmurs of her clandestine efforts with the Underground Railroad circulated orally before the war among some enslaved populations and abolitionists, Bradford's biographies *Scenes* and *Moses* played an essential role in concretizing this vision of Tubman. Providing a written account of Tubman's life, these biographies have directly contributed to contemporary memories of her and, more generally, to social perceptions of Black women. But while Bradford's biographies broadly influence how Tubman is remembered, these base layers of memory are inevitably rhetorically selective. In ways similar to autobiographical accounts, which I take up more fully in other chapters, biographies are constructed to convey a particular impression about a particular person, but in the case of this latter genre, the narrative is not composed by the subject of the book. Inevitably informed by the writer's prejudices and proclivities, biographies carry the DNA of those who composed them. Written by Sarah Hopkins Bradford, both *Scenes* and *Moses* are imbued with the author's subject position as a white woman from the northeast corner of the United States and the specific circumstances of the historical moment in which they were composed. As such, the impression of Tubman that emerges from the pages of these discrete accounts is notably different. Analyzing these divergences, I trace in this section how Tubman is depicted in both *Scenes* and *Moses,* focusing primarily on how her war labors are characterized in each book. Illustrating how meaning changes with each addition to a text, Bradford's second account flattens recollections of Tubman's service to the Union, exemplifying how commemorative acts of layering function rhetorically to diminish particular memories. While both biographies discuss her service to the Union, even repeating several passages verbatim, *Moses* omits crucial details relating to Tubman's service, reflecting the white reconciliationist values that informed its publication. The enduring legacy of this specific vision of Tubman, I ultimately suggest, is at once connected with the popularity of *Moses* but also the ways that reconciliationist views have continued to drive public memory of the Civil War.

Due to her "unusual career" and "her ability to form and keep close relationships with a group of well-connected white antislavery activists in the North," Tubman "was a celebrity in her own day," as historian Jean M. Humez maintains (5). But to protect Tubman from retribution, stories of her exploits primarily circulated by word of mouth in the years preceding the war.[2] While oral traditions constitute distinct layers of memory, without continuously practiced customs, habits, routines, and rituals that ensure longevity, such visions of the past are made ephemeral, leaving only traces, if that, of their existence. But after Abraham Lincoln issued the Emancipation Proclamation, guaranteeing liberation for all enslaved populations not residing in border states, written accounts of Tubman began to appear with greater frequency.[3] Exemplifying the power of the written word, these accounts allowed stories of her abolitionist efforts to reach a greater and more diverse readership, inspiring hope, resilience, and defiance in those who learned about her incredible endeavors. But these accounts also helped preserve and grow her memory.

Composing the first two book-length accounts of Tubman's life, Bradford first published *Scenes,* which she later revised into *Moses.* A white woman who supported abolitionist causes, Bradford has come to be seen by many as a questionable choice for this undertaking (Humez 148–150; Larson 243; Sernett 129). The sister of Reverend Samuel M. Hopkins, a professor of theology at the Auburn Theological Seminary who "took a lifelong interest in Harriet Tubman," Bradford became acquainted with Tubman's parents, Ben and Harriet Ross, during her stay in Auburn (Sernett 112). As Bradford explains in the preface to *Scenes,* she "*wrote letters for the old people to commanding officers at the South, making inquiries about Harriet, and received answers telling of her untiring devotion to our wounded and sick soldiers, and of her efficient aid in various ways to the cause of the Union*" (3, emphasis in original).[4] Though she had some publication experience, as Larson reports, Bradford's work primarily focused on "moralistic topics as overindulgent parents and naughty children who 'owe their origin to the criminal neglect of proper parental discipline,' dead mothers and orphaned children, impoverished widows and at least one story of a fugitive slave, 'Nina'" (240). In conducting research for *Scenes,* Bradford met with Tubman to learn more about her past. While this gave Bradford the opportunity to create an invaluable, though highly imperfect, written record of Tubman's life, she notifies readers that "*Much has been left out which would have been highly interesting, because of the impossibility of substantiating by the testimony of others the truth of Harriet's statements. But whenever it has been possible to find those who were cognizant with the facts stated, they have been corroborated in every particular*" (*Scenes* 4, emphasis in original). In addition to Tubman's personal history, Bradford also draws from letters, newspapers articles, and other personal testimony to compose *Scenes.* But preparing to travel abroad, she had limited time to assemble these materials, resulting in "the very desultory and hasty manner in which this little book is written," as she abruptly notes in the middle of the biography (*Scenes* 47). An amalgamation of outside sources loosely woven together by Bradford's retelling of Tubman's life, *Scenes* helps make visible the ways in which fragments of memory combine to make a new commemorative project.

Hinting at the kinds of challenges many Black Americans faced in the years following the war, *Scenes* was published in response to Tubman's great financial need. Specifically written to "raise funds, a common tactic from antislavery days," as Catherine Clinton explains, Bradford's book was intended to provide Tubman and her family with some economic relief (*Harriet Tubman* 195). Bradford makes clear in the opening pages of *Scenes* that the income generated from the sale of her book would "ai[d] [Tubman] in ministering to the wants of her aged parents, and in the hope of securing to them the little home which they are in danger of losing from inability to pay the whole amount due"

(*Scenes* 2). The Tubmans's insolvency was related to their daughter's service to the Union, as Bradford also communicates, for the debt was only "partly paid when our heroine left them to throw herself into the work of aiding our suffering soldiers" (*Scenes* 2). Though Tubman made considerable sacrifices to provide much-needed assistance to the Union, she was denied a pension in the years following her service, contributing to her economic precarity. In his introduction to *Scenes,* Hopkins publicly speaks to this issue, writing that "Harriet Tubman's services and sufferings during the rebellion, which are acknowledged in the letters of Gen. Saxton, and others, it was thought by many, would justify the bestowment of a pension by the Government. But the difficulties in the way of procuring such relief, suggested other methods, and finally the present one" (quoted in Bradford, *Scenes,* N.P.). Speaking to the book's success, *Scenes* generated over $1,200 in profit, all of which was given to Tubman (Clinton, *Harriet Tubman* 196).

Adding a new layer of memory to Tubman's legacy, Bradford published *Moses* in 1886 in the post-Reconstruction United States. As she remarks in the preface of the revised edition, *Scenes* "ha[d] been long out of print, and the facts stated there are all unknown to the present generation" (*Moses* 6). But in addition to this commemorative exigency, Tubman had renewed financial need. Though she would finally be granted a pension in 1890,[5] prior to the publication of *Moses,* Tubman's case was repeatedly rejected "because it did not come under any recognized law," as Bradford explains to readers (6). But as she makes clear in the preface, the revenue generated from the sale of *Moses* was not intended to help Tubman herself, but rather fund a new endeavor in service of others: "the building of a hospital for old and disabled colored people" (78). Spurred by this motivation, Bradford undertook rewriting the story of Tubman's life. Larson explains the revision this way: "Though in many ways a reprint of the first edition, [*Moses*] was [a] less demanding and less detailed biography with a milder and more stereotypical image of a former slave than the Harriet Tubman of the 1869 book" (265). Though it is over two thousand words longer, Bradford's second book smooths over some of the more controversial passages of Tubman's war experiences, particularly as they concern Tubman's service to the Union and her experiences with racism in the North.

Revealing how sites of memory are comprised of different pieces of the past, both *Scenes* and *Moses* reprint an article written by Franklin Sanborn. An acquaintance of Tubman's, Sanborn served as the editor of the Boston *Commonwealth,* an anti-slavery newspaper that primarily circulated in the Northeast. Titled "Harriet Tubman," this piece was originally published on 17 July

1863. A highly influential document, Sanborn's article provided key details of Tubman's early life. Born into slavery as Araminta Ross around 1820 or 1821, Tubman spent the early years of her life on the Eastern shore of Maryland. At the age of six, she was taken from her mother and sent away to learn how to weave cloth, but as Sanborn writes, Tubman resisted this path. She was eventually hired out as a field hand, performing many labors that were typically assigned to men: she "drove oxen, carted, plowed," but also "cut wood, haul[ed] logs, etc." (*Scenes* 75–76; *Moses* 111). But in addition to highlighting her physical strength in his article, Sanborn captures her bold and uncompromising character: when Tubman was ordered to tie up an enslaved man who left his work post to go to the village store, "[s]he refused, and as the man ran away, she placed herself in the door to stop the pursuit" (*Scenes* 74; *Moses* 109). The slaveholder then threw a two-pound weight that struck Tubman in the head, resulting in injuries that left "her subject to a sort of stupor or lethargy at times; coming upon her in the midst of conversation, or whatever she may be doing, and throwing her into a deep slumber, from which she will presently rouse herself, and go on with her conversation or work" (*Scenes* 75; *Moses* 109). Adding to the mythos of her supernatural abilities, this incident, as reported in both Bradford biographies, gave Tubman clairvoyant powers that helped her make many successful trips on the Underground Railroad.

Helping to cement Tubman's legacy as "Moses," Sanborn offers one of the first published accounts that publicly discusses Tubman's work on the Underground Railroad. Republished in both biographies, the article explains that Tubman fled slavery in 1849, when she "walked away one night alone" in search of liberation (*Scenes* 76; *Moses* 111). Eventually landing in Philadelphia, she secured work and earned enough money to help her loved ones escape slavery. To this end, Tubman made several trips back to Maryland over the course of the next decade. But revealing an internal discrepancy within Bradford's books, Sanborn's article differs from the narrative that Bradford provides. While Sanborn reports that Tubman escorted dozens of people to freedom, including her elderly parents, Bradford inflates these numbers, writing that Tubman rescued more than three hundred (*Scenes* 53; *Moses* 6). Though most contemporary sources of memory suggest that Tubman helped around seventy people, roughly aligning with Sanborn's account, sources will still cite Bradford's figures, exemplifying how her biographies shaped public memories of Tubman.

When the Fugitive Slave Bill was passed in 1850 and subsequently enforced in cities like Philadelphia and Boston, Tubman and her cohort went to Canada where they would be safe "'under the paw of the British Lion'" (*Scenes* 77;

Moses 112). Taking notice of their loss of human property, slaveholders offered a "great reward" for her capture (*Scenes* 79; *Moses* 114), but Tubman's liberatory endeavors also attracted the attention of abolitionists from around the country. Sanborn explains:

> She became known to Thomas Garrett, the large-hearted Quaker of Wilmington, who has aided the escape of three thousand fugitives; she found warm friends in Philadelphia and New York, and wherever she went. These gave her money, which she never spent for her own use, but laid up for the help of her people, and especially for her journeys back to the "land of Egypt," as she called her old home. By reason of her frequent visits there, always carrying away some of the oppressed, she got among her people the name of "Moses," which it seems she still retains. (quoted in *Scenes* 78; *Moses* 114)

Recorded in Sanborn's article and then recirculated in Bradford's two biographies, the foundation of Tubman's reputation as "Black Moses" was laid.

While Bradford republished Sanborn's article in its entirety in *Scenes,* she made some consequential edits to it in *Moses.* Illustrating how written text can modify memory, Bradford excised the last third of the piece, making her second book more palatable to a late nineteenth-century white audience. Tempering some of Sanborn's more contentious discussions of pre-war politics, Bradford omits his critique of William Henry Seward, the Secretary of the State who served under President Abraham Lincoln. The likelihood of conflict between the North and South increased exponentially after Lincoln was elected to office, prompting Republican politicians to go to extraordinary lengths to persuade their Democratic colleagues to remain in the Union. Though Tubman and Seward had been acquaintances for several years, Tubman's supporters were concerned that he would turn Tubman over to authorities to appease Southern politicians and preserve the Union. Though Seward believed that slavery was immoral and actively fought against it throughout his political career, working for the newly elected President Lincoln, he proposed a federal bill that preserved slavery in the Southern states in an effort to assuage the Democratic contingent. Interpreted as a betrayal to abolitionist causes, Seward's political maneuverings damaged his reputation with those fighting for emancipation, as portrayed in Sanborn's article:

> The hunting of fugitive slaves began again. Mr. Seward went over to the side of compromise. He knew the history of this poor woman; he had

given his enemies a hold on him, by dealing with her; it was thought he would not scruple to betray her. The suspicion was an unworthy one, for though the Secretary could betray a cause, he could not surely have put her enemies on the track of a woman who was thus in his power, after such a career as hers had been. But so little confidence was then felt in Mr. Seward, by men who had voted for him and with him, that they hurried Harriet off to Canada, sorely against her will. (Sanborn quoted in *Scenes* 84)

In documenting Seward's attempts to preserve the Union at the expense of the enslaved, Sanborn's article captures the Republican party's initial hesitancy to support the abolitionist movement, an event that received renewed attention when Bradford reprinted the article in its entirety in *Scenes* in 1868. But layering over the complexities of pre-war politics, Bradford omits this passage of Sanborn's article in the publication of *Moses,* contributing to a more stream-lined narrative of emancipation and Republican support of liberation in the face of the divided nation.

Paring back her coverage of war refugees, historically referred to as "contrabands," Bradford cuts the last portion of Sanborn's letter from *Moses,* an excision that aligns with late-nineteenth-century emancipationist trends that buried Black experiences of the war. As historian Amy Murrell Taylor explains, "the nation's descent into civil war set in motion hundreds of thousands of men, women, and children—entire families, neighborhood, and communities— in a mass exodus from slavery that would strain and then destroy the institution once and for all" (5). In the early stages of this unanticipated diaspora, Federal officials forced many refugees to return to Southern slaveholders in accordance with fugitive slave laws, but realizing that the Confederate forces were using slave labor to advance their cause, Union Major General Benjamin Butler proposed a contraband policy that would benefit the Union and debilitate the South. Because the Confederate units extracted manual labor from enslaved men, Butler argued in May 1861 that the Union should retain these men as human "contraband," a "'species of property'" that were "confiscated from the enemy" (McCurry 76). Butler's model helped inspire the Confiscation Act of 1861, a federal policy that permitted the Union to seize any property, including enslaved people, that supported Confederate efforts. While some Union officials disregarded the law because they were not sympathetic to the plight of the enslaved, others found it challenging to manage the large groups of enslaved people who flocked to Union bases. But the Union was faced with different circumstances when, in November 1861, they captured South Carolina's

Sea Islands and gained possession of a significant harbor between Virginia and Florida. White residents fled the islands, leaving behind over 10,000 enslaved men, women, and children. In January 1862, General Thomas W. Sherman requested that Northern teachers be sent to help educate this population, thus beginning the Port Royal Experiment. As Sanborn explains in a part of his article that was redacted in *Moses,* Tubman "[i]nstantly . . . conceived the idea of going there and working among her people on the islands and the mainland. Money was given her, a pass was secured through the agency of Governor Andrew [of Massachusetts], and she went to Beaufort" (quoted in *Scenes* 85).

Illustrating how different vestiges of memory coalesce to form new commemorative sources, a letter that Tubman wrote Sanborn, which he published in the context of the *Commonwealth* article, is also reprinted in *Scenes* but cut from *Moses.* Dated 30 June 1863, Tubman's epistle was composed by an amanuensis, though it reads as though it were written by Tubman herself. When taking dictation, the recorder typically aims to document the reciter's spoken words with precision and accuracy. To this end, the scribe usually strives for neutrality, but transcription is inevitably a mediated undertaking that is informed by the writer and their positionality. Written in a standardized, white-coded dialect, the letter was likely composed by a missionary from New England who travelled south during the war to support the war refugees (Humez 60). Leaving their mark on this retelling, the writer helps to shape the narrative conveyed in the letter, adding another coat of memory to consider when peeling back the layers of the past. While the missive describes the aid that Tubman offered the men, women, and children fleeing slavery, it also captures the dire circumstances that the newly freed faced in the early days of freedom. "Among other duties which I have, is that of looking after the hospital here for contrabands," Tubman explains. "Most of those coming from the mainland are very destitute, almost naked. I am trying to find places for those able to work, and provide for them as best I can, so as to lighten the burden on the Government as much as possible, while at the same time they learn to respect themselves by earning their own living" (Bradford, *Scenes* 87). As reported in the letter, war refugees had very few resources to help them transition to life as free individuals in a wage-labor economy. But reprinted only in *Scenes,* this context is buried by the publication of *Moses.* As discursive fragments of these postslavery experiences fall away in Bradford's second biography, the story that the book tells about "contrabands" is inevitably altered.

Though the harsh realities that the refugees faced are somewhat mitigated in *Moses,* Tubman's devotion to this population is clearly conveyed in both books. As previously noted, she was compelled to move south during the war to help the newly freed. While the aid that Tubman provided in this context took many forms, Bradford specifically foregrounds Tubman's service as a nurse in both *Scenes* and *Moses.* Though *Scenes* reports that she cared for both Black and white soldiers (23), Tubman primarily worked at the "contraband" hospital in Beaufort before briefly serving as the "matron" of the "Colored Hospital" in Fort Monroe, Virginia toward the end of the war. By detailing Tubman's labors, Bradford offers an overview of Tubman's everyday routine while stationed in Beaufort. Told from Tubman's perspective, using a dialect intended to intimate her speech patterns, the following passage is repeated verbatim in *Scenes* and *Moses:*

> "Well, Missus, I'd go to de hospital, I would, early eb'ry mornin'. I'd get a big chunk of ice, I would, and put it in a basin, and fill it with water; den I'd take a sponge and begin. Fust man I'd come to, I'd thrash away de flies, an' dey'd rise, dey would, like bees roun' a hive. Den I'd begin to bathe der wounds, an' by de time I'd bathed off three or four, de fire and heat would have melted de ice and made de water warm, an' it would be as red as clar blood. Den I'd go an' git more ice, I would, an' by de time I got to de nex' ones, de flies would be roun' de fust ones black an' thick as eber.' *In this way she worked, day after day, till late at night . . . (Scenes* 37; *Moses* 98, emphasis in the originals)

Offering a glimpse into her experiences as a nurse in a contraband hospital, this passage hints at the limited resources available to the newly freed and the sanitation challenges that Tubman and others faced as a result, but before expounding on this point, Bradford's transcription of Tubman's nursing exploits and its rhetorical impact warrant discussion.

Though "related by [Tubman] herself" (Bradford, *Scenes* 38; *Moses* 7), the nursing excerpt and others of a similar nature exhibit "white writers' ideas about 'authentic' black vernacular speech," as Vivian May rightly asserts (42). In contrast to Tubman's letter to Sanborn, which was written in a white dialect, Bradford's use of a Black dialect leaves "contemporary readers . . . to wade through the rhetorical and historical muck" (42). While Bradford supported Tubman and, more generally, the anti-slavery movement, the dialect is reflective of her positionality as a nineteenth-century American white woman and, as such, is imbued with common racial prejudices of the period that persist today. Echoing features of local color literature that was popular after the war, Bradford's parlance attempts to capture the cadence of Tubman's speech, but indicative of a misalignment between intent and impact, it reads as a "caricature" (May 42). Presupposing a white-coded linguistic standard, Bradford's dialect is constructed to connotate intellectual and cultural inferiority. Discursively linked to a Black woman's body, Tubman's speech is racialized as "other" as it racializes "other," a co-constitutive process that contributes to the formation of race and gender. Woven throughout Bradford's books, these passages subtly diminish her in the eyes of her predominantly white readers.

While problematic, such nursing passages document Tubman's care for the sick—service that she long performed without "pay or pension" (*Scenes* 38; *Moses* 98)—but they also call attention to the impact of disease during the war. As historian Jim Downs elucidates, "The Civil War . . . produced the largest biological crisis if the nineteenth century, claiming more soldiers' lives and resulting in more causalities than battle or warfare and wreaking havoc on the population of the newly freed" (4). Illness and infection disproportionately impacted war refugees, plaguing them with greater severity "since ex-slaves often lacked basic necessities to survive" (Downs 4). Providing much-needed care and relief, Tubman used her considerable knowledge of herbal medicines to attend to help the sick, as Bradford relates in both books:

> At one time she was called away from Hilton Head, by one of our officers, to come to Fernandina, where the men were "dying off like sheep," from dysentery. Harriet had acquired quite a reputation for her skill in curing this disease, by a medicine which she prepared from roots which grew near the waters which gave the disease. Here she found thousands of sick soldiers and contrabands, and immediately gave up her time and attention to them. At another time, we find her nursing those who were down by hundreds with small-pox and malignant fevers. (*Scenes* 38; *Moses* 98)

Further shrouding her in mysticism, Bradford notes that Tubman "never had these diseases" and didn't fear them. Again using a racialized dialect, Bradford writes that "'De Lord would take keer of her till her till her time came, an' den she was ready to go'" (*Scenes* 38; *Moses* 98). Consistent with the general impression that Bradford cultivates in her books, Tubman is characterized in these passages as a devoted and selfless nurse, committed to advancing racial equality, even as Bradford undercuts those efforts in her delivery.

While Tubman worked closely with newly freed populations in hospital contexts, she also participated in militaristic ventures too. While both biographies discuss her experiences with the 2nd South Carolina Volunteer Infantry Regiment, an all-Black unit, these endeavors are covered in greater detail in

FIGURE 4. *Harriet Tubman.* The lithograph is featured in *Scenes in the Life of Harriet Tubman* by Sarah H. Bradford, 1869; J. C. Darby, illustrator; W. J. Moses, printer. This image is reprinted in the NPS article "Harriet Tubman and the 54th Massachusetts." Courtesy Tennessee State Library and Archives.

Scenes (fig. 4). Visually, this observation is represented in a picture of Tubman featured in the frontispiece of *Scenes.* Highlighting her military contributions, the engraving depicts Tubman wearing her scout uniform and wielding a long rifle as she stands in front of army tents. Created by John G. Darby, the woodcut functions as an example of what Sarah Lewis calls representational justice. Discussed in greater detail in chapter 4, representational justice can be broadly defined as the use of images to advance positive views of Black life. Visually depicting Tubman's service to the Union, the wood cut interrupts white-centered recollections of the war in its depiction of a Black woman's fight against slavery. Citing Samuel Hopkins Adams's *Grandfather Stories,* Sernett reports that Tubman "'was inordinately proud of that woodcut. Reference to it never failed to loosen her tongue'" (75). Despite Tubman's approval of the illustration, the woodcut is conspicuously missing from *Moses.* Though Bradford's second biography does not include any images, perhaps suggestive of budget and/or printing limitations, the absence of the woodcut further deepens the commemorative chasm between Tubman and the Civil War that is observed in Bradford's second book.

Discursively, Bradford's biographies offer textual records of Tubman's militaristic expeditions that document her contributions to the Combahee River Raid. Though the event is covered in greater depth in *Scenes, Moses* addresses this facet of her service, too. In a passage that is repeated in both editions, Bradford writes that Tubman was asked "if she would go with several gun-boats up the Combahee River, the object of the expedition being to take up the torpedoes placed by the rebels in the river, to destroy railroads and bridges, and to cut off supplies from the rebel troops" (*Scenes* 39; *Moses* 99). As conveyed in Bradford's accounts, Tubman agreed to undertake the mission, as long as Colonel Montgomery, "one of John Brown's men," spearheaded it (*Scenes* 39; *Moses* 99). But elucidating how Tubman's militaristic contributions were eroded through a textual layering process, Bradford's second book fails to include Tubman's description of what the 2nd South Carolina Volunteer Infantry Regiment accomplished during the raid. Also addressed in the letter to Sanborn that was excluded from *Moses,* Tubman conveys a sense of pride in such mission successfully undertaken by the regiment in her missive: "We weakened the rebels somewhat on the Combahee River, by taking and bringing away seven hundred and fifty-six head of their most valuable live stock, known up in your region as 'contrabands,' and this, too, without the loss of a single life on our part, though we had good reason to believe that a number of rebels bit the dust. Of these *seven hundred and fifty-six* contrabands, nearly or quite all the able-bodied men have joined the colored regiments here" (quoted in Bradford, *Scenes* 87, emphasis in original). As Sanborn's piece suggests, the raid marked a significant turning point in the war, showcasing what African Americans could do when given the opportunity to pick up arms against the Confederacy and the legalized structures of oppression that it endorsed. Prior to the Militia Act and the Emancipation Proclamation, Black men were prohibited from enlisting in the US military, but these legal changes gave Black men, both enslaved and free, the opportunity to become soldiers. Following this revision of military policy, Union Colonel James Montgomery assembled the 2nd South Carolina Volunteer Infantry Regiment. Capturing Black troops' active fight against slavery, Tubman's letter documents the regiment's notable achievements with the Combahee River Raid, though it also records her dissatisfaction in how the event was discussed in the newspapers. "You have, without doubt, seen a full account of the expedition I refer to," she wrote to Sanborn. "Don't you think we colored people are entitled to some credit for that exploit, under the lead of the brave Colonel Montgomery?" (quoted in Bradford, *Scenes* 42). Because such portrayals of the war shaped public perceptions of Black citizenship and, relatedly, impacted wages and pensions, recognition of these labors had both social and material implications. Exposing the ways that the coverage of the raid was whitewashed, Tubman calls attention to the occlusion of Black contributions to the Union. But paving over her critique, Bradford cuts this passage from *Moses*. Altering perceptions of Tubman, this exclusion inevitably softens her legacy as it oversimplifies her complicated relationship with Federal forces.

Though Bradford, a white woman, supported abolition, *Scenes* and *Moses* still exhibit racial biases common to the period. Sernett assesses the matter this way: "If Bradford consciously wrote for a black audience as well as a white one . . . she missed the mark. *Moses* is flawed by racist and stereotypical language and imagery" (126). Particularly illustrative of Sernett's point is a passage that appears in both *Scenes* and *Moses* that describes Tubman's role in escorting enslaved populations to freedom during the Combahee River Raid. Largely unaware of Lincoln's Emancipation Proclamation, the enslaved who lived in the region were frightened by the Union vessels coming up the river, but as Bradford remarks, Tubman helped persuade them that "Lincoln's gun-boats come to set them free" (*Scenes* 40; *Moses* 100). While slaveholders tried to stop them from fleeing, using whips to corral them back toward the plantations, enslaved inhabitants ran to the boats seeking freedom. Echoing the troubling dialect used to recount Tubman's work in the hospital, Bradford's transcription is constructed to entertain her readers:

> "I nebber see such a sight," said Harriet; "we laughed, an' laughed, an' laughed. Here you'd see a woman wid a pail on her head, rice a smokin' in it jus' as she'd taken it from de fire, young one hangin' on behind, one han' roun' her forehead to hold on, 'tother han' diggin' into de rice-pot, eatin' wid all its might; hold of her dress two or three more; down her back a bag wid a pig in it. One woman brought two pigs, a white one an' a black one; we took 'em all on board; named de white pig Beauregard, and de black pig Jeff Davis. Sometimes de women would come wid twins hangin' roun' der necks; 'pears like I nebber see so many twins in my life; bags on der shoulders, baskets on der heads, and young ones taggin' behin', all loaded; pigs squealin', chickens screamin', young ones squallin'." And so they came pouring down to the gun-boats. (*Scenes* 41; *Moses* 101)

Bradford's problematic characterization of the enslaved in this passage is rendered more perceptible when juxtaposed with an excerpt from Tubman's letter to Sanborn that references the same event. According to Tubman, as relayed by the anonymous amanuensis, "I was carrying *two pigs* for a poor sick woman, who had a child to carry" while helping liberate enslaved populations along the Combahee River (*Scenes* 86, emphasis in original). Though couched in a conversation about the impracticality and disfunction of her female-coded clothing, this particular excerpt conveys a greater sense of empathy for Tubman and the enslaved women described therein.[6] Redolent of the ways in which biographical mediators rhetorically shape the subjects they depict, these two excerpts create notably different impressions of Tubman and the enslaved people that she helped. While Bradford's retelling is generally more jocular in nature, written with a larger white readership in mind, the letter has a more serious quality, reflective of the realities that Tubman faced while away at war.

Though there are several differences that can be observed between Bradford's biographies, another notable deviation captures the complex relationship that Tubman had with the North.[7] Exemplifying how memory can be layered over to occlude particular features of the past, *Moses* omits the passage recorded in *Scenes* that describes how Tubman was violently attacked on the train from New Jersey to New York while traveling home from the war. As Bradford explains, Tubman bought a "half-fare ticket, as she was told she must do," but taking issue with this purchase, the white conductor said "'Come, hustle out of here! We don't carry n***ers for half-fare'" (Bradford, *Scenes* 46). Although Tubman explained that she worked in service of the Union army, he threw her into the baggage car, severely injuring her. "She supposed her arm was broken, and in intense suffering she came on to New York," as Bradford writes, noting that "Harriet remained all winter under the care of a physician in New York" (*Scenes* 46–47). Exposing the racial prejudices that persisted in the North, this excerpt was omitted from *Moses,* aligning with post-Reconstruction sensibilities that prioritized white reconciliation, commemorative patterns that can still be observed today.

Reflecting the affordance of print biographies as a source of memory, *Scenes* and *Moses* and the material records that they provide—however flawed they may be—function as the bedrock of memory from which a concatenation of sites arises. Inevitably mediated through Bradford's positionality, these accounts are infused with the distinct brand of whiteness that was common to the moment in time that they were produced, many subsequent expressions of which carry with it this residue. But these accounts also offer a discursive map that illustrates how memories evolve. While *Scenes* places more emphasis on Tubman's military pursuits and documents the racism that she experienced in the North as well as the South, these experiences are noticeably expurgated in *Moses,* reflecting reconciliationist traditions that disregarded how the Union failed to advance civil rights for people of color in the years following the war and Reconstruction. Adding a new layer of memory, *Moses* offered Bradford's white readers a less militaristic and divisive vision of Tubman. Focusing more on her experiences with the Underground Railroad, this way of remembering Tubman has continued to hold prominence throughout the twentieth century as an ever-growing number of material and digital sites further grow this vision and the values associated with it.

The NPS's Digital Layers of Harriet Tubman

Echoing reconciliationist trends observed in *Moses,* many sites of memory continue to focus on Tubman's labors with the Underground Railroad. But demonstrating how sociocultural priorities inform visions of the past, as calls to remove Confederate monuments and memorials were renewed following the murder of George Floyd in 2020, there was a discernible effort to cultivate a more inclusive vision of the war, as readily exemplified by Klein and Criqui's projections onto the Lee monument in Richmond, Virginia. Some progress was made in this regard, resulting in a number of new Civil War monuments and memorials that focused on Black contributions to the war, but generally speaking, physical sites of remembrance remain predominantly white androcentric spaces; limited by the constraints of material sources and political support, monuments, memorials, and other public places of memory are often slow to arise and slow to change, perpetuating outdated ways of seeing the past. But the World Wide Web, with its relative ease of use, potential for instant updates, and general accessibility, allows for the possibility of greater commemorative intervention. Exemplifying how digital sites can nimbly be adapted to a rapidly changing cultural climate—in ways both socially progressive and regressive—a notable number of web sources began to amplify Tubman's service to the Union as calls to remove Confederate iconography grew more vocal. Exploring this memorializing trend in greater detail, in this section I turn to the National Park Service (NPS) and its digital coverage of Tubman. In its main biographical account of Tubman, internally called a "person asset" (Linger, "Harriet Tubman"), the multimedia composition titled "Harriet Tubman" utilizes hyperlinks, images, and alphabetic text to provide site users with a brief overview of Tubman's life. Though the site bears traces of Bradford's narratives, it also draws from historical sources that expand and sometimes correct Bradford's work. But while the person asset includes only a general discussion her service to the Union, the supplemental article titled "Harriet Tubman and the 54th Massachusetts" offers a more nuanced account of Tubman's experiences during the war, exemplifying how digital layers can texture status quo narratives and help counter petrified public memories.

The NPS has long been a significant force in cultivating remembrances of the Civil War. As Paul A. Shackel observes, "The control for the memory of the Civil War has been an ongoing struggle, and national parks have been the arena for some of this debate" (21). Born out of the National Park Service Organic Act of 1916, the NPS was originally appointed to "conserve the scenery and the natural and historic objects and wildlife therein, and to provide for the enjoyment of the same in such manner and by such means as will leave them unimpaired for the enjoyment of future generations" ("Organic Act of 1916"), but its purview broadened dramatically when newly elected President Franklin D. Roosevelt suggested in 1933 that the NPS assume oversight of "all federally owned national parks, monuments, military battlefields, sites under the control of the War Department, eleven national cemeteries, and national capital parks," as John Bodnar recounts (170–71). "Suddenly the owner of numerous battlefield sites and national cemeteries in 1933," Bodnar continues, "the park service . . . was faced with the prospect of promoting historical symbols that were formulated by an earlier generation" (194). While this new charge gave the NPS the authority to select, create, and shape sites of memory that attended to national interests, including those related to the Civil War, the organization largely propagated reconciliationist views until social pressures demanded commemorative change. Reminiscent of the power of vernacular sources on memory, historian Robert Cook asserts that "only concerted action by previously disempowered groups and their allies to recover and disseminate their history can reshape the stories that nations tell themselves and others about their past. National Park Service officials at sites like Harpers Ferry and Gettysburg only tell visitors today about the significance of slavery and African Americans in the Civil War era because of the civil rights and Black Power movements of the 1960s" (212).

Nudging the diversification of Civil War memories along, in 1999, Congress approved legislation for a Special Resource Study "to determine the appropriateness of establishing a unit of the National Park Service to honor Harriet Tubman" ("Various National Parks Bill"). This initiative, Sernett maintains, "stimulated greater public interest in locating her in the American memory" (256), an observation which is confirmed by the many statues and monuments that were erected around this time in cities such as Boston, Massachusetts (1999); Ypsilanti, Michigan (2006); Bristol, Pennsylvania (2006); New York City, New York (2007); and Wilmington, North Carolina (2012), among others.[8] While the Special Resource Study would continue for years, in March

2013 President Barack Obama issued a presidential proclamation under the Antiquities Act to create the Harriet Tubman Underground Railroad National Historical Park in Maryland. A year later, Congress approved this site and the 480-acres surrounding it as a national historic park, legislation that also included the creation of the Harriet Tubman National Historical Park in Auburn, New York.[9] This sister site features the Harriet Tubman Visitor Center, the Harriet Tubman Home for the Aged, the Harriet Tubman Residence, and the African Methodist Episcopal Zion Church.

Forging connections between physical sites of memory and digital ones, the NPS developed informative web pages that describe these material sites, advancing its goals of helping "virtual visitors loo[k] to plan trips to parks" and "learn more about our nation's natural and cultural heritage" ("NPS.gov"). Though these pages can be accessed through the "Find a Park" link on the main menu of the NPS site, they are also hyperlinked at the top of person asset pages. Creating what Jay David Bolter calls "a network of interconnected writings" (27), hyperlinks help publicize the physical sites under the purview of the NPS, but they also shape site users' impressions of the subject discussed—whether that be Tubman or other notable American figures the NPS takes up in these accounts, including Belle Boyd, Sarah Emma Edmonds, and Susie King Taylor, whose legacies are also analyzed in this study of memory circulation. Though, as Wendy Morgan observes, "it is the reader who determines . . . the reading order which is performed on any one occasion of reading" (219), even if the user never clicks on the attendant sites, hyperlinks, often denoted by their blue color or underline, graft meaning onto the subject under discussion. Acknowledging and reinforcing Tubman's place in American memory, the links to the "Harriet Tubman National Historical Park" and the "Harriet Tubman Underground Railroad National Historical Park" featured on the person asset page amplify Tubman's historical significance. Of the sixty-three designated NPS historical parks, the Tubman sites constitute only two of the three that are dedicated to the legacy of African American women.[10] While this rarity amplifies the significance of Tubman's parks, it also exemplifies how whiteness shapes and structures official sites of memory. But further connecting the physical with the digital, links to "Fort Sumter and Fort Moultrie National Historical Park" and "Reconstruction Era National Park" are also found on Tubman's person asset page. Located in South Carolina, where Tubman spent considerable time during the Civil War in service of the Union, these parks were designed to foster memories of the war and its political and social aftermath. As such, these links suggest that there is a connection between Tubman and the war. Tubman spent time in Beaufort, South Carolina, where one of four Reconstruction Era National Park properties is located, but her association with Fort Sumter and Fort Moultrie National Historical Park is less clear. While the Confederate attack on Fort Sumter in Charleston, South Carolina traditionally marks the beginning of the war, both locations were primarily occupied by Confederate forces during the Civil War. Contributing to the ambiguity of this particular connection, Tubman is neither mentioned in the park websites nor are links to her person asset and park sites featured on these pages, so while these links fortify Tubman's association with the war, dominant memories of this event still often reflect and perpetuate whiteness.

While Tubman's person asset helps publicize the NPS's physical sites of memory, it also aims to educate the public about noteworthy historical figures. Exemplifying how different sources of memory collide and amalgamate to form new layers, this particular account bears traces of Bradford's narratives while also drawing from other historical sources that expand and nuance how Tubman is remembered. Though the NPS strives "to ensure and maximize the quality, objectivity, utility and integrity of information disseminated by the National Park Service," deciding what to cover and how to cover it is not a neutral undertaking ("About Us"). Indicative of the ways that whiteness informs digital sites of memory, even when organizations and the individuals who work for them are well-intentioned, the person asset tends to center Tubman's exceptional experiences. Reflecting the values and priorities of the NPS and its intended audience, the entry—last updated in spring 2023 as of this analysis—is a visual and textual composition that largely downplays her experiences as an enslaved woman. This rhetorical trend can be observed by tracing the ways that different artifacts of memory are remixed to create new layers that give rise to visions of the past.

Putting a new face to Tubman's name, the person asset includes a photograph of Tubman that was only recently circulated publicly (fig. 5). In 2017, the Library of Congress purchased an album that belonged to Emily Howland, a Quaker abolitionist and school teacher who lived in Auburn, New York, where Tubman and her parents resided. Taken by photographer Benjamin F. Powelson after the war between 1868 and 1869, around the time that *Scenes* was published, the sepia-colored image can now be found widely on the web, even appearing in the StoryMap of Susie King Taylor discussed in chapter 4; as recirculated on the NPS person asset page, however, the photo necessarily acquires new rhetorical meaning and purpose. As displayed on the NPS's person asset page, the photo is cropped. Determining for audiences what is "rhetorically available,"

FIGURE 5. *Portrait of Harriet Tubman,* taken by Benjamin F. Powelson in 1868 or 1869. This image of Tubman is featured on the NPS person asset page. Credit: Library of Congress, Prints & Photographs Division, LC-DIG-ppmsca-54230.

in the words of Cara A. Finnegan, this reframing excises visual clues that help situate the photograph in *carte de visite* tradition ("What's This a Picture Of?" 116).[11] Relatively inexpensive and easy to produce, *carte de visites* were pocket-sized photographic calling cards that were popular in the 1860s. While there are countless artistic renditions of Tubman, only a handful of photographs are known to exist, reflective of a symbolic annihilation that disproportionately affects women of color. Extant images tend to depict her as an older woman, but in the NPS photo Tubman appears youthful—somewhere in her 40s. Though she wears an au courant dress, her countenance is solemn, capturing the promise of new possibilities while hinting at old wounds.

Running about 500 words in length, the NPS's person asset is inevitably limited in what it can cover, but what makes the cut (or not) reflects the priorities of the NPS. While the person asset commences by stating that Tubman was "[b]orn into slavery," it tempers its discussion of the violence that she experienced as a result. Using passive voice to circumvent blame, the passage simply states that Tubman was "[n]early killed at the age of 13 by a blow to her head" ("Harriet Tubman"). Though no specific sources are named in the person asset, the language used strongly suggests that this passage was heavily influenced by Larson's 2004 biography *Harriet Tubman: Portrait of an American Hero.* As Larson writes, "Working a field hand as a young teen, she was *nearly killed by a blow to the head* from an iron weight thrown by an angry overseer at another feeling slave" (xvi, emphasis added). Exposing memory's layers, Bradford's books offer even more detail about the incident. As she relays in both accounts, Tubman was hit by a white man who threw a two-pound weight at her when she refused to help tie up an enslaved man (*Scenes* 74–75; *Moses* 109). But in an act of rhetorical selection, the NPS excludes these details, subsequently distancing Tubman from slavery and the physical, emotional, and mental damage it caused. But this omission also detracts from the agency that Tubman is afforded through her act of defiance. Despite the punishment she would most certainly face, she rejected the command to do harm against the enslaved man, a move that is representative of her uncompromising commitment to Black lives. While rhetorical deflection is an inevitability, as Kenneth Burke teaches us, it also exemplifies that accuracy is not only a matter of fact, but also what is said (or not) about a subject that is determined by the architects of memory and the power afforded to them.

Further illustrating how the trauma of slavery is rhetorically softened in the passage, the person asset attributes Tubman's extraordinary success with the Underground Railroad to her experiences as an enslaved woman, divorcing acts of necessity and courage from the brutal reality of slavery. Though the NPS rightly notes that Tubman fled Maryland "when her enslaver died and she was to be sold," the retelling attributes her success with this endeavor to "the skills she had learned while working on the wharves, fields and woods, observing the stars and natural environment and learning about the secret communication networks of free and enslaved African Americans to affect her escapes" ("Harriet Tubman"). While such phrasing hints at Tubman's resiliency and resourcefulness, it also echoes the "positive good" view articulated by John C. Calhoun in the 1830s that advanced the idea that slavery benefited the enslaved in material, social, and physical ways. As reimagined in contemporary contexts, this myth maintains that human bondage helped enslaved populations, providing them with opportunities to cultivate skills that were used for their personal gain. While the physical and psychological violence that Tubman and other enslaved people encountered is well documented in Bradford's biographies and Larson's book, these experiences are excised from the NPS person asset. Offering only a partial view of the past, this retelling distances Tubman from what drove her to undertake this dangerous work with the Underground Railroad, adding a layer of memory that both reflects and reifies whiteness.

Suggestive of the NPS's narrative priorities, while the person asset omits meaningful discussion of Tubman's experiences in slavery, it devotes considerable attention to quantifying Tubman's efforts with the Underground Railroad, but attending to the layers of this narrative exemplifies how memory can mutate. Though long contested by historians, Bradford reports that Tubman helped 300 enslaved people flee slavery (*Scenes* 52; *Moses* 3), a figure still widely circulates today in online spaces. While the NPS does not cite a specific number of "passengers," it reports that Tubman "[v]ow[ed] to return to bring her family and friends to freedom . . . spen[ding] the next ten years making about 13 trips into Maryland to rescue them. She also gave instructions to about 70 more *who found their way to freedom independently*" ("Harriet Tubman," emphasis added). As noted in Larson's book, "Over the next eleven years, Tubman returned to the Eastern Short of Maryland approximately thirteen times to liberate family and friends; in all, she personally brought away about seventy former slaves, including her brothers and other family and friends. She also gave instructions to approximately fifty more slaves *who found their way to freedom independently*" (xvii, emphasis added). Some language is repeated verbatim without appropriate acknowledgment citation; a more important shortcoming, however, is that the person asset does not accurately relay Larson's claim: instead of reporting that Tubman helped *liberate* seventy enslaved people, the person asset claims that Tubman *shared information* with seventy people. Although historians have differing views on the number of enslaved people Tubman freed, this particular retelling is rhetorically consequential, ultimately downplaying Tubman's noble efforts. But refracting a distorted version of Larson's claims, this retelling also reveals how information can shift as it is picked up and deployed in new contexts, an effect that can ripple outward as site users recirculate this flawed retelling of Tubman.

Similar kinds of numeric corrections can be observed in the NPS's discussion of the reward offered for Tubman's capture, further alluding to the narrative priorities of the person asset. In Bradford's books, this remuneration is cited as $40,000 dollars (*Scenes* 23; *Moses* 33), but consistent with Larson's take, the person asset reports that "[o]ne hundred dollars was offered for her capture" ("Harriet Tubman"). Pointing to a copy of a "wanted" ad which is copied in her book, Larson argues that the return of "Minty" and her brother would yield $100. Unearthing the source of Bradford's error, Larson explains that an abolitionist named Salle Holley fabricated the $40,000 bounty to help Tubman secure a war pension from the Union Army (241). Published in an 1867 newspaper article, Holley's figure was picked up by Bradford and subsequently disseminated in her highly influential biographies. Because this number was shared with greater frequency, it gained wider acceptance and influence, becoming a common point of discussion in narratives of Tubman. While the

NPS's recirculation of this point helps to correct the long-established exaggeration perpetuated by Holley and then Bradford, the person asset obscures the harsh realities of slavery by failing to discuss in detail Tubman's experiences in bondage.

Further illuminating its rhetorical priorities, the NPS devotes a full paragraph to listing Tubman's famous acquaintances, drawing attention to her considerable social standing. Described as a "lifelong humanitarian and civil rights activist," who "formed friendships with abolitionists, politicians, writers and intellectuals," Tubman was acquainted with Frederick Douglass and "was close to John Brown and William Henry Seward," as explained in Bradford's books and Larson's biography. In addition, she was also "particularly close with suffragists Lucretia Mott, Martha Coffin Wright, and Susan B. Anthony" and "New England's progressive circles," including Ralph Waldo Emerson, William Lloyd Garrison, Harriet Beecher Stowe, Franklin Sanborn, and Mrs. Horace Mann ("Harriet Tubman"). While this entry brings novel information about Tubman to the fore, highlighting her celebrity, its inclusion is prioritized over her more traumatic experiences as an enslaved woman.

Adding another layer to remembrances of Tubman, the NPS embedded a hyperlink to an article titled "Harriet Tubman and the 54th Massachusetts" on the bottom of Tubman's person asset page. Further demonstrating how this technological affordance textures digital sites of memory, this article is one of several on a growing list including "Harriet Tubman and the Underground Railroad," "Re-Imagining Harriet Tubman," and "Determining Harriet Tubman's Birth Year" that, if clicked, drill down into particular facets of Tubman's life. Focusing on her experiences during the Civil War, "Harriet Tubman and the 54th Massachusetts" specifically discusses Tubman's contributions to the Combahee River Raid. While this aspect of Tubman's service to the Union is addressed in the person asset, this retelling offers only a limited account of her contributions. Drawing on information found in the latter half of Sanborn's article reprinted in *Scenes,* the person asset reports that Tubman "joined Colonel James Montgomery and the 2nd South Carolina Infantry, composed of emancipated slaves to rescue more than 700 enslaved people, many of whom later enlisted in the Union army." Commenting on the success of the mission, the site explains that the raid severely damaged "the Confederate economy," reiterating the point that the event "provid[ed] the Union army with more soldiers" ("Harriet Tubman"). Exemplifying the elastic potential of online acts of memorialization, "Harriet Tubman and the 54th Massachusetts" augments this general overview, offering greater detail of Tubman's role in the Combahee River Raid and her relationship with the 54th regiment, the African American unit led by Colonel Robert Gould Shaw.

Written by seasonal park guide Theo Linger, "Harriet Tubman and the 54th Massachusetts" was published in August 2020. Though whiteness and androcentricity still function as the "normative force . . . in conventional public memories," as Mitchell G. Reyes asserts, there are notable efforts to confront, challenge, and change these expressions and the recollections that they evoke (2). As Linger explains in a personal interview, though plans for the piece preceded this tragic event, the composition of the article was "informed" by the George Floyd protests, though "that wasn't the original intention at all." Rather, Linger continues, the NPS was trying to generate more content on the 54th Massachusetts Regiment specifically, but also the 55th Massachusetts Regiment and the 5th Massachusetts Calvary—all African American units—for its website. As such, regional Massachusetts NPS employees were given topics on these regiments to research. As Linger described it, "the Harriet Tubman topic on [the] list really caught my eye because I knew that they were in the same part of South Carolina at the same time, but before I dug into it I didn't know just how much overlap there was." Drawing from a range of primary and secondary sources, all of which are footnoted at the bottom of the NPS page in contrast to the person asset, Linger offers site users a nuanced discussion of Tubman's experiences during the Combahee River Raid while exploring her relationship with Gould and the 54th Massachusetts regiment. Making visible the connection between digital and material sites of memory, "Harriet Tubman and the 54th Massachusetts" serves the dual purpose of sharing information about key events and actors in the Civil War while also publicizing NPS-sponsored physical sites.

In ways similar to the person asset, the article also includes links to other NPS sites; in this case, it connects audiences with the "Boston African American National Historic Site" web page. Specifically focusing on the wide range of opportunities in Boston that celebrate Black accomplishments during the 1800s, the digital site shares information about the various experiences "remarkable men and women . . . [who] were leaders in the Abolition Movement, the Underground Railroad, the Civil War, and the early struggle for equal rights and education" ("Boston African American"). Of particular relevance, the site discusses the Robert Gould Shaw/54th Regiment Memorial created by Augustus Saint-Gaudens ("Boston's Continuing Revolution"). Unveiled in 1897, this monument was the first official site in the United States to honor Black Union soldiers, but suggestive of its original purpose, only the names of the white officers killed were originally engraved into it; the Black soldiers' names were only added in the early 1980s at a time when the city working through racial hostilities. A stop on the NPS's Black Heritage Trail and the Freedom Trail in Boston, the Robert Gould Shaw/54th Regiment Memorial is both referenced and hyperlinked in Linger's discussion of Tubman and the Combahee River Raid, further increasing exposure to this physical site. Drawing from a *Boston Herald* article published in 1905, Linger reports that Tubman went to visit the monument and "gazed long and tenderly on the magnificent work of the sculptor and dropped a silent tear for the departed." Foregrounding her "matronly role as 'Shaw's nurse,'" the 1905 *Herald* article, as summarized by Linger, only briefly mentions Tubman's scouting work while generally omitting the discussion of the Combahee River Raid. Like the publication of *Moses,* such omissions participated in reconciliationist visions that systematically neglected Black contributions to the war, distancing Tubman from the historic labors that she undertook as a Black woman planning and executing this martial venture.

Serving as a corrective to this common occlusion, Linger centers Tubman's military contributions in "Harriet Tubman and the 54th Massachusetts," a perspective that is most visibly observed in the recirculation of the illustration of Tubman holding a rifle. Published in *Scenes* but excised from *Moses,* the image is located at the top right of the page, optically setting the tone of Linger's article. Informing site users' perceptions of the image, Linger comments on persistent memories of Tubman, noting that "[r]elatively few know the entirety of [Tubman's] story, including her groundbreaking Civil War Service." Acknowledging that some parts of Tubman's life were "trimmed out or simplified" to create a more palatable version of her, Linger explains that typical retellings have "discard[ed] the strong, assertive military and underground railroad operative that defied pro-slavery laws and challenged 19th century assumptions about the female sphere." Calling attention to fossilized memories of Tubman that fail to take up her active fight against slavery, these opening lines signal a desire to tell a different story of Tubman.

To this end, Linger uses a range of primary and secondary historical sources in "Harriet Tubman and the 54th Massachusetts." While the person asset leans on Larson's account, Linger draws extensively from Catherine Clinton's 2005 biography of Tubman, *Harriet Tubman: The Road to Freedom.* Offering new insight, Clinton's book aims to tell a fuller, more accurate account of Tubman's life, but in doing so, clashes with other accounts of the past. Citing Clinton, Linger asserts that Tubman first volunteered for the Union in

1861 to assist Major General Benjamin Butler at Fort Monroe in Virginia where "enslaved people rushed to sanctuary" at Union bases. But exposing the kinds of historiographical discrepancies that can live beneath the surface of a text, this detail contrasts the NPS person asset, informed by Larson's biography, as well as Bradford's books, all of which assert that Tubman's service commenced with her arrival in Port Royal, South Carolina in 1862. Though new historical accounts tend to expand the scholarly contributions of their predecessors, the ways that such narratives of the past may compete with or contradict each other are not always captured in the popular media that references them, as these NPS pages illustrate. Tracing the way that history is recirculated in digital sites brings these differing perspectives more clearly into focus. But of note, Clinton's particular take on Tubman's service gave Linger an opportunity to link to other NPS sites, including an informative page on Fort Monroe and a person asset of Butler. Further highlighting the connection between physical and digital sources of memory, these links add dimension to how Tubman is remembered while exposing readers to other sites in the process. While at Fort Monroe, Linger explains, Tubman "provided humanitarian aid as a cook, laundress, and nurse." Though she performed similar duties while in South Carolina, the rhetorical effect of inserting her in the early days of the war deepens her commitment to "contraband" populations and, more broadly, the abolition of slavery.

Further nuancing memories of Tubman's contributions to the Combahee River Raid, Linger draws on Clinton but also other secondary sources to describe what he aptly calls "the most notable achievement of her Civil War service." Transpiring between 1–2 June 1863, this mission, which she performed in collaboration with Colonel James Montgomery and the 2nd South Carolina Infantry, resulted in the destruction of Southern property and the liberation of hundreds of formerly enslaved people, as also noted on the NPS person asset page. But fleshing out the circumstances of this experience, Linger reports that this mission was commanded by Montgomery, who "fought proslavery settlers alongside John Brown in the Bleeding Kansas conflict of the 1850s," which offers necessary context for understanding Tubman's relationship with Montgomery. Although Brown is perhaps best known for his role in the Harper's Ferry uprising, as explained in Brown's person asset page hyperlinked from Linger's article, his connection to Montgomery hints at the latter's own steadfast abolitionist principles. This association offers an implicit explanation as to how a white man came to collaborate with a Black woman on a Union mission.

Of significance, the NPS site maintains that Tubman helped "pla[n] [the Combahee River Raid] *alongside . . .* Montgomery" (Linger, emphasis added). While Bradford advances similar claims, most notably in *Scenes,* many subsequent sources of memory neglect this facet of her service or minimize it. Although Black women contributed to the Union cause in a range of ways, Tubman took the unusual step of engaging direct military in action against the South. While this aspect of Tubman's labors is also documented in Bradford's biographies, it has a long history of erasure that the NPS article amends through its retelling of the event. Although Linger acknowledges that the mission was executed "[o]n Montgomery's orders," it was Tubman who "led a raiding party up the Combahee." She did not have previous military experience, but her "talents for stealth and reconnaissance . . . [were] honed during her years on the Underground Railroad." Foregrounding the financial ramifications of the raid, Linger comments that Tubman's efforts on the Combahee "damage[d] the economic power of the South by burning wealthy plantations." Spotlighting the damage inflicted upon Confederate-supporting citizens at the hands of a Black woman again represents a significant departure from traditional accounts of Tubman that only offer a perfunctory review of her war work. Complementing Linger's retelling of the raid is a wood-engraved illustration that specifically highlights the liberatory nature of the mission. Published in *Harper's Weekly* on 4 July 1863, this sketch is captioned "Raid of Second South Carolina Volunteers (Col. Montgomery) among the rice plantations on the Combahee, S.C." It depicts two boats pulling away from the shores, while houses burn in the distance, and enslaved men, women, and children run after the boats. Aligning with Bradford's narrative, the NPS article notes that Tubman helped liberate more than 700 enslaved people on this mission. Underscoring just how exceptional this was, Linger reports that it was one of the largest groups to secure their freedom in a single event, and of import, many of those rescued "later enlisted in the Union army."

To contextualize the Combahee River Raid and, more generally, foreground Black Americans' contributions to the war, Linger compares this event with the 54th Massachusetts Infantry Regiment's attack on Darien, Georgia, which occurred a few days later. Creating an opportunity to link to other NPS pages, this approach brings greater attention to the physical sites of memory located in Boston that honor the labors of Black Americans, but this particular pairing also rhetorically pits Tubman against Shaw. As Linger maintains, "Shaw and Tubman had different ideas of what constituted acceptable warfare, and their reactions to Montgomery's orders reflected that difference." Illustrating again the connection between published historical accounts and public memory, Linger draws from Clinton's book to help substantiate this point, noting that several days after the Combahee River Raid, Montgomery asked Shaw and the 54th to lead an attack on the mostly deserted Darien. Despite his documented objections to the destructive nature of the mission, Shaw reluctantly "sack[ed] and burn[ed]" the Confederate town (Linger). Echoing passages from Clinton's book, Linger comments on the widespread denunciation of the unit, writing that "even the abolitionist newspaper *The Commonwealth* condemned the burning of Darien at the hands of 'Yankee negro vandals' and 'brigands.'" While Linger leans extensively on Clinton's account, unique to his own retelling is the explicit comparison between the Combahee River Raid and the 54th Massachusetts Infantry Regiment's attack on Darien. "While *The Commonwealth* had praised Tubman's Combahee River raid in previous weeks, the destruction of an entire town crossed a line," Linger hypothesizes. Despite acknowledging this important difference, Linger invites questions about the ethics of Tubman's contributions to the Combahee River Raid through this critical juxtaposition: "Whereas Tubman enthusiastically led Montgomery's raid up the Combahee River, Shaw felt troubled when he received similar orders a week later." Linger's article deepens collective memories of Tubman and the war, specifically her role with the Combahee River Raid, but it also prompts concerns about the ethical dimensions of this mission. Concluding his discussion of the relationship between Tubman and Shaw, Linger explains that Tubman, after returning to Beaufort, resumed the gendered labors of nursing and cooking for the regiment. Again evincing the distinct influence of Clinton's narrative, Linger notes that Tubman served Shaw his final meal before he met his death during the Battle of Fort Wagner, which is hyperlinked to an NPS page describing how this clash "paved the way for more African Americans to enlist" (Zack).

Though Black Americans contributed in significant ways to the Union cause, their efforts were not always welcomed, appreciated, or compensated. Addressing this latter point in particular, Linger comments on Tubman's repeated requests for a Union pension, a major exigency driving the publication of Bradford's biographies. As Linger explains it, Tubman "struggled to receive recognition and compensation from the United States government for her wartime service." It was only in 1898, after the publication of Bradford's books, that Congress finally approved Tubman's request. Illustrating an affordance of digital memory remediation, the NPS article links to the National Archives site, which features a digital copy of the general affidavit that Tubman filed in 1898 and the bill that was introduced to increase Tubman's pension. Complementing Linger's discussion of Tubman's momentous victory is a grainy, black and white image of Tubman. Appearing in the *Boston Herald* in 1905, this photograph was taken near the 54th Massachusetts war memorial and features an elderly Tubman wearing a war medal on her coat. Though often erased from public memories of the war, Tubman played a notable role in this influential occasion and worked tirelessly to ensure that she be documented in its historical record. Circling back to the problem of "simplified" stories of Tubman that excise elements of Tubman's story "deemed inconvenient," Linger concludes the article by reflecting on how traditional sites of memory have centered more maternal visions of Tubman, eclipsing her service to the Union, particularly her role in the Combahee River Raid. Reiterating the constructed nature of memory, Linger reiterates that Tubman is "a household name today, but only rarely do we glimpse the full picture."

The Many Layers of Harriet Tubman

As discussed throughout this chapter, layers of memory accumulate through the suasive mechanisms that shape the past. While the analog and digital sources examined herein constitute only a few layers in the stratum of memory that gives rise to recollections of Tubman, each addition is distinct, born of the circumstances in which they emerge, but collectively, they do the important work of making Tubman a true public figure. Interconnected, these commemorative sites share common DNA, which is carried forward in the mechanisms that subsequently follow. Reflecting on the work of Maurice Halbwachs, Lewis A. Coser writes "the present generation may rewrite history but it does not write it on a blank page" (34). This phenomenon can be observed in the ways that Bradford's biographies continue to inform new sources of the past. Mirroring the contexts in which they were written, Bradford's accounts absorb her white social and political realities and the distinctly nineteenth-century white American audience for whom she wrote. *Scenes* offers a fuller view of Tubman's contributions to the war, even as she criticized the Union, but revised after Reconstruction, *Moses* pares back on its discussion of Tubman and the war, reflective of reconciliationist trends that focused on white reunion that papered over Black experiences in the process. Because these accounts, particularly the latter, were picked up and retold over time, they continue to inform many contemporary sites of memory. But as recollections of the American Civil War have been reconsidered in the wake of intersectional concerns born out of white supremacist violence, Tubman's service to the Union has been brought into greater focus, particularly in digital spaces, where such texturing practices are fairly fast and easy to implement, though they often leave no record of revisions made, ablating the digital layers that mark this evolution.

Combining alphabetic, visual, and hypertextual elements, multimodal compositions such as those featured on the NPS site contribute to an ever-growing and changing assemblage of biographical accounts that shift memories of Tubman. Illuminating the transformative power of the digital, the NPS sites challenge common conceptions of Tubman in noteworthy ways. Drawing from historical sources that both extend and correct Bradford's biographies, the NPS person asset muffles the realities of slavery in its account of Tubman while centering her more extraordinary experiences, as they concern the Underground Railroad. But linked to this site, Linger's article textures common ways of remembering Tubman, bringing greater awareness to the ways she supported enslaved populations as they transitioned into life as free individuals and to her collaboration with Montgomery on the Combahee River Raid, which resulted in significant economic damage to Southern resources. While Linger's comparison of Tubman and Shaw prompt questions about the ethics of such endeavors, his overall take on Tubman's contributions help rescript memories of the war and the ways in which Black men and women contributed to the fight against slavery but also, more broadly, the noble experiment that is the United States.

Spanning time and space, mechanisms of memory work in tandem to shape impressions of the past. While bearing the imprint of those who created it, each individual marker functions as a brick that gives rise to public memory. As ways of remembering shift and that change is made manifest in material, discursive, and otherwise symbolic ways, collective views of the past evolve, even as residual perspectives remain. Capturing this evolution in action, though the Robert E. Lee Monument in Richmond stood for 131 years, it was finally removed from the premises on 8 September 2021. Adding another layer of memory to this story, the "Emancipation and Freedom Monument" was unveiled that same month, approximately two miles from the former site of the Lee Monument. It features a 12-foot-tall Black man with outstretched arms and a Black woman with a baby in one hand and a piece of paper dated 1 January 1863, in the other. Celebrating emancipation and the long road to freedom, the monument aims to tell a different story of Virginia's past. Names and faces of ten Black Virginians who fought for the abolishment of slavery and racial justice, including Mary Elizabeth Bowser, William Harvey Carney, Nat Turner, among others, are located on the pedestal where the woman stands, honoring their legacy and the fruits of their labors. Restorying the Lost Cause narrative that was evoked through Confederate monuments, this new installation helps pave the way for bringing emancipationist memories of the Civil War that highlight the ways in which Black men and women served the Union and saved the nation.

CHAPTER 3

Questionable Memories

*Mapping Recollections of Sarah Emma Edmonds and
Loreta Janeta Velazquez on Wikipedia*

Someone has stated the number of women soldiers known to the service
less than four hundred. I cannot vouch for the correctness of this estimate,
but I am convinced that a larger number of women disguised themselves
and enlisted in the service, for one cause or other, than was dreamed of.
Entrenched in secrecy, and regarded as men, they were sometimes revealed as women, by accident or casualty. Some startling histories of these
military women were current in the gossip of army life; and extravagant
and unreal as were many of the narrations, one always felt that they had a
foundation in fact.

    —Mary Livermore, *My Story of the War*

As illuminated in the previous chapter, memory arises from an assemblage of
commemorative enterprises representing the values and beliefs of a particular
community. Given the multitudinous ways of seeing the past, all shaped by
rhetorical selection, discrepancies will invariably arise. Writes Barbie Zelizer,
there is not "one memory at one place and one time that retains authority over
all others. Memory studies presume multiple conflicting accounts of the past"
("Reading the Past" 217). As broadly exemplified by the competing ways of
remembering the Civil War, divergent recollections are an inevitable character-
istic of commemorative landscapes. But these different ways of seeing bring to
the fore questions about memory: When presented with competing memories,
how do we choose what to believe? What do our memories convey about us as
individuals and as communities? And what are the social, cultural, and material
repercussions of these choices?

    In this chapter, I take up this line of inquiry, analyzing the collaboratively
composed Wikipedia entries that circulate the stories of Sarah Emma Edmonds
and Loreta Janeta Velazquez. Participating in an established tradition of female

fighters, including the Amazons, Hua Mulan, Joan of Arc, Molly Pitcher, and Deborah Sampson, Edmonds and Velazquez are best known for dressing as male soldiers to fight in the American Civil War: Edmonds for the Union and Velazquez for the Confederacy. While historian Elizabeth Leonard estimates that anywhere between 500 and 1,000 women from both sides of the Mason-Dixon line dressed as men to engage in battle, Edmonds and Velazquez feature particularly prominently in these conversations (*All the Daring* 165). Unlike their lesser known sisters in arms, both women wrote personal narratives about their war experiences that have helped keep them in the public eye: Edmonds's book, most commonly known as *Nurse and Spy in the Union Army,* was published during the war in 1864, while Velazquez's *The Woman in Battle* was composed toward the end of Reconstruction in 1876.[1] Although the veracity of these accounts has long been called into question, they nonetheless serve as fertile sources that influence how Edmonds and Velazquez are remembered in the present.

While a range of sites comprise the strata of memory that give rise to recollections of Edmonds and Velazquez, in this chapter, I focus on how stories of their lives have been retold on Wikipedia, the "free encyclopedia that anyone can edit" ("Welcome to Wikipedia"). A powerful and influential source of public memory, it is the largest and most commonly used reference site in the world. Inviting the general public to create, add, and otherwise revise text in its collaboratively produced web pages, Wikipedia functions as what Ekaterina Haskins refers to as a participatory site of memory. Though all acts of remembrance necessitate human involvement, participatory sites, as Haskins elucidates, specifically concern "the *production* of memory artifacts . . . [that] reflects the desire and ability of nonelite actors to coproduce narratives of public memory, not merely to experience them as spectators, or interactive extras" (*Popular Memories* 3–4, emphasis in original). Ostensibly more inclusive and democratic, Wikipedia enables the public to contribute to the social construction of memory, but the resulting product, as the pages covering Edmonds and Velazquez suggest, still mirrors the values of dominant culture and the ideologies to which it gives rise. Like other mechanisms of memory, Wikipedia entries are shaped by those who create them, in this case, white, cishet men from Western countries, and the policies by which they abide. Collectively absorbing their biases, the entries that comprise this high-traffic website quietly reinscribe status quo ways of thinking, being, and doing. But following the fluctuations of culture, Wikipedia pages are dynamic and ever-evolving. While many sites do not publicly document how their content changes, Wikipedia is unique in that it makes this process visible through the "View History" tab located at the top of the page. Preserving all modifications made to site entries, this feature offers a detailed record of how web pages have developed over the course of their existence, giving us a map to track the ebb and flow of information and the culture it helps produce.

Turning to the Wikipedia entries of Edmonds and Velazquez, I chart these societal shifts, examining how these accounts have been retold and textured over time. But since their inception in 2003 and 2005 respectively, their pages have focused on their experiences dressing as men to fight in the war. While disputes over the reliability of their narratives feature prominently, especially in more recent editions of their pages, Edmonds's and Velazquez's discussions of race and slavery are conspicuously absent in these retellings, following the general rhetorical patterns identified in other case studies presented in this book. In theory, the collaborative nature of Wikipedia and the option to immediately publish edits make it a productive place for engaging with complicated entanglements of the past, but as suggested by Edmonds's and Velazquez's pages, even participatory sites are infused with the ideology of dominant white culture.

Wikipedia as a Participatory Site of Remembrance

"The spread of participatory culture," Haskins rightly notes, "is credit in no small measure to the ubiquity and accessibility of new media technologies" (*Popular Memories* 44). Though the collective production of memory has long existed in analog form, projects such as crowdsourced transcriptions (Enoch, Bramlett, and Novara), interactive multimodal histories (Enoch and Bessette), even social media curation (VanHaitsma and Book), just to cite a few examples, point to some of the novel ways participatory memory has been reimagined in digital contexts. But extending rhetorical considerations of Wikipedia, I explore in this chapter how this widely used site contributes to the national and even global memoryscape. Now the largest and most commonly utilized reference site in the world, Wikipedia functions as what Christian Pentzold calls as "a place of the discursive fabrication of memory" (264). Hosting over sixty-four million articles in more than 300 languages, including almost 7 million written in English, Wikipedia boasts about 1.7 billion unique visitors monthly, shaping how its users think and understand life around them ("Wikipedia: About").[2]

Taking inspiration from the Libraries of Alexandria and Pergamum, which endeavored to collect the sum of the world's knowledge in one location, as well as Denis Diderot's efforts with collaboratively constructed printed encyclopedia ("History of Wikipedia"), Wikipedia aims to function as "a widely accessible and free encyclopedia; a comprehensive written compendium that contains information on all branches of knowledge" ("Wikipedia: Purpose"). While it originally began as a supplement to Nupedia, a free digital encyclopedic endeavor spearheaded by Jimmy Wales and Larry Sanger in October 1999, it quickly "became the tail that swallowed the dog," to borrow the phrasing of Roy Rosenzweig (121). Nupedia relied on volunteer writers to create content, but entries had to undergo a rigorous and slow peer review process before they were published online. Because of this, only a few dozen articles were produced by the end of Nupedia's first year of existence (Lih 40–41). But the WikiWiki-Web technology developed by Ward Cunningham promised to accelerate the production process. Capitalizing on the connotations of the Hawaiian word "wiki" for "to hurry; fast, quick," wiki software enables an infinite number of people to immediately edit a site without knowledge of coding or even use of a password. Using Cunningham's program to augment their work with Nupedia, Sanger and Wales created Wikipedia, "a silly name for what was at first a very silly project," as Sanger describes it (quoted in Lih 45). Officially launched on 15 January 2001, two days after the domain name was registered, Wikipedia.com attracted "legions of folks" after only a few weeks of its existence, Andrew Lih reports, making clear that the collaboratively-written encyclopedia "was going to be more than just a small silly project" (65).

In contrast to print encyclopedias like Britannica, World Book or even digital versions such as Microsoft's Encarta that rely on experts to produce and shape knowledge, Wikipedia invites the general public to create, add, and otherwise revise its pages. While such a space encourages more participation and interaction, as Haskins observes, "The intersection of contemporary remembrance culture and new media technologies presents a mixed bag of promises and problems" (*Popular Memories* 52). Of particular concern, Wikipedia has long struggled with diversity of authorship, which affects the kind of knowledge it produces and how it is framed. As well established, there is a notable lack of women editors (Menking and Erickson; Wagner et al). A recent assessment from the Wikimedia Foundation estimates that women constitute only 15–20 percent of total contributors (Balch). Though racial and ethnic demographics of its editors have been less systematically reviewed, it is roundly acknowledged that the majority of the roughly 120,000 active editors are white men who are "technically inclined," "formally educated," and live in the Northern Hemisphere ("Wikipedia: Systemic Bias"). Because, as Sara Ahmed observes, "Spaces acquire the 'skin' of the bodies that inhabit them,"

Wikipedia is steeped in whiteness, which is replicated and reproduced through the vast majority of entries composed and consulted (157). "This is not to say that Wikipedia is 'bad' or that the editors are 'bad,'" as Zachary J. McDowell and Matthew A. Vetter assert, though they do acknowledge some "bad actors." But rather, as they elaborate, the homogeneity of authorship helps explain why Wikipedia "succumbs to and participates in perpetuating information biases that often ignore underrepresented groups and continues to marginalize non-white, non-male, non-Western ideas, subjects, and people" (63). Because our identities prime us for some perspectives while desensitizing us to others, a variety of editors are needed to close the gaps of knowledge, especially in a powerful source of information like Wikipedia.

But Wikipedia's guidelines and policies also influence what is discussed and how that information is presented and shared, further contributing to the propagation of whiteness. The "fundamental principles of Wikipedia may be summarized in five 'pillars,'" as declared on the site: "Wikipedia is written from a neutral point of view," "Wikipedia is free content that anyone can use, edit, and distribute," "Wikipedia's editors should treat each other with respect and civility," and "Wikipedia has no firm rules" ("Wikipedia: Five Pillars"). All of these pillars, as observed by Maja van der Velden, are "connected with sets of policies, guidelines, templates, classifications, and category systems, which further shape and are shaped by the structures of Wikipedia knowledge," but for the purposes of this chapter, I want to focus on the principle of neutrality, which overlaps with Wikipedia's core content policies (310). When composing "fairly, proportionately and without bias," and when using direct quotations or referencing material that is likely to be challenged, they need to attribute their contributions to "a reliable, published source" ("Wikipedia: Core Content Policies"). Expanding on this latter point, entries should neither include "original research" that has not been appropriately vetted nor offer "new analysis or synthesis of published material that serves to advance a position not clearly advanced by the sources" ("Wikipedia: Core Content Policies"). These policies, as is explained, are designed to encourage the use of verifiable sources that allow for the inclusion many notable though often divergent viewpoints. But though they are meant to foster objective and impartial contributions and the exchange of differing ideas, they can also be exclusionary, shaping what is covered in a given entry.

To illustrate the potential effects of systemic bias in Wikipedia, I turn to the pages of Edmonds and Velazquez. While Wikipedia hosts over twenty pages that discuss women who presumably fought in the American Civil War, the entries on Edmonds and Velazquez are some of the most frequently viewed sites in this category. A testament to the cumulative effect of memory, their popularity can largely be attributed to the personal accounts that they published about their war experiences, further demonstrating how life-writing genres function as rhetorical mechanisms that generate public memory. As Elizabeth Young observes, "The image of the cross-dressed woman soldier appears in a surprisingly large number of Civil War texts, consistently cited in journalism, memoirs, and fiction about the war from the 1860s onward," but the narratives of Edmonds and Velazquez are unique because they are often circulated as *true* autobiographical accounts (149). "Because of the interpretative nature of any autobiographical act," posit Sidonie Smith and Julia Watson, "the distinction between autobiographical narrative and fiction remains elusive. Autobiography is always a story in time interweaving historical fact and fiction" (5). But while all personal narratives are inevitably informed by the bents and biases of the writers, some have taken greater liberties when composing their life.

Although there is a long list of published accounts that have been proven to contain factual errors and exaggerations, questions of accuracy and authenticity can be more difficult to answer for those belonging to historically marginalized populations. Exemplifying how power informs what we can know of the past, traces of their lives are less typically preserved and made accessible to the public, the effect of which is even more acutely felt when such subjects act in secrecy. Scant evidence and the passing of time may make it impossible to determine conclusively the verity of Edmonds's and Velazquez's claims, but as exemplified by the editorial records located on their "View History" pages, there is considerable interest in debating them. To be sure, questions of accuracy and authenticity warrant a place in contemporary retellings of Edmonds's and Velazquez's lives, especially in a moment plagued by false information, but accuracy is a matter of inclusion as much as it is exactitude. Directly related to the Civil War, deep-seated tensions over the legality and economics of human bondage were pressing matters of the moment. Reflective of that reality, Edmonds and Velazquez both take up these topics in their books. When retellings, then, focus on their espionage and soldiering claims and ignore their discussions of slavery, they actively depoliticize their inherently political texts. As a collaborative site, Wikipedia has the potential to correct these oversimplified retellings, but rendering perceptible how whiteness informs even participatory sources of memory, as of spring 2023 when I concluded this analysis, there was no movement on this front.

Sarah Emma Edmonds

Created on 1 December 2003, the first Wikipedia entry on Edmonds constituted one sentence that read "Sarah Edmonds was a spy in the American Civil War" (1:04), though by the end of the day, six users had collectively made more than thirty-five documented edits. The resulting three short paragraphs offered a broad strokes overview of Edmonds's life following generic conventions of encyclopedias: it included basic biographic information about her birth in New Brunswick, Canada, her journey to the United States, her marriage to L. H. Seeyle and their three children, as well as her death in La Porte, Texas in 1898, but it is her experiences as Franklin Thompson, a field nurse and spy for the Union army, that make her a notable addition to Wikipedia.

Though an imperfect source of the public memory, Edmonds's book *Nurse and Spy in the Union* has been instrumental in making visible her service to the Union. First published near the end of the war, this wildly popular book captured the attention of Edmonds's contemporaries, selling over 50,000 copies within the first four months of its release ("A Printer in Luck"). By the end of its run in 1900, it went through five editions, including one German translation, totaling more than 175,000 copies sold ("Sarah the Soldier"). Written "almost immediately after leaving the army," Edmonds "left it in the hands of good, faithful men, to publish and sell for the benefit of . . . those poor suffering men, whom I had learned to love as brothers," as explained in an interview that she gave in 1883 ("The Female Volunteer of Company F"). Dedicated to the "sick and wounded soldiers of the army of the Potomac," it was written "mostly in the interests of the sanitary commission," an organization that provided relief to injured Union soldiers ("The Female Volunteer of Company F").[3]

Hinting at its positive reception, initial reviews of *Nurse and Spy in the Union Army* were generally favorable, but at least one early review, "Fraud in Authorship," called the accuracy of Edmonds's account into question. Though the author identifies several anachronisms and discrepancies in Edmonds's timeline, they painstakingly point out passages she plagiarized from Horatio Hackett's *Memorials of War,* asserting that readers "will recognize, in the 'Nurse and Spy,' many incidents with which they are already familiar. They will find them in most instances unchanged in either word or form" (17). While the author's accusation has merit, more common criticisms of Edmonds's book concern the legitimacy of her claims.[4] Compounding this doubt, when Edmonds was asked in an interview if the book could "be regarded as authentic," she replied, "Not strictly so. Still," she continued, "most of the experiences there recorded were either my own or came under my own observation" ("The Female Volunteer of Company F"). Though she did not comment further on what parts were based on her own lived encounters, her war story continues to live on in the many retellings that shape how she is remembered.

Despite the historical uncertainty of her narrative, Edmonds's book has proven to be instrumental in the preservation of her memory as captured online. While a handful of physical sites and television programs have been created in Edmonds's honor, the web has enabled site users from around the world to learn more about her should they so choose. An internet search of her name reveals the kaleidoscope of ways that her story has been retold online, confirming her notability factor. While official organizations such as the American Battlefield Trust, the National Park Service, and the National Archives share brief biographies of Edmonds on their sites, those expressly dedicated to women's, transgender, and LGBTQ histories, including the *History of American Women, TG Forum,* and *Outhistory,* also offer accounts of Edmonds's life.[5] But those interested in her story can also turn to regional sources, such as *Canada's History, Texas State Historical Association,* and *Michigan Women Forward,* and general reference pages like *Brittanica.com, Encyclopedia.com,* and of course, Wikipedia. While not an exhaustive list, these sites typically focus on her experiences dressing as a man and working for the Union army. Fighting on the "right" side of history, she is often cast in a favorable light. Capturing this sentiment, as one blog post phrases it, "if Sarah Emma Edmonds were my contemporary she would often sport a t-shirt saying, 'This is what a feminist looks like'" (Jensen). Centering her gender transgressions, such retellings are often characterized by a progressive ethos. While traces of this commemorative trend can be observed in even the most recent revisions to the Wikipedia entry on Edmonds, an analysis of the evolution of her page reveals how this theme has morphed as selections from new popular and academic sources are incorporated into the Wikipedia retelling as other pieces fall away.

While the influence of *Nurse and Spy* can be observed in a multitude of digital sites, these mechanisms of memory tend to remain relatively static, and when they are revised, there is often no record of changes made. But tracking how its entries have evolved, Wikipedia allows site users to review edits, confirming that early iterations of Edmonds's page foregrounded her experiences as a crossdressing nurse and spy. Undergoing very little revision in the first few years of its existence, the first entry states that Edmonds was "disguised as a man named Frank Thompson, and served as a male nurse, participating in several campaigns, including the Battle of First Bull Run" (1 Dec. 2003, 21:18).

While historical evidence corroborates the claim that Edmonds assumed the identity of Franklin Thompson to serve as a field nurse for the Second Michigan Volunteer Infantry Regiment, or "Flint's Union Greys" (Leonard, "Introduction" xxii), she withholds these details in her book, disclosing neither the name of her regiment nor her nom de guerre. In fact, if the "Publisher's Notice" that prefaces her book didn't explain that she "laid aside, for a time, her own costume, and assumed that of the opposite sex" (xxvii), readers would likely assume that she presented as female. Only after one hundred or so pages does Edmonds hint that she was dressed as a man the whole time. In discussing a friend that she knew prior to the war, she writes "When we met in the army we met as strangers. The changes which five years had wrought, and the costume which I worse, together with change of name, rendered it impossible for him to recognize me" (52). But after her friend was killed in battle, she was moved to leave her nursing post to become a spy. In undertaking her first mission, as recounted in her book, she assumed the appearance of Black man. For other assignments, she disguises herself as an Irish woman, a Black woman, and then again as a white man. These details, too, are discussed in the earliest versions of her Wikipedia entry that reports "she also served as a spy, occasionally disguising herself as an African American or a woman, or sometimes both. At one point, she disguised herself as an Irish peddler with the name of Bridget O'Shea" (1 Dec. 2003, 21:18). Though presented as fact in many online sources, including early retellings of Edmonds's story on Wikipedia, her espionage claims continue to be questioned in the present.

Instituted in the earliest years of Wikipedia, core content policies require editors to consult and cite credible sources, which can be observed in the very first additions made to Edmonds's page. Leaning on primary sources to help verify her story, editor "AlexPlank" added one of the only known photographs of Edmonds to the site on the very first day of its existence (fig. 6). In the picture, Edmonds wears cropped hair and dons a colonial tie and suit jacket, offering optic proof of her life as Franklin Thompson. While seeing is believing, "AlexPlank" also references Edmonds's pension records to confirm her service (1 Dec. 2003, 01:49). Vetted by the US Congress, her application was approved in 1884; she was allocated $12 a month for her work as Franklin Thompson, a private in Company F, Second Regiment of Michigan Infantry Volunteers. Edmonds's service earned her several posthumously awarded honors, further legitimizing Edmonds's story. "GabrielAPetrie," for example, adds that Edmonds was "inducted into the Michigan Women's Hall of Fame in 1992" (7 Jan. 2005, 21:05), and "Steelbeard1" shares that, in 1897, Edmonds "became the

FIGURE 6. Left: *Seelye, Sarah Emma Edmonds*. Taken
in 1867. Right: *Seeyle, Sara Emma Edmonds as Franklin
Thompson*. Taken between 1861 and 1863. These are the
only two known photographs of Edmonds. The image on
the right appears on Edmonds's Wikipedia page. Both
images are used with permission from the Archives of
Michigan, Item No. 129 and No. 130.

only woman admitted to the Grand Army of the Republic, the Civil War Union
Army veterans' organization" (12 June 2011, 18:23), a contribution that was later
amended to acknowledge other women honored by the Grand Army.[6]

While the core content guidelines help ensure the reliability of entries, the
directive also brings into greater focus how source accessibility impacts the
construction of Wikipedia pages. What an editor can retrieve determines what
information can be incorporated into a particular entry. Speaking to this point,
McDowell and Vetter rightly observe that "many important sources of secondary information (particularly academic journals but also many newspapers)
lie behind often cost-prohibitive paywalls," preventing numerous editors from
consulting relevant and meaningful materials (64). But of the sources available
to a given editor, what actually makes its way into an entry is a reflection of
what they selectively mine from those materials, which is informed by their
own values and priorities. Illustrative of this phenomena, editor "Risnerkr"
draws from Bonnie Tsui's accessible popular history book titled *She Went to
the Field: Women Soldiers of the Civil War* (2006), which provides details of

Edmonds's early life not covered in her monograph. Attempting to explain how Edmonds came to dress as a man, "Risnerkr" reports that she was inspired to assume the identity of Thompson after reading Maturin Murray Ballou's American novel, *Fanny Campbell, the Female Pirate: A Tale of the Revolution* (1844). In this fictional adventure story, Fanny's fiancé is taken hostage on a British ship; in an effort to rescue him, she enlists as a male deckhand named Channing on the same vessel. But even after saving him, "Fanny remained dressed as a man in order to take other adventures," "Risnerkr" reports, "which Edmonds attributes to her desire to crossdress" (17 Dec. 2010, 02:55). "[T]o make things easier for herself" when she left her family in Canada, "Risnerkr" continues, Edmonds "wore men's clothes, cut her hair and changed her name to Franklin Thompson" (17 Dec. 2010, 00:48).

While Edmonds's early history helps contextualize her crossdressing experiences, as "Risnerkr" comments, again citing Tsui, there is "no proof in her military records that she actually served as a spy" (17 Dec. 2010, 02:55). Additional discussion about the authenticity of Edmonds's narrative can be found on Wikipedia's "Talk" page, which records editorial deliberations and debates. Not beholden to the core content policies, the exchanges captured here are far less formal and regulated. "Veritas109," for example, takes issue with Edmonds's Wikipedia entry, remarking that it is "typical of the combination of a little truth and a lot of myth that surrounds the Sarah Emma Edmonds/Franklin Thompson tale" (12 Feb. 2013, 17:34). Though Edmonds's book is often used as evidence of her war experiences, "Veritas109" asserts that "Quoting 'Nurse and Spy' regarding Emma's adventures is akin to quoting a Superman comic book." (12 Feb. 2013, 17:34). Informed by Edwin Fishel's extensively researched *The Secret War for the Union: The Untold Story of Military Intelligence in the Civil War* (1996), "Veritas109" condemns Edmonds's book as "a work of propaganda, the sales of which were used to benefit sick and wounded Union soldiers" (12 Feb. 2013, 17:34). The concern about factual accuracy is echoed by an unsigned contributor, who writes that though Edmonds "is enshrined in popular history and Civil War lore . . . only a fraction of this story is accurate, and her espionage tales are fiction" (23 Aug. 2014, 18:04). Also referencing Fishel's account, this editor concedes that "Edmonds did join the 2nd Michigan Infantry Regiment in Detroit, posing as a man" and she "was assigned to work first as a hospital attendant; then as a regimental mail carrier/postmaster and then as her brigade's mail carrier; and lastly as an orderly to her commanding officer," but as the editor asserts, she was not a spy: "Only the most naïve modern reader would believe this farfetched adventure" (23 Aug. 2014, 18:04).

Carrying over to her Wikipedia entry proper, questions about the authenticity of Edmonds's claims have grown more prominent in the last decade. In October 2014, "Basie" added a "disputed" tag, notifying readers that the "factual accuracy" of the content was questionable. Located in a textbox at the top of the site, this warning remained in place until May 2021. In order to delete "maintenance templates" on Wikipedia, editors need to address the problem identified. To this end, "Therealcivilwar" added a section to Edmonds's page in March 2021 titled "Controversy," which was later renamed "Disputed Accuracy" by "Anne MacGall" (18 May 2021, 18:19) and then "Veracity of Claims" by "Sangdeboeuf" just days later (25 May 2021, 00:34). Reviewing common points of concern, "Therealcivilwar" reminds site users that Edmonds herself acknowledged in an interview that her book was "not strictly" true. But indicative of how editors' interpretations of sources also affects the construction of a Wikipedia entry, "Therealcivilwar" selectively references several different publications to build a case against Edmonds's espionage claims. Citing Betty Fladeland, "Therealcivilwar" writes that historians have explored "fraudulent aspects of her pension file" (6 Mar. 2021, 21:59). While Fladeland does concede that witnesses may have "protected [Edmonds] in order not to jeopardize her chance to obtain a pension," the article primarily focuses on information gleaned from the journal of Jerome John Robbins, a doctor who worked in the army hospital with Edmonds when she was disguised as Thompson (362).[7] And like "Veritas109," "Therealcivilwar" also references Fishel's study, claiming that the author "debunk[ed] Edmonds's claim of having been a spy" (6 Mar. 2021, 21:59). But Fishel only briefly mentions Edmonds in his book, using a footnote to outline a handful of reasons why he thinks she "almost certainly was never a spy at all" (624).[8] Finally, to close out the "Controversy" section, "Therealcivilwar" cites *By Her Available Means: The Sensational Rhetoric of Women's Civil War Memoirs,* my dissertation, as evidence of Edmonds's fabrication. Exemplifying how editor interpretation can inform the construction of Wikipedia entries in misleading ways, "Therealcivilwar" inaccurately suggests that my project positions Edmonds's account as "fiction" (6 Mar. 2021, 21:59). But concerned with the social function of women's Civil War memoirs, my analysis examines the rhetorical implications of their accounts, not their factual accuracy. Quoting from my abstract, the only publicly accessible part of my dissertation, "Therealcivilwar" does acknowledge that my research explored how "disenfranchised nineteenth-century women used sensational rhetoric to circumvent obstacles that prevented them from publicly discussing issues related to the American Civil War," but as framed in this section, the editor misrepresents the purpose of the project.

While "Therealcivilwar" exemplifies how source selection and interpretation can inform Wikipedia entries and the memories they subsequently inspire, the call for "verifiable accuracy" is a necessity, particularly in this age of misinformation. But in addition to using "reliable, authoritative sources," accuracy is also shaped by what editors choose to include and omit in the entries they compose. Though slavery very much at the heart of the Civil War, human bondage is not discussed on Edmonds's Wikipedia page, yet as she conveys in her book, it is deeply interconnection to her experience and understanding of the war. Similar acts of selective omission can be observed in retellings of Confederate women, but Edmonds, in notable contrast, opposed slavery. Still, her exceptional stories take textual priority over her documented anti-slavery commitments.

Evidence of Edmonds's abolitionist views are first witnessed in her account of the "contraband" camp that she visited at Fortress Monroe in Virginia. Reflecting on her interactions with these war refugees, she wrestles with arbitrary racialized taxonomies, posing the question, "why should blue eyes and golden hair be the distinction between bond and free?" (36). Though Edmonds does not directly respond to this query, she follows with a story about a group of enslaved men who approached the fort late one night, asking for admittance and protection. After their request was approved, they were given food and blankets, and then, seated around a fire, they shared their experiences of enslavement and their long journeys to the camp. Moved by their trials and tribulations, Edmonds confirms her abolitionist commitments to her readers, writing that "Resolved, although my brother be a slave,/ And poor and black, he is my brother still;/ Can I, o'er trampled 'institution' save/ That brother from the chain and lash, I will" (37).

As the book progresses, it becomes clear that Edmonds, a devout Christian, found slavery to be incongruous with her religious beliefs. This point is brought into particularly sharp relief through her account of a dying Confederate soldier named Allen Hall. While on a espionage mission, she came across Hall in an abandoned house, where he sought cover after falling behind during a battle. Sick with typhoid fever and nearly starving, he was on the precipice of death. Feeling sorry for the soldier in his time of need, Edmonds cared for him, staying with him until he passed. In describing her experiences with Hall, she asked him as he lay dying about his views of slavery: "Can you, as a disciple of Christ, conscientiously and consistently uphold the institution of Slavery?" (88). Although he did not reply verbally, he "fixed those mournful eyes on my face with a sad expression as much to say—. . . you have touched a point upon which my own heart condemns me, and I know that God is greater than my heart, and will also condemn me" (88). While Edmonds's question highlights the disconnect between professed Christian values and human bondage, this scene also suggests that Confederate supporters inwardly recognized the depravity of slavery. Though intuitively aware of this cognitive dissonance, they continued to fight on behalf of the Confederacy and the causes for which it stood.

But even some Union soldiers supported slavery, as Edmonds makes clear in her book. Exemplifying the cruelty of the institution, she shares an example of the kinds of physical violence that enslaved populations faced, stirring the sympathies of Northern readers who often had little exposure to slavery. While in Kentucky, a border state where slavery remained legal until the end of the war, Edmonds recounts how members of two local Union regiments "amuse[d] themselves by throwing stones at every poor Negro who had occasion to pass" (196). When soldiers from a Michigan unit were sent south, they brought with them their Black servants, who were targeted by the proslavery Union soldiers. When members of a Michigan regiment tried to put an end to this hostile treatment, a skirmish ensued, resulting in "the Kentuckians sw[earing] they would hang every "n****r" that came into their camp" (196).[9] Attempting to make good on their promise, when a Black boy later entered the camp to sell food, they immediately attacked him. In a particularly brutal passage, Edmonds describes how "four of the soldiers took hold of him, each one taking hold of a hand or foot, and pulled him almost from limb to limb. . . . When they threw him on the ground he could neither speak, cry, nor walk, but there he lay a little quivering, convulsive heap of pain and misery" (196). Such violent behavior, especially when directed toward children, demonstrates that even Union soldiers were not exempt from barbarity. But exposing such atrocities, Edmonds helps advance an abolitionist agenda, calling attention to the depravity of slavery and the dehumanizing ideology that engendered it.

While Edmonds's opposition to slavery is rarely mentioned in common retellings, the disguises that she assumed are discussed with considerable regularity, though this is one facet of her book that is frequently called into question. In particular, her appearance as a Black "contraband" man is referenced in many digital accounts of her life. Suggestive of the ways that whiteness informs what memories are called into question, this facet of Edmonds's war story is frequently circulated as fact, despite its spurious nature. An established feature of Edmonds's Wikipedia page, the very first iteration of this entry noted that she "disguise[d] herself . . . as an African American" (1 Dec. 2003,

01:32). Augmenting this description in late 2007, a contributor identified only by an IP address shared more details about Edmonds's disguise, directly quoting from a passage in her book: "Having to travel into enemy territory in order to gather information required Frank Thompson to come up with a disguise. In fact, Thompson established several. For example, for the first disguise, Edmonds used silver nitrate to dye her skin black, shaved her head, and walked into the Confederacy disguised as a black man by the name of Cuff" (6 Dec. 2007, 17:13). Since this addition, retellings of Edmonds's disguise, to date, have undergone only minimal change. Some editors debated whether to call Edmonds's character "Ned" (3 Apr. 2008, 1:50) or "Cuff" (29 May 2008, 16:42), but both are used in her book. Commonly associated with minstrel shows, these names generally referred to enslaved men. Another editor revised the section to read that Edmonds "used a black wig" as part of her disguise (7 Apr. 2010, 21:12), again referencing the experience described by Edmonds herself. And in summer 2011, "Lamro" created a hyperlink to silver nitrate so that users could better understand the nature of this substance (28 Jul. 2011, 09:58). But even as more editors broadly acknowledge the hyperbolic nature of *Nurse and Spy*, this particular dimension of Edmonds's narrative generally goes unchallenged. Exemplifying how the questions we ask about authenticity are informed by dominant culture, a closer examination of this oft-referenced passage further elucidates its troubling nature.

Although Edmonds makes clear her anti-slavery beliefs, her depictions of people of color often played into common racial stereotypes of the era. As Henry Louis Gates Jr. explains, "Being an advocate of the abolition of slavery was not the same thing as being a proponent of the fundamental equality of black and white people, or the unity of the human species" (*Stony the Road* 11). Suggestive of such a position, Edmonds's account of her experiences in Black face bear traces of the minstrel tradition that lampoons the "supposed . . . racial characteristics of black Americans" and "graph[s] difference as inferiority," in the words of Eric Lott (101). Functioning as a kind of a textual minstrel show, Edmonds's tale of a white woman presenting as a Black man was meant to amuse and entertain readers. Capitalizing on the sensational possibility of her double-passing, she takes great care in discussing her "contraband" costume: "I purchased a suit of contraband clothing, real plantation style," she recounts, "and then I went to a barber and had my hair sheared close to my head" (57). A postmaster helped her procure a wig of "a real negro wool" (57), and to darken her skin, she applied silver nitrate (63), a substance commonly used during the war "to treat venereal disease, eye infections, skin ulcers and infected wounds"

FIGURE 7. *Disguised as a Contraband*, engraved by R. O'Brien. Featured in *Nurse and Spy in the Union Army*, 1865.

("Silver Nitrite"). While literary scholars have noted that this scene speaks to the "extraordinary mobility possible for white women" (E. Young 150) and "symbolizes how "boundaries of race, class, and gender . . . are permeable, easily crossed and recrossed" (Laffrado 115), historian Alice Fahs observes that passing narratives, which were commonly published during the war, "also had specific pleasurable and transgressive connotations within a white Northern culture that celebrated and enjoyed putting on 'blackface' in minstrelsy" (*The Imagined Civil War* 247). In assuming the appearance of a Black man, Edmonds participates in this tradition, entertaining white readers with adventures of her life in camp. Though various scholarly interpretations of this highly questionable scene exist, they have yet to be incorporated into Edmonds's Wikipedia page.

As Edmonds describes in the chapter titled "My First Secret Expedition," she donned the disguise to embark on a mission to a Confederate camp in Yorkstown, Virginia, as a "contraband" (fig. 7). The term, as she employs it in this scene, warrants clarification. While "contraband" generally refers to men and women who fled slavery and sought refuge with Union army, in this particular context, Edmonds uses it to describe the enslaved individuals who were *forced* to work for the Confederacy. After infiltrating the camp without incident, Edmonds joined one hundred war refugees who were made to build a defense wall (60). The arduous labors that she describes are indicative of the considerable undertakings that enslaved men were made to perform in support of rebel forces. Tasked with wheeling gravel up a single plank to the top of the eight-foot wall, she writes, "I need not say that this work was exceedingly hard for the strongest man; but few were able to take up their wheelbarrows alone, and I was often helped by some good-natured darkie when I was just on verge of tumbling off the plank" (60). Unaccustomed to these kinds of physical demands, Edmonds was blistered and bruised at the day's end, so she convinced the man assigned to carry water to swap positions with her. Adopting what Lott calls a "ventriloquized dialect" and exaggerated mannerisms, Edmonds describes how her "true" identity as a white person was almost discovered while fulfilling the duties of her new role (18–19). After bringing water to her "sable friends," one enslaved man noticed that the color had started to fade from her hands, remarking, "I'll be darned if that feller ain't turnin' white; if he ain't then I'm no n****r" (63). Edmonds makes light of the situation, joking that "Well, gem'in I'se allers 'spected to come white some time; my mudder's a white woman" (63). Amplifying the comedic effect of this scene, she describes how she checked her complexion in a mirror, and "sure enough, as the Negro had said, I was really turning white. I was only a dark mulatto color now, whereas two days previous I was black as Chloe" (63). For Edmonds, a white woman disguised as a Black man, such a problem was easily remedied through another application of silver nitrate. The simple solution to this complicated problem further elucidates how this scene seeks to delight white readers through its superficial discussion of racial difference.

But as recorded in her book and recirculated in many online sites, including Wikipedia, Edmonds assumed other disguises, including that of a female "contraband," again used here to refer to an enslaved individual who was put to work at Confederate camps (fig. 8). This facet of Edmonds's narrative first appeared on Wikipedia in 2007 when an editor reported that Edmonds dressed as a Black laundress to infiltrate Confederate territory and gather information about their military plans. While on this particular mission, as limned in the entry, "a packet of official papers fell out of [a Confederate] officer's jacket. When Thompson returned to the Union with the papers, the generals were

FIGURE 8. *Disguised as Female Contraband,* engraved by R. O'Brien. Featured in *Nurse and Spy in the Union Army,* 1865.

quite pleased" (6 Dec. 2007, 17:13). This brief passage, which has undergone minimal revision since it was originally published on the site, recirculates the most extraordinary scenes of Edmonds's book. But a critical examination of this account as narrated by Edmonds reveals the ways that it, too, participates in textual minstrelsy.

Though Edmonds dedicates far less space to her "female contraband" costume—only noting that she "procured a disguise"—she regales her readers with her story of working at a Confederate camp (156). Failing to acknowledge the significant constraints that enslaved women, in particular, experienced during the war, Edmonds remarks on how easy it was to "pas[s] through the enemy's lines in company with nine contrabands, men, women, and children who *preferred* to live in bondage with their friends, rather than to be free without them" (156–57, emphasis added). Fleeing the physical, mental, and emotional traumas of slavery was far from a simple endeavor, but this reality was further complicated for enslaved Black women who had fewer options than their male counterparts, as discussed in greater detail in the next chapter. When the Confiscation Act of 1861 was passed, Union contraband camps became a legal refuge for Black men who would be otherwise forced to work on behalf of the Confederacy, but contraband women were not consistently afforded the same protection. As historian Stephanie McCurry explains, the Union "had no legal rationale for holding women and children" who did not serve the same military function as their male counterparts (76). If an enslaved woman, then, fled her captors, her place at a Union contraband camp was not guaranteed. As a white woman dressed as a Black woman, Edmonds moved freely between the Union and Confederate territories, in sharp contrast to *actual* enslaved women who faced a harsher and more brutal existence. Though highly suspect, Edmonds's experiences as a contraband are a source of amusement for readers; as such, there is minimal conversation about the realities of female war refugees. In a platform like Wikipedia that has considerable reach, such priorities are particularly consequential, demonstrating how participatory sites haunted by invisible biases of whiteness that inform their construction and the memories they induce.

Loreta Janeta Velazquez

At the bottom of Edmonds's Wikipedia page there is a hyperlink that directs site users to the entry on Loreta Janeta Velazquez. Though they fought on opposing sides, they are often taken up together in the various mechanisms that collectively give rise to how they are remembered. In ways similar to Edmonds, Velazquez's lasting fame can be traced back to her published personal narrative, *The Woman in Battle: A Narrative of the Exploits, Adventures, and Travels of Madame Loreta Janeta Velazquez, Otherwise Known as Lieutenant Harry T. Buford, Confederate States Army*. Written eleven years after the Civil War ended, Velazquez's book recounts her time as assuming the identity of Lieutenant Harry T. Buford, a Confederate soldier and spy. While the exact sales record of Velazquez's memoir is unknown, newspapers throughout the country advertised her account, suggestive of its popularity. Excerpts from her memoir also later appeared in Ménie Muriel Dowie's *Women's Adventures* (1893), a collection published in England that focused on the stories of women who dressed as men to undertake various kinds of military pursuits. Although Velazquez claims that her 600-page monograph is based on lived experiences, she is also upfront in her desire to generate income. As she writes in the "Author's Prefatory Notice," "I care little for laurels of any kind just now, and am much more anxious for the money that I hope this book will bring in to me" (5–6). Written to sell, Velazquez's book focuses on her most extraordinary experiences, the effect of which still bears out today.

Serving as the primary source of information about her life, *The Woman in Battle* has propagated new sites of memory, steadily increasing Velazquez's celebrity. While both Velazquez and Edmonds are the subjects of the History Channel's film *Full Metal Corset* (2007) and podcasts such as *The Exploress* and *Stuff You Missed in History Class*, Velazquez was the sole focus of María Agui Carter's documentary *Rebel* (2013), a film that explores Velazquez's identity as a Latina and questions of citizenship, myth, and memory. But also like Edmonds, retellings of Velazquez's story also circulate on a range of websites, including the *American Battlefield Trust, Hispanics in the U.S. Army, Latino Genealogy & Beyond, Documenting the American South, Tennessee Civil War Trails, Encyclopedia of Arkansas, TG Forum*, and the *Digital Transgender Archive*, among others. Though only a smattering of examples, these sites exemplify the significant interest that Velazquez's story has generated in the contemporary moment.

Preceding many of these sites, Velazquez's Wikipedia page was created by "Skysmith" on 7 November 2005. Drawing from *The Woman in Battle*, the 600+ word entry describes Velazquez's early life, commenting on her Castilian lineage, her birth and early life in Cuba where her father owned a plantation, and her move to New Orleans, Louisiana when she was a teenager, although the bulk of the page focuses on her experiences as a Confederate soldier and spy named Harry T. Buford. As "Skysmith" explains, when Velazquez's first husband joined the Confederacy, she wanted to accompany him on his mission. When he disapproved of this idea, Velazquez took matters into her own hands and acquired two Confederate uniforms, transforming herself into a soldier named Harry T. Buford.

While this disguise in many ways defines Velazquez, her Wikipedia entry does not delve much into it, quietly conveying a sense of narrative authenticity (fig. 9). Still, Velazquez discusses the matter at length in her book, describing in one passage her longstanding desire to dress as a man:

> I was especially haunted with the idea of being a man; and the more I thought upon the subject, the more I was disposed to murmur at Providence for having created me a woman. While residing with my aunt, it was frequently my habit, after all in the house had retired to bed at night, to dress myself in my cousin's clothes, and to promenade by the hour before the mirror, practicing the gait of a man, and admiring the figure I made in masculine raiment. I wished that I could change places with my brother Josea. (42)

Like Edmonds, Velazquez found inspiration to dress as a man in the examples that came before her, including Deborah, Catalina de Eranso, Appolonia Jagiello, most notably, Joan of Arc, all of whom fought for noble causes.

FIGURE 9. Left: *Harry T. Buford C.S.A.* Right: *Madam Velazquez in Female Attire.* Engraved by REA, John Rea Neill, and featured in *Woman in Battle,* 1876, and on Wikipedia.

Establishing a pattern of interest that makes her sensational claims seem more legit, Velazquez attempts to clarify the motivation behind her crossdressing choices, though many of these the details are not covered in her Wikipedia entry. Further exemplifying how source accessibility influences the construction of a Wikipedia entry, "Jdimaggio1," also drawing from Tsui's book, does write that Velazquez "took to fairy tales and stories of heroism, citing Joan of Arc as a particular inspiration," but to date, says nothing more about it (2 Feb. 2017, 19:02).

But the primary source of contention regarding Velazquez's narrative is not her Buford disguise, at least not explicitly, but rather her claims that she fought and spied for the Confederacy. As "Skysmith" retells her story, Velazquez disguised as Buford recruited troops to bring to her husband, but he died shortly after their arrival. Continuing the mission, she "supposedly fought" in the First Battle of Bull Run and at Fort Donelson and Shiloh, taking up arms in service of the Confederacy (7 Nov. 2005, 12:34). After it was discovered that Buford was a woman, Velazquez retired her uniform permanently and became a spy. Highlighting the more remarkable missions as recorded in her book, "Skysmith" reports, for example, that Velazquez was hired by Union officials to search for herself on one undercover mission. Another passage from the entry notes that she attempted to organize a rebellion of Confederate prisoners in Ohio and Indiana. But making clear the questionable nature of her book, "Skysmith" remarks that "How much of it is true is unknown. Various historians have doubted its veracity for lack of any concrete evidence" (7 Nov. 2005, 12:34).

Far more suspect than Edmonds's account, *The Woman in Battle* has long been the subject of intense criticism. While Reverend J. William Jones, for example, understood that her book would "be read by those who are fond of the marvelous," as his review in the *Southern Historical Society Papers* indicates, he wondered how Velazquez could "be at so many battles fought by different armies in different sections of the country . . . [and] manag[e] to accomplish various other physical impossibilities" (208). Upon learning of Jones's review, Velazquez wrote to him, insisting that her account was accurate, noting, though, "the book was not intended as a history of the late war between the States" (Letter to Jones, 27 October 1876). She further addressed Jones's criticisms by clarifying the timeline of events that she provided in her narrative. In concluding her letter, she offered Jones the names of several Confederate men who would verify her account. Concerned by Jones's lack of response to her first letter, Velazquez wrote him again reiterating that she believed his review to be "unfair and unjust" and implored him to reread her book (Letter to Jones, 12 November 1876). She noted in the letter that she included stamps so that he might be more compelled to respond.

But Velazquez's most vehement criticism came from Confederate General Jubal Early, who helped propagate Lost Cause narratives that sought to reconcile the values of the antebellum South with the Confederate defeat. He was so offended by *The Woman in Battle* that he accused Velazquez of being a white Northern man ridiculing the South. In his letter to Representative William F. Slemons of Arkansas, Early attacked her book, noting "There are many . . . statements which I could point out to show that the writer of the book is not telling the truth" (Letter to William H. Slemons 7). As Early concluded in his letter, Velazquez is not a "true type of Southern Woman," those "fair specimens of the pure and devoted women who followed with their prayers the armies of the Confederate states through all their struggles and trials" (8). If *The Woman in Battle* was "intended as a work of fiction," he continues, "then it is one which ought not to be patronized by Southern men or women, as it is a libel on both" (8). Responding to these accusations, Velazquez vehemently defended the authenticity of her account. Upon learning of Early's complaint, she wrote him a letter explaining that the flaws in her story are due to a loss of notes but also a desire to protect those who might be adversely affected by her disclosures. While she "might have been more explicit in some points," she offered Early a list of military references who would vouch for her and her labors that she performed in support of "our glorious . . . South" (Letter to Jubal Early 2). She closed the missive by asking Early to consider the repercussions of his criticisms: "my Book and Correspondence with the Press is my entire support of my self and little Son. (My health is failing,) and my whole soul's devotion is the Education of him who is to live after I have passed away. . . . [A]ll I now ask from you is Justice to my *child*. I live for him and him alone" (3). In response, Early dropped the matter, explaining to Slemons:

> I have no disposition to injure the alleged author of that book, and still less to deprive her of the means of training and educating her child; but I cherish most devotedly the character and fame of the Confederate armies, and of the people of the South, especially the women of the South, and when a book affecting all these is sought to be palmed on the public as true, and bears on its face the evidence of its want of authenticity, then I have the right to speak my opinion and will speak it, whether the author be man or woman. (9)

Although Early did not publicize his suspicions, his letters have been preserved in the Southern Historical Collection at the University of North Carolina, Chapel Hill. Exemplifying the rhetorical power of the archive, these letters are widely referenced in historical and popular works about Velazquez, including Wikipedia.

Also attending to concerns of authenticity, Wikipedia editors went to work revising "Skysmith"'s initial post, amplifying the doubt cast on Velazquez's Confederate service. In 2007, "PhD~enwiki," for example, writes that many historians had misgivings about the book because of "the improbability of many of her adventures, her frequent vagueness or inaccuracy about names and places, and the absence of any evidence to corroborate her sensational claims" (11 May 2007, 15:18). In alignment with Wikipedia verifiability guideline, the editor references General Early's letters, remarking that he "denounced the book as a complete fiction shortly after its appearance" (11 May 2007, 13:14). Nodding to Velazquez's response to Early, "PhD~enwiki" adds that Velazquez had "written the book primarily 'for money' so she could support her child" (11 May 2007, 13:14). But "PhD~enwiki"'s revisions also call out the influence of popular media on collective memory, illustrating up close the "entangled" relationship between history and memory (Sturken, *Tangled Memories* 5). Critiquing the

History Channel's *Full Metal Corset,* "PhD~enwiki" takes issue with how the program presents Velazquez's story as verified fact, contributing to the belief that her story is legitimate, but as they ultimately point out, "the overall truthfulness of her account remains indeterminate and highly questionable" (11 May 2007, 15:18).

Concerns of credibility become even more centralized on Velazquez's page following the publication of William C. Davis's *Inventing Loreta Velasquez: Confederate Solider Impersonator, Media Celebrity, and Con Artist* in 2016. The first full-length historical investigation of Velazquez, Davis uses newspaper articles, census records, letters, and journals, among other sources, to expose the discrepancies and contradictions in her book. As Davis argues, Velazquez was not a Confederate soldier, but rather a thief, prostitute, and fraud, who was likely born in New York—not Cuba. Making perceptible the ways that at least some scholarly sources can be fed into popular sources of memory, Davis's work has since been referenced at length in the Wikipedia entry. While this in accordance with core content policies, it further exemplifies the ways that editors and source selection impacts the construction of an entry. Though first mentioned on Velazquez's page by "TeriEmbrey," this editor only listed Davis's book in the bibliography (7 Sept. 2016, 15:56). But less than a month later, "Bebe Jumeau" adds that Davis took to task "feminist and Hispanic historiographical approaches as well as post modernist [*sic*] literary theory, all of which he says have failed to accurately evaluate Velasquez and have perpetuated her lies to promote their own agenda" (1 Oct. 2016, 13:44). Over time, Davis's claims were selectively developed into a full section on Velazquez's Wikipedia entry. Currently titled "Revisionist Biography," this portion of the page outlines Davis's arguments that attempt to settle the debate on Velazquez.

While Wikipedia editors have called attention to the validity of Velazquez's claims, other significant details of her book have been omitted from these participatory retellings, indicative of editorial priorities. Though Wikipedia promises to be more democratic, as this particular entry reveals, it still reproduces dominant white cultural values. While her Cuban identity, disguises, military service, and espionage work most typically drive common retellings, Velazquez's book also documents her racist and colonialist impulses, though these facets of her book are rarely broached in Wikipedia, an omission that drastically alters how she is publicly perceived. While entries debate whether she served as a Confederate soldier or spy, they rarely take up the ways she supported slavery, what prompted her to take up arms in the first place.

Though popular sites regularly highlight Velazquez's Cuban origins, they consistently fail to interrogate her colonialist relationship to the island that is documented in her book. For over ten years, between February 2010 to March 2020, the first sentence of Velazquez's Wikipedia page reported that she was "a Cuban-born woman." Disrupting the Black/white binary that most typically defines the war, Velazquez's ethnicity is characterized as an exceptional attribute of her story, repeated with great regularity in the multitude of sites. Of significance, though greatly underacknowledged, Latine communities were active participants in the war. While 4,000 soldiers with Spanish surnames have been identified (Thompson xv), the National Park Services estimate that up to 20,000 Hispanics fought both for the Union and Confederacy (National Park Service 1). But while nuancing public recollections of the war and its players is an important endeavor, Velazquez's connection to Cuba stems directly from Spanish colonialism, which decimated the cultures of the people who inhabited these lands. With pride, Velazquez asserts in her book that "Both in Spain and in the Spanish dominions on this side of the Atlantic, is the name Velazquez well known and highly honored" (39). In a passage that is frequently recirculated in popular retellings, including Wikipedia, Velazquez describes her familial relationship to Don Diego Velázquez de Cuéllar, whom she describes as "the conqueror and first governor of Cuba, under whose superintendence the expedition which discovered Mexico was sent out" (39). Playing a significant role in Spain's colonial enterprises, particularly in the Americas, de Cuéllar helped overtake Cuba in 1511 under orders from Diego Columbus, son of Christopher Columbus. After defeating the indigenous Taíno, which culminated with the burning of chief Hatuey at the stake, the Spanish developed a permanent settlement in Baracoa under the direction of de Cuéllar.[10] This settlement contributed to the colonization of the island and was instrumental in Spain's exploratory efforts, eventually leading to the acquisition of Mexico.

While Velazquez's association with de Cuéllar demonstrates distant familial connections to the colonization of Cuba, her discussion of her immediate family's relationship with the island is indicative of how they directly participated in this oppressive system, though the repercussions of this arrangement are seldomly interrogated in common retellings, including Wikipedia. In the centuries that followed de Cuéllar's governorship, Cuba became a major producer of sugar and tobacco, crops that were largely maintained by enslaved peoples who were both indigenous inhabitants and imported from various part of Africa. Directly benefiting from Spain's colonial rule, Velazquez's Spanish-born father was assigned "an official position in Cuba," as she explains in her book (40). His French-American wife and their five children accompanied him on this move in 1840; two years later, Velazquez was born in Havana. Eventually settling in Puerto de Palmas, her father "engaged actively in the sugar, tobacco, and coffee trade," she records. "The profits on these articles being very large, he speedily acquired great wealth, and was able to surround his family with every luxury" (41). Worked by enslaved populations, her family's plantations offer some explanation as to why she supported the Confederacy. Born into a household that profited extensively from enslaved labor, Velazquez readily identified with Confederate values that sought to preserve human bondage.

Elizabeth Young points out that Velazquez believed that "Cuba and the Confederacy [were] similarly enslaved by tyrannical powers" (191). Subscribing to the persistent narrative that located the origins of the Civil War in a denial of states' rights, Velazquez proudly took up arms to fight against the Union. But, as she asserts, "if there was anything that could have induced me to abandon the cause of the Southern Confederacy, it would have been an attempt on the part of the Cubans to have liberated themselves from the Spanish yoke" (248). Though the Civil War had ended years before Velazquez published her work, Cuba, at that time of her writing, was fighting for its independence against Spain in the Ten-Years' War (*Guerra de los Diez Años*).[11] In 1868, Carlos Manuel de Céspedes, a wealthy sugar plantation owner, and his associates declared independence from Spain, thus beginning the conflict. Drawing connections between the Confederacy and Cuba, Velazquez locates liberty and independence as the common factors inciting these rebellions, but more specifically, it was the freedom to preserve slavery that impelled these conflicts. As Jesse Alemán explains, "Cuba's landed class increasingly embraced a contradictory anticolonial break with Spain for the possibility of United States annexation as a way of protecting slave interests in Cuba" ("Introduction" xxxi). In championing the Confederacy and the revolt in Cuba, Velazquez actively supported slavery and advocated for its expansion.

Velazquez's view of slavery is made more explicit in her discussion of Bob (fig. 10), "a smart and mannerly negro boy . . . about eighteen years of age" (89). Though he is rarely acknowledged in typical retellings, Velazquez enslaved Bob during the war in a gesture that, in the words of Alemán, "legitimates Buford's white Southern masculinity, harkens back to Velazquez's Spanish colonial heritage, and connects them both to an ideology of whiteness propped up by black slave labor" ("Introduction" xxxv). Bob was an "excellent servant," Velazquez reports, "taking care of my clothing in good style, and when we were in camp, attending to my two horses in a very satisfactory manner" (89). Although he joins Velazquez on several military missions, which is a common point of contention on her Wikipedia page, he has not, to date, been named in the entry. While contemporary audiences might assume that "a true Southern sympathizer" like Velazquez would support slavery, thereby negating the necessity of explicitly discussing Bob, his occlusion from Wikipedia and other digital sites participate in a tradition of Civil War stories that, as writer Lorraine Hansberry pointedly asserts, take great pains to discuss "which army was crossing the river at five minutes to two and how their swords were hanging," but says nothing about slavery.

Echoing Lost Cause ideology that rendered slavery as "positive good," a way of life that people of color actually preferred to emancipation, Velazquez characterizes Bob as loyal to her and, more generally, to the Confederacy. While she records that she threatened to "kill him" if he abandoned her, this warning is otherwise lost in a sea of affectionate depictions of Bob as a steadfast and dependable companion (96). After they had been temporarily separated, Velazquez, for example, notes how "delighted [he was] to see me again, as he had been apprehensive, from my long absence, that something had happened, and that I might never return" (143). Such scenes reinforce the Lost Cause myth that depicted the enslaved as happy and faithful servants. Velazquez further participates the perpetuation of this ideology when she describes how she and Bob got separated from one another shortly after the battle of Shiloh. "My boy had not put in an appearance," she writes, failing to acknowledge that he may have purposefully left, "and suspecting that he must have lost himself, I started out to search for him" (223). Although it took some time and effort, she eventually found him in Grenada, Mississippi. "[H]eartily glad to see me again after such a long separation," Velazquez writes, "Bob . . . had gone plump into a Federal camp, having missed his road . . . but not liking the company he found there, had slipped away at the earliest opportunity, and had wandered about in a rather aimless manner for some time, seeking for me" (271). Depicting him as her steadfast servant, even when freedom is in reach, Velazquez contributes to the Lost Cause sensibilities that painted slavery as a loving institution that people of color preferred to freedom.

As characterized in Velazquez's book, Bob is ardently devoted to Velazquez, but also, more broadly, to the Confederacy. Resembling Edmonds's account of the labors she performed disguised as a Black man in the Confederate camp, Bob helped maintain Confederate horses, dug entrenchments, and buried the dead, but according to Velazquez, her also took up arms against the Union. Such stories contribute to highly erroneous narratives of the Black Confederate soldier, though white masculinist notions of war strictly forbade this possibility. Such a proposal, Kevin M. Levin argues, was only considered near the end of the war when Confederate loss was imminent, but it "undercut the very rationale for waging war, namely the protection of slavery and white supremacy" (39). But flying in the face of this Confederate code, Velazquez depicts Bob as an active and willing combatant. During the heat of the Ball's Bluff battle, she writes, "[m]y darkey had his fighting blood up too, and was, apparently, as anxious as I was to have a crack at the enemy; for he said, 'Give me a gun, Mas' Harry. I want to shoot, too'" (120). After the battle had ended, Velazquez commented on Bob's performance, noting that "having possessed himself of a gun, he fought as well as he knew how, like the rest of us. When the enemy gave way, I could hear Bob yelling vociferously; and I confess that I was proud of the darkey's pluck and enthusiasm" (121–22). Although Velazquez's account of Bob blatantly contrasts Confederate values that distinctly forbid enslaved men from taking up arms, the narrative concurrently speaks to his devotion to her, perpetuating paternal notions Lost Cause notions of slavery that attempt to mitigate its reality.

But not only does Velazquez support slavery in her book—she actively looks to expand its reach even after the Union victory. Again, this point tends to be omitted from contemporary retellings of her exploits.[12] Though Velazquez's Wikipedia page, for example, acknowledges that she went to Venezuela after the war's end, it is framed as mere adventure, yet her travels to this South American country had far more nefarious intentions. After the Confederacy lost the war, pockets of Southerners left their homeland in order to, as Velazquez explains, "start life anew under better auspices than were then possible within the limits of the late Confederacy," inspiring an exodus that brought thousands of Confederates to places such as Mexico, Brazil, and Belize, then British Honduras (535). Scouting out potential Confederate colonies, Velazquez traveled south, documenting this journey in her book. As she explains, Venezuela "was one of the countries which it was proposed to colonize, and representation were made, to the effect that the Venezuelan government would extend a cordial welcome to emigrants, and would aid them in establishing themselves" (536–37). Ultimately, she found Venezuela to be an unsuitable place to build a new Confederate homeland. After several encounters with Black Venezuelan officials, she writes, "A good many of the emigrants . . . seemed to think that if the negroes were of as much importance as they seemed to be in Venezuela, it would have been just as well to have remained at home and fought the battle for supremacy with the free negroes and carpet-baggers on familiar ground"

FIGURE 10. Velazquez disguised as Buford with Bob in *Starting to the Front,* engraved by REA, John Rea Neill, and featured in *Woman in Battle,* 1876.

(543). Though such consequential details are documented in her text, they are rarely addressed in the descriptions of her travels to Venezuela, foreclosing this particular way of remembering.

Rhetorical Possibilities of Participatory Public Memories

Though a democratic source of memory, Wikipedia is largely maintained by those who edit the site, the majority of whom are technologically savvy white men from the Western world. Though collaboratively constructed, the entries that they create tend to reproduce dominant ideologies. While this way of seeing the world generally infects the whole of Wikipedia, we can see how it is specifically manifested in the entries of Edmonds and Velazquez. Because retellings such as those featured on Edmonds's and Velazquez's Wikipedia pages are necessarily pared down to meet the generic demands of the site, it is inevitable that a considerable amount of nuance present in the original core text will be lost. While such omissions are expected, the trends that emerge from this sifting process are revealing. Though issues of veracity are generally worthy of acknowledgment and debate, there is a preoccupation with the authenticity of Edmonds's and Velazquez's "women warrior" stories because their documented discussions of race and slavery are omitted. At present, there hasn't been any discussion of these topics on their Wikipedia pages, an exclusion that points to the biases that haunt those who have collectively compiled these entries. Showing us who we are, contributors are culturally primed to ignore slavery especially in the context of white and Latina women, in accordance with ways of remembering the war that excise motive from action. Replicating familiar ways of knowing, being, and seeing, these editors subsequently focus on Edmonds's and Velazquez's military records and questions of authenticity while ignoring the social realities of slavery that are etched into their published accounts.

While exploring the veracity of their accounts warrants consideration, especially on the internet where misinformation runs rampant, participatory sites such as Wikipedia can complicate how Edmonds and Velazquez are remembered, subtly disrupting dominant ideologies that reinforce white, masculine, cishet culture. As a collaborative, immediately editable, and widely accessible source, Wikipedia holds great promise for broadening ways of remembering. While any act of interpretation is subject to the aperture of identity, as editors become more attentive to intersectional concerns, they revise differently, a rhetorical trend that is exemplified by entries on key Confederate politicians and officers, such as Jefferson Davis and Robert E. Lee, that do address their views on slavery. As editors concerned with social justice come to revise Edmonds's and Velazquez's Wikipedia pages, they can better attend to the ways that race and slavery haunt their stories. In this way, sites like Wikipedia can help teach us who we want to be. In offering more complex, nuanced views of subjects like Edmonds and Velazquez, we take responsibility for past wrongs with the goal of building a more equitable world.

CHAPTER 4

Visual Memories

Ways of Seeing Susie King Taylor

There have always been Black women activists—some known, like Sojourner Truth, Harriet Tubman, Frances E. W. Harper, Ida B. Wells Barnett, and Mary Church Terrell, and thousands upon thousands unknown—who have had a shared awareness of how their sexual identity combined with their racial identity to make their whole life situation and the focus of their political struggles unique.

—Combahee River Collective

While Abraham Lincoln is revered by many, some statues erected in honor of the sixteenth president have been the source of considerable debate. The Emancipation Memorial is one such site. Located in Washington, DC, the sculpture depicts Lincoln standing tall over a stooping Black man dressed in a loincloth.[1] After seeing its unveiling in 1876, Frederick Douglas remarked, "The negro here, though rising, is still on his knees and nude. What I want to see before I die is a monument representing the negro, not couchant on his knees like a four-footed animal, but erect on his feet like a man" (qtd. in White and Sandage). Probing the connection between oppression and visual representation, Douglass believed "the astonishingly large storehouse of racist stereotypes that had been accumulated in the American archive of antiblack imagery, the bank of simian and other animal-like caricatures . . . undermine[d] the Negro's claim of a common humanity, and therefore the rights to freedom and citizenship and economic opportunity," explains Henry Louis Jr. ("Frederick Douglass's Camera Obscura" 28, emphasis in original). Participating in this troubling visual tradition, the hunkering Black man in the Emancipation Memorial reinforces a culture of white supremacy that placed a Black man on unequal footing with his white counterpart.

But if images can be employed to dehumanize African Americans, they can also be used to transform socially constructed conceptions of racial difference, as Douglass was acutely aware. The most photographed man in nineteenth-century America, Douglass lived out the rhetorical possibility of the visual (Gates, "Frederick Douglass's Camera Obscura" 28). In contrast to the image of the subservient enslaved man in the Emancipation Memorial, photographs of Douglass speak to the great power and potential of the African American man. Making explicit his theory of the visual, Douglass discussed his views of photography and pictures in several lectures, asserting that images "exert a powerful, though silent influence upon the ideas and sentiment of present and future generations" ("Lecture on Pictures" 130).[2] Inspired by Douglass, art historian Sarah Lewis explores the connection between "vision and justice" in her special edition of the photography magazine *Aperture* (11). In discussing the ways that images expanded notions of Black citizenship, Lewis offers the concept of "representational justice," what she describes as "[t]he centuries-long effort to craft an image to pay honor to the full humanity of black life . . . for which photography and cinema have been central, even indispensable" (11). More than a mere act of optical inclusion, representational justice attends to the role that the visual plays in changing social perceptions of race with a specific focus on how depictions of Black individuals contribute to, in ways both exceptional and everyday, American society—past, present, and future.

Lewis's articulation of representational justice offers a productive framework for examining how images function rhetorically to shape public memories of the American Civil War and the ways that those visuals, in turn, inform constructions of race, gender, and citizenship. While the continued visual whitewashing of American history illuminates the need for representational justice, it proves particularly difficult in the commemorative landscape of the war. Broadly reflecting how marginalized populations have historically been documented in official archival collections, visual representations of Black men and women during the war are scant—if present at all. While the rhetorical repercussions of these representational *in*justices ripple outward in a multitude of consequential ways, in this chapter, I specifically examine how the photographs and images that comprise the Prints & Photographs Division at the Library of Congress (LOC) are repurposed in a StoryMap project titled "Susie King Taylor: An African American Nurse and Teacher in the Civil War," an award-winning multimedia composition that aims to bring greater attention to Taylor and the labors that she performed on behalf of the Union.[3] After fleeing slavery when the war first erupted, Taylor came to serve the Union as a cook, laundress, teacher, and nurse, documenting these experiences in *Reminiscences* *of My Life in Camp with the 33rd United States Colored Troops, Late First S.C. Volunteers* (1902).

Taylor's book serves as the narrative blueprint for the StoryMap project that Elizabeth Lindqwister, the 2019 Liljenquist Family Fellow, worked on in collaboration with Karen Chittenden and Micah Messenheimer, Library of Congress (LOC) Prints & Photographs Division staff members, to "bring [Taylor's] story to the foreground" (Lindqwister et al.).[4] Linked from the LOC website, this highly visual endeavor combines passages from Taylor's memoir with images from the LOC's Digital and Physical Prints & Photographs Collection to bring greater attention to Taylor and her service to the Union. Both stunning and informative, their StoryMap does the important work of disrupting dominant white androcentric narratives of the war through its retelling of Taylor's story, but as I argue in this chapter, it falls short of advancing representational justice, particularly for women of color. Although this may seem like an indictment of Lindqwister et al.'s project, it more broadly illuminates the repercussions of archival scarcity. While the StoryMap focuses on Taylor, a Black woman, images of Black women are conspicuously sparse in the project.[5] To offset this dearth, Black men feature more prominently in the StoryMap, but even these visuals often bear the imprint of the particular brand of racism common to the period. Reflecting the limitations of the archive, this discernable discrepancy between the discursive elements of the StoryMap and the visuals employed in this retelling points to a pressing need to think more capaciously about how visualizations of Black women, in particular, are rendered legible in public memory projects.

The Rhetorical Dimensions of Representational Justice

As is well documented, the connection between memory and the visual has deep roots in rhetorical studies. Because the fourth canon traditionally focused on how an orator could improve recall, mnemonic strategies were regularly discussed in ancient rhetorical treatises. As described in *Rhetorica ad Herennium*, for example, the memory palace invited practitioners to associate specific details with familiar physical locations. Also called the Method of Loci, this place-based visualization exercise links abstract information with spatial imagery, improving recall. Animating this concept is the story of Simonides of Ceos, taken up by both Cicero in *De Oratore* and Quintilian in *Institutio Oratoria*. A Greek poet, Simonides was invited to perform at a banquet in honor of a nobleman, but when he had stepped outside for a moment, the hall roof collapsed and everyone inside was killed. The bodies were so mangled that they couldn't be identified, but relying on his visual memory of the guests' seating arrangements, Simonides remembered where everyone was sitting and could thus identify the victims based on their locations.

But the rhetorical possibilities of the ocular concern more than mere recall. The visual plays an essential role in shaping human understanding of the world, as famously illustrated by Plato in his allegory of the cave. In this excerpt from the *Republic*, Plato describes a group of people who, since infancy, were bound in chains in a cave located deep underground. Unable to move, they can only see the silhouettes of objects that flit in front of them, as their captors parade "all kinds of artifacts" in front of a fire behind a screen (514b). Through sight, these shadows shape the prisoners' memory, informing how they understand and navigate life as they know it. It is only when one prisoner escapes and sees the world in its fuller reality does he come to understand how they have all been deceived. While this narrative is used to describe Plato's theory of the forms and the limitations of the senses, it also speaks to how the visual, what Laurie Gries defines as "that which we *think* we see," informs human perceptions of the world (*Still Life with Rhetoric* 9, emphasis added). Though "[t]he way we see things is affected by what we know or what we believe," what we visually consume concomitantly contributes to what we know and what we believe (Berger 8).

Visual and material artifacts help shape social constructions of race, as Lewis rightly theorizes, but taking up how images have historically been used to degrade and dehumanize Black populations, bell hooks discusses the damage done in *Black Looks: Race and Representation*:

> There is a direct and abiding connection between the maintenance of white supremacist patriarchy in this society and the institutionalization via mass media of specific images, representations of race, of blackness that support and maintain the oppression, exploitation, and overall domination of all black people. Long before white supremacists ever reached the shores of what we now call the United States, they constructed images of blackness and black people to uphold and affirm their notions of racial superiority, their political imperialism, their will to dominate and enslave. From slavery on, white supremacists have recognized that control over images is central to the maintenance of any system of racial domination. (2)

Harnessed in service of white supremacy, images have long been used to oppress people of color. Situating this phenomena squarely in the realm of rhetoric, Ersula J. Ore animates this theory through her analysis of lynching images. A kind of visual epideictic, these depictions, Ore argues, helped define white citizenship. "Like all iconic images," she explains, "lynching photographs reproduced dominant ideology and communicated social knowledge that instructed citizens in the 'ordinary habits' and 'deep rules' of democratic citizenship. Within this context, photographs of a degraded black body flanked by crowds of smiling white faces depicted the contract of racial exploitation and eradication that secured democratic promise" (57). To this end, Ore concludes, "the lynching photograph, by way of its resonance as an irrefutable representation of 'the real,' ideologically naturalized lynching as an esteemed practice of white citizenship" (57).

Exploring the flip side of this coin, Lewis focuses on the transformative potential of images in her work on representational justice, asserting that images can disrupt white supremacist logics that undermine Black humanity and equality. Writes Lewis, "the foundational right of representation in a democracy, the right to be recognized justly, has historically and is still urgently tied to the work of visual representation in the public realm" (7). Though Lewis doesn't explicitly describe this as a rhetorical enterprise, her theory of representational justice can also be understood as a type of epideictic rhetoric for reasons similar to Ore's: the visual mirrors and reproduces the sociocultural values and priorities of those with the most power, shaping constructions of race and gender. Highlighting its transformative potential, Lewis underscores how images can also disrupt white-centered and otherwise problematic representations, but as exemplified by Lindqwister et al.'s StoryMap, archival constraints limit this possibility. Because "[a] crowd thinks in images" (Le Bon 15), stories of Black women and the war continue to exist on the periphery because they remain largely unseen in a vast sea of whiteness.

Developments in photography and print technology allowed the Civil War to be documented in ways that previous martial conflicts had not. "Approximately a thousand photographers worked separately and in teams to produce hundreds of thousands of portraits," Jeff L. Rosenheim explains, creating a "national visual library of sorts" that influences our collective memory of the war (1). Circulating in primary source collections, these "visual materials," what the Society of American Archivists defines as a "generic term used to collectively describe items of a pictorial nature, including prints, paintings, photographs, motion pictures, and video" help give rise to visual memories of the war. But illustrative of what K. J. Rawson calls "the rhetorical power of archives," these repositories are anything but neutral sites ("The Rhetorical Power of Archival

Description" 2). Shaped by the availability of sources as well as those who assemble, arrange, and describe them, these collections are a "reflection of and often justification for the society that creates them," as Joan M. Schwartz and Terry Cook maintain (12). Howard Zinn puts it this way: "The existence, preservation, and availability of archives, documents and records in our society are very much determined by the distribution of wealth and power. That is, the most powerful, the richest elements in society have the greatest capacity to find documents, preserve them, and decide what is or is not available to the public" (20). As such, many archival collections have historically excluded artifacts that document the experiences of marginalized populations. This "archival violence," as Amalia S. Levi calls it, has dire consequences: "What gets into the archives gets to be preserved 'forever' and is enhanced with access tools through archival description and metadata that usually reinforce Western assumptions. These records are then retrieved and used in scholarship, and eventually become part of historical narrative in a process that shapes what we remember and what we forget" (131). Though Levi is specifically discussing textual records, her point is applicable to visual collections as well: because many archival images were produced by and for dominant white groups, they often advance a relatively homogenous view of the past, impeding representational justice on a broad public scale.

To illustrate how archives inform representational justice, I turn to the StoryMap of Taylor. Similar to other case studies offered in this book, the mechanisms that evoke memories of Taylor, including the LOC-sponsored StoryMap, are largely born from her own writings. Suggestive of the social constraints of the period, it is "the only published account by an African American woman who served with the Union army, and one of less than a score of eyewitness black Civil War memoirs," as historian Catherine Clinton confirms ("Susie King Taylor" 130).[6] While she was "asked many times by my friends, and also by members of the Grand Army of the Republic and Women's Relief Corps, to write a book of my army life, during the war of 1861–65," as Taylor explains in the preface, she self-published the eighty-three-page book in 1902 (ii). While "military memoirs of the Civil War were particularly in vogue" at the time, she focused on the contributions of African Americans, complicating and nuancing common recollections (Clinton, "Introduction" vii). In her discussion of Black women specifically, Taylor highlights some of the ways they supported the Union, while also confronting their erasure from this contentious event: "There are many people who do not know what some of the colored women did during the war," she writes. "There were hundreds of them who assisted the Union soldiers by hiding them and helping them to escape. Many were punished for taking food to the prison stockades for the prisoners. . . . Others assisted in various ways the Union army. These things should be kept in history before the people" (67–68). In documenting their efforts, Taylor does her part to keep Black women's service to the Union in the public eye, illustrating the active role that they took in fighting for freedom and citizenship.

When first published, *Reminiscences of My Life in Camp* primarily circulated in the Boston area where Taylor resided in the later years of her life. But as civil rights and the feminist movements advanced in the 1960s and 1970s, greater attention was given to more diverse perspectives of the war, particularly in response to the largely white-centered centennial celebrations of the era. During this period, Taylor's book was reissued and additional articles and biographies that shared her story began to circulate with more regularity.[7] As acknowledgment of her efforts took greater hold, physical monuments were erected in her honor, changing the visual topography of the war: in 2015, the Susie King Taylor Community School opened in Savannah, Georgia; in 2019, a historical marker in Midway, Georgia was erected in honor of her accomplishments as educator, nurse, and author; and in 2021, a memorial celebrating Taylor's labors was unveiled in the Mount Hope Cemetery in Boston, Massachusetts. And more commemorative projects are on the horizon: the Susie King Taylor Women's Institute and Ecology Center is actively pursuing fundraising efforts to build the Susie King Taylor Escape to Freedom Underground Railroad Park. Though the growing number of material markers speak to her emerging eminence, so too does her notable web presence. Taylor is featured on numerous sites, including web pages sponsored by the National Park Service and the American Battlefield Trust as well as popular sources such as Wikipedia.

Though Taylor's book has helped propagate her memory, it was a photo of her, held in the LOC's Liljenquist Family Collection of Civil War Photographs, that inspired the StoryMap project (fig. 11). Among the 5,000 special portrait photographs of mostly white Union and Confederate soldiers, the image of Taylor is one of the few depicting an African American woman. As Lindqwister explained in an interview, "Susie was one of the only non-white nurses in the collection, and after reading her memoir, *Reminiscences of My Life in Camp,* I came to understand that her time serving with a black Union regiment contributed to a wartime experience that was not well-documented in this period" (quoted in Lindberg). Using Ersi StoryMaps, a web-based application that encourages users to "[c]reate inspiring, immersive stories by combining text, interactive maps, and other multimedia content" ("ArcGIS StoryMaps"),

FIGURE 11. *Susie King Taylor, Known as the First African American Nurse,* photographed by Elmer Chickering. Published in 1902 in Taylor's memoir, *My Life in Camp,* and circulated on the LOC StoryMap. Credit: Library of Congress, Prints & Photographs Division, LC-USZ61–1863.

Lindqwister et al. fused alphabetic text from Taylor's book with visual artifacts from the LOC's extensive collections.

A significant source of national memory, the LOC was established in 1800, earning the designation of "the nation's oldest federal cultural institution" ("Introducing . . ."). Though it is the official library for the US Congress, the LOC also serves the general public as one of the largest libraries in the world, counting among its collection over 171 million items, including 40 million books and other print materials in 470 languages ("General Information"). Its physical presence spans three buildings on Capitol Hill in Washington, DC, in addition to the High-Density Storage Facility in Maryland and the Packard Campus for Audio Visual Conservation in Virginia. The LOC also has a strong web presence, recording 805.1 million views on the Library's web page in 2020 ("General

Information"). Complementing its physical collections, the LOC hosts a range of digital archives and databases, including several focused on the American Civil War. But despite its massive holdings, the LOC contains only a dearth of images featuring Black women during the conflict. Because visuals are what Laurie Gries describes as ongoing "events" with endless "dynamic, unfolding, and unforeseeable becomings," this archival scarcity has implications that ripple outward ("Iconographic Tracking" 335).[8] As the StoryMap illustrates, these absences and limitations are often reproduced when visual materials are picked up and recirculated in subsequent sites of memory, exemplifying the limitations of the archive to advance intersectional representational justice.

Archival Scarcity and Black Women's Civil War Work

While the LOC's collection of visual materials tends to reflect a white male perspective of the Civil War, there are a handful of images featuring Black women that are repurposed in the StoryMap of Taylor. But even as these visuals are absorbed into the project, pushing back against whitewashed narratives of the war, photographs and illustrations that document the kinds of experiences that women of color endured during this momentous occasion are scarce. As my analysis of the StoryMap reveals, repurposing such images, particularly from a digital collection like the LOC that is easily accessible to the general public, can create a loop of imagistic repetition that inevitably stunts representational justice. Additionally, my study of this digital site of memory illuminates how long-standing archival descriptive practices that promote seemingly neutral physical accounts of visual materials can also impede representational justice. Omitting visual materials' relevant historical context can shape how images are interpreted and thus recirculated in new contexts, as I discuss in this section and throughout the chapter.

Acknowledging the ways that whiteness has historically informed visions of the war, Lindqwister et al. include a sepia-colored photograph in an early segment of the StoryMap titled "Narratives of War." Taken by James F. Gibson during the Peninsula Campaign, the image titled *Group—Brigade Officers of Horse Artillery Near Fair Oaks* depicts a group of men in Union uniforms, all of whom are named and ranked in the LOC's description of the photo. Although the specific image is likely unfamiliar to site users, the visual theme it advances is widely recognizable: white men valiantly fought in the Civil War. Using a "scrolling narrative panel" called a "sidecar"(Wilber),[9] Lindqwister et al. explain that "[i]n the postwar 19th century, publications primarily commemorated the war by writing about white soldiers, generals, and presidents—heroic figures celebrated for their bravery in battle or brilliance in war strategy." This combination of the visual and the textual helps drive home the point that the labors performed by women and people of color have been historically ignored and overlooked. As attempts to diversify memories of the Civil War came into vogue, Lindqwister et al. explain, "the achievements of most African American women surfaced slowly."

To help diversify common memories of the war, Lindqwister et al. use the StoryMap platform to visually "retell" Taylor's story. Centering her as the main subject of the project, the opening image depicts Taylor wearing a nurse's veil and a dark-colored uniform. But because there is only one known photograph of her, it is also embedded in the first section and the conclusion. Taken after the war by Elmer Chickering, a Boston photographer known for his portraits of famous individuals, the image was first published as the frontispiece to Taylor's book.[10] Acting as what Roland Barthes calls "certificate of presence," it exemplifies how the visual can help create memory (87). As Barbie Zelizer explains, "images work in patterned ways, concretizing and externalizing events in an accessible and visible fashion that allows us to recognize the tangible proof they offer of the events being represented" ("The Voice of the Visual in Memory" 160). Offering visual evidence that Black women fought for their freedom through their service to the Union, the photo of Taylor helps counter what Glymph describes as "erasure [that] surround[s] the story of enslaved women who pinned the U.S. flag to their chests and fought for the nation and their freedom" (10).

Housed in both the LOC's physical and digital collections, the photograph of Taylor is now "detached from the place and time in which it first made its appearance and preserved," to borrow the language of John Berger (9–10). More accessible to a wider public, artifacts in digital collections have more potential for virality, what Gries describes as "the tendency of things to spread quickly and widely . . . [as] a consequence of a thing's design, production, distribution, circulation, transformation, collectivity, and consequentiality" (*Still Life with Rhetoric* 87). In addition to its appearance in the StoryMap, the photo of Taylor is now reproduced in a variety of online spaces and features prominently in a Google image search of "Black women and the American Civil War." Though the photo's circulation on the web (and, writ small, on the StoryMap) advances representational justice through amplifying Taylor's service to the Union, it also has come to function as a visual synecdoche, signifying the broader swath of African American women who performed similar labors but whose contributions to the war were not visually or textually documented. While the

FIGURE 12. A screenshot of Harriet Tubman as featured in the LOC StoryMap.
Left: *Portrait of Harriet Tubman,* taken by Benjamin F. Powelson in 1869. Right:
Harriet Tubman Escape, Disguised as a Man, composed by Bernarda Bryson
in ink and watercolor in 1934 or 1935. Original images can be found at the
Library of Congress, Prints & Photographs Division, LC-DIG-ppmsca-54232
and LC-DIG-ppmsca-06782.

photograph of Taylor helps disrupt traditional visions of the war as it solidifies
her own legacy, it also runs the risk of tokenizing her image as one of the few
Black female faces of the war. The repetition of the image, then, invites questions about the role of visual variety in the broader landscape of representational justice.

To visually diversify the ways that Black women actively served the Union,
the StoryMap also includes two images of Harriet Tubman from the LOC collections: a photograph and a watercolor painting. Though both artifacts bring
an important intersectional optic to the project, Tubman is one of the most
widely recognized women of color in the United States, featuring prominently
in public sites of memory and popular media. But as I take up more fully in
chapter 2, she is primarily remembered for her work with the Underground
Railroad. Calling attention to her service to the Union nuances memories of
Tubman and her abolition efforts while further exemplifying the ways in which
Black women actively fought for their freedom. But Tubman's association
with the war is not readily discernable in these images. Offering a more femi-
ninized view of Tubman, the *carte de visite,* a small calling card of sorts that was

popular during and after the American Civil War, taken by Benjamin Powelson in Auburn, New York around 1868. The image depicts a youthful Tubman wearing a stylish dress. Contrasting this photo is the ink and watercolor illustration, which depicts Tubman dressed as a man while on an Underground Railroad mission, the abolitionist work for which she is more typically remembered. Created in 1934 or 1935 by Bernarda Bryson, an American painter and lithographer, the piece was to be included in a children's book on the Underground Railroad, though it was never published ("Harriet Tubman Escape"). Suggestive of just one way to advance representational justice in the face of archival annihilation, its presence in the StoryMap expands how Black women are remembered in the context of the Civil War, but exemplifying the necessity of contextualization, both the photo and illustration are made relevant to Taylor and Black women's Civil War experiences more broadly through Lindqwister et al.'s textual intervention. Demonstrating how description can alter "'that which we think we see,'" to harken back to Gries's definition of the visual (*Still Life with Rhetoric* 9), the StoryMap explains that Tubman was "[o]ne of [the] many women working with the regiment . . . .[s]he served as a nurse, scout, and spy for the 1st South Carolina Volunteers." Though "[i]t is unclear whether she and Taylor knew each other," there has been considerable speculation that their paths did cross (Lindqwister et al). Adding a layer of meaning to this image, Lindqwister et al.'s discussion of Tubman speaks to how representational justice can be enhanced through discursive means. Imbued with new meaning as they are recirculated, the images of Tubman as displayed in the StoryMap alter conventional ways of seeing and remembering Tubman, the war, and more broadly, Black women's place in US history.

A corollary to archival scarcity, Black women appear in only one other photograph in the StoryMap. Paired with a discussion of Taylor's service to the First South Carolina Volunteer Infantry Regiment, later reorganized into the 33rd US Colored, the photo *Smith Plantation Port Royal Island SC* (fig. 13) was taken on property that eventually acquired the name Camp Saxton, which was the training grounds for the unit.[11] Foregrounding Black women's experiences as they transitioned from slavery to liberation, Lindqwister et al. discuss Taylor's work as a laundress for the regiment. While they comment on the physical challenges of this work, they also note that women who typically performed such labors "were not often literate and were stereotyped as 'loose women.'" Such characterizations, they explain, did not accurately capture Taylor and her service to the Union. In juxtaposing the discursive and the visual, Lindqwister et al. invite site users to think more capaciously about the parameters of the

FIGURE 13. *Smith Plantation Port Royal Island SC,* photographed by Hubbard & Mix between 1863 and June 1866. Featured on the LOC StoryMap. Credit: Library of Congress, Prints & Photographs Division, LC-DIG-stereo-1s07100.

conflict, but this example also illuminates a key tension that can potentially hamper the execution of representational justice. Though text and images work in tandem to create meaning, misalignments can emerge when these connections are muddled. In focusing on Taylor's labors and foregoing discussion of the Black women and children featured in the photo, Lindqwister et al. prompt questions about the circumstances in which this photograph was originally taken.

While the StoryMap provides a link to the LOC entry for *Smith Plantation Port Royal Island SC,* in accordance with standard archival descriptive practices, the digital record offers little additional context. Though the description of visual materials vary from institution to institution, it generally aims to "captur[e] and communicat[e] knowledge about the broad administrative and documentary contexts of records creation within an organization as a whole as one move further away from the original circumstances of creation. Its purpose is to preserve, perpetuate, and authenticate meaning over time so that it is available and comprehensible to all users—present and potential" (MacNeil 30). But as critical archive scholars have noted, applying such principles to visual materials proves challenging. Joan Schwartz explains it this way: "without adequate contextual information about their functional origins and provenance, or clear links to such contextual information . . . photographic archives [are transformed] into stock photo libraries, reducing photographs to their visible elements, and conflating photographic content and photographic meaning" (157). The general concerns that Schwartz raises can be specifically observed in the LOC's entry on *Smith Plantation*. Though the LOC includes some accession information, acknowledging that the image was purchased from Russell Norton in 2016, and offers some details about the photographers, its summary constitutes a physical description of the image. Shot by Hubbard & Mix between 1863 and 1866, the stereoscope card features "a group portrait of African American women and children, former slaves, now considered Freedman" ("Smith Plantation").[12] While description and metadata make the photograph discoverable to site users searching for images of Black women and the Civil War, notably missing from the LOC depiction is a discussion of this relationship, further occluding the ways in which Black women experienced the war. Such an omission invites questions about how visual materials in the archive should be articulated to best "educat[e] the public, suppor[t] social justice, and facilitat[e] scholarly research" (Holterhoff, para. 31). Description, as Wendy Duff and Verne Harris remind us, plays an essential role in "the construction of meanings and the exercise of power" (264). Attending to these dynamics, recent efforts to adopt general reparative and anti-oppressive descriptive practices have gained momentum (Frick and Proffitt; Hughes-Watkins; Tai), but these suggestions often forgo specific discussions of visual materials and the necessity of providing situational context. Yet as the *Smith Plantation* demonstrates, attending to the scene of an image is often needed to understand its significance and how it might enact representational justice.

Once a cotton plantation owned by John Joyner Smith, the property in the photo was confiscated by the Union during the early years of the war. As Smith and over two hundred enslavers fled the area, the thousands of men, women, and children they enslaved remained, eventually joined by others who sought Union protection in the contraband camps established there (Willis 63). Because many of the emancipated men worked in service of the Union, women and children largely remained on site, a reality captured in the LOC photograph. As several historians have argued, Black women and children faced considerable obstacles in these ostensible places of refuge. Amy Murrell Taylor explains that "the nation's descent into civil war set in motion hundreds of thousands of men, women, and children—entire families, neighborhood, and communities— in a mass exodus from slavery that would strain and then destroy the institution once and for all" (5). But initially, there was no policy in place to address this unanticipated diaspora, so Federal officials forced many to return to their Southern enslavers in accordance with the Fugitive Slave Act. Recognizing the

FIGURE 14. *View on Smith Plantation, Near Beaufort, SC,* photographed by
E. W. Sinclair between 1862 and 1864 for Sam. A. Cooley, photographer Tenth
Army Corps. Credit: Library of Congress, Prints & Photographs Division, LC-
DIG-stereo-1s04463.

great disadvantage of such an approach, Union Major General Benjamin Butler
proposed a contraband policy that enabled the Union to retain the enslaved, as
discussed in chapter 1. Initially, though, this policy did not include women and
children, whose labors were not highly valued. But as Stephanie McCurry observes, Black women resisted these legal obstacles by "turn[ing] military posts
into refugee camps, confront[ing] commanders like Butler, Henry Halleck, and
Grant with a humanitarian crisis, and perpetually challeng[ing] the limited parameters of the government's military emancipation policy" (80). While several
issues regarding the legal status of enslaved women and children were resolved
with President Abraham Lincoln's Emancipation Proclamation that went into
effect in 1863, Black women encountered unique challenges on their road to
freedom that are often neglected in common visual and discursive narratives
of the war. While archival scarcity has contributed to this general elision, descriptive practices also play a role. As illustrated by the *Smith Plantation* photo
and its circulation in the StoryMap, description informs how an image is understood and repurposed. When visuals are stripped of relevant context, pictorial content runs the risk of being misunderstood, hindering representational
justice.

A similar contextual omission emerges in Lindqwister et al.'s repurposing
of *View on Smith Plantation, Near Beaufort, SC* (fig. 14). A stereograph image
taken by E. W. Sinclair between 1862 and 1864, the image "shows a group of

men and women standing on the road in front of John Joyner Smith's cotton plantation in Port Royal, South Carolina. Four African American children stand in the field behind them. From November 1862 to January 1863, the house was used as Union Camp Saxton, and was the location of Emancipation Day activities on January 1, 1863," as the LOC entry reports ("View on Smith Plantation"). Located in the first sidecar panel in a section titled "Words from the Battlefield" in the StoryMap, *View on Smith Plantation* discusses the First South Carolina Volunteer regiment and their movement throughout the region. Prioritizing the setting of the photo, Lindqwister et al. use the image to bring to life their discussion of the regiment's training grounds, explaining that the unit "left from St. Simons Island to start training at Camp Saxton, located on the Smith plantation, or 'Old Fort,' in Port Royal, South Carolina." While the sidecar panel that follows acknowledges the "little school" that Taylor oversaw on St. Simons Island, the majority of the section focuses on the regiment, a predominantly Black male experience, which runs in discursive contrast to the photograph.

The lack of Black women in *View on Smith Plantation* invites questions about how description and contextualization might be used to better attend to archival scarcity. While discursive solutions cannot fully address the problems of visual absence, they can encourage us to look differently at what we see before us and ask questions about what is missing. Port Royal, where the Smith Plantation is located, and the Sea Islands more generally, was the site of a government initiative intended to "propagate industry, religion, and education" in the newly emancipated (Moore, *The Rebellion Record* 224). Part of a larger endeavor to integrate the formerly enslaved into white society, over fifty Northerners, many of whom were white abolitionist women, went to the region to help with this transition. While some newly freed Black women went to school during this time, they also performed a range of roles providing much-needed services. Some, like Taylor, worked as laundresses and cooks for the Union (Manning 172; 184). Others were domestic servants for the Northern teachers and missionaries (Glymph 174–79). Still others tended the land, caring for the gardens that helped feed the island inhabitants and picking cotton to fund the Union cause. These—and the many other labors that Black women undertook for the Union, their local communities, and families—helped "reinvent citizenship" for African Americans, in the words of Chandra Manning (174). Though there are only a limited number of images in the LOC archives that document Black women at this time, descriptive practices can make their experiences more textually visible. While such reparative endeavors are limited in terms of their capacity to advance representational justice, they can help mitigate the "archival violence" that has been inflicted upon women of color in these spaces.

Blurred Visions of Black Union Soldiers

While only a few visuals of Black women are featured in the StoryMap project and the LOC more generally, photographs of Black men appear with greater regularity, indicative of personal and official interests in documenting Civil War soldiers. Writing specifically about African American soldiers, Deborah Willis explains that "[h]aving a photograph taken was indeed a self-conscious act, one that shows the subjects were aware of the significance of the moment and sought to preserve it. Photographs were a luxury," she continues; "their prevalence shows their importance as records of family, position, identity, and humanity, as status symbols" (9–10). For Black soldiers in particular, donning the Union uniform marked a momentous point in the march toward racial equality. Though a federal law precluded Black men from enlisting in the military, that changed with the Emancipation Proclamation. As a result, roughly 180,000 Black men came to volunteer as soldiers ("African-American Solders"). While their service inspired many to have their photographs taken, as Willis acknowledges, there is a general "lack of images of black soldiers" in Civil War archives (viii). Though more additions have been made to the LOC holdings over the last decade, there are far fewer images of Black men in these collections than their white counterparts. This archival limitation inevitably constrains how Black soldiers are visually depicted in the commemorative landscape of the war. But while Lindqwister et al. had more options of visual materials featuring Black men of the period set this scene, their selections tend to highlight a noteworthy distinction between visual diversity and representational justice. In contrast to the work of Willis, who collated images that "engage that sense of activism and highlight the various acts of courage by black men, both bonded and free, during the Civil War," the photos of Black soldiers included in the StoryMap often reflect the racial inequities that haunted the moment (6). Informed by Taylor's memoir and her descriptions of her service to the First South Carolina Volunteers, such images typically center the authority of white officers, a sentiment that is often reinforced through archival description and metadata.

Highlighting the social and political significance of the First South Carolina Volunteers, the regiment which Taylor served and wrote about extensively in her book, the StoryMap commences the section titled "At War" by explaining that "[t]he creation of this regiment was made not solely because of a need

FIGURE 15. *Dress Parade of First South Carolina, (U.S.C.T.), Beaufort, SC,* taken between 1862 and 1864, printed between 1880–1889. Featured on the LOC's Story-Map. Credit: Library of Congress, Prints & Photographs Division, LC-DIG-ppmsca-35307.

for increased troops; its existence reflected the Union Army's slowly-changing mindset toward African American soldiers" (Lindqwister et al.). The photograph *Dress Parade of First South Carolina, (U.S.C.T.), Beaufort, SC* (fig. 15) is used to illustrate this point, but the content of the image is visually unclear, prompting site users to ponder what Finnegan calls a "deceptively simple question 'What is this a picture of?'" ("What Is This a Picture Of?" 118). While the barren trees, tents, and buildings in the background offer some contextual clues, the figures in the photograph are nearly illegible, even when users zoom into the digitized image linked to the LOC site. Further exemplifying the rhetorical power of description, those who encounter the image have to rely on the discursive context to understand that image documents "the 1st South Carolina Volunteers, a regiment of African American soliders [*sic*] formed in the fall of 1862 in Beaufort, South Carolina" ("Dress Parade"). Though this summary helps site users understand what they are seeing, in ways similar to the limitations of the *View on Smith Plantation* photo, its optical ambiguity diminishes its suasive punch. While the mere existence of such an image, however imperfectly executed, offers an important visual record of racial progress, the general indecipherability of *Dress Parade* limits how it advances representational justice.

While *Camp Brightwood, D.C. Contrabands in 2nd R.I. Camp* (fig. 16) is sharper, it captures the racialized inequities that characterized the moment.

FIGURE 16. *Camp Bright-wood, D.C. Contrabands in 2nd R.I. Camp,* taken around 1863. Featured on the LOC StoryMap. Credit: Library of Congress, Prints & Photographs Division, LC-DIG-ppmsca-11198.

Appearing in a sidecar panel that passes over *Dress Parade,* the photograph accompanies a brief review of contraband war politics. As Lindqwister et al. explain, "the Union usually sent escaped African Americans back to their slave owners," but by designating Black men "contraband" of war, "the Army [could] . . . conscript former slaves as military laborers, without being legally obliged to return them to the Confederates" (Lindqwister et al.). Depicting this reality, *Camp Brightwood, D.C. Contrabands in 2nd R.I. Camp,* taken between 1861 and 1863 by an unknown photographer, features Union Captain Beriah Brown, Captain John P. Shaw, and Lt. James B. Fry, all of whom are named in the finding aid, while the Black individuals are described as "African American men and boy" ("Camp Brightwood"). But exemplifying how, in the words of John Tagg, "the camera is never neutral," the image hints at the ways in which white supremacy informed these camps, and more broadly, the social and political epoch (63). Although all in the photo wear uniforms, the white officers' attire is more ornate; their swords are also in full view in contrast to the contrabands

FIGURE 17. *2nd Rhode Island Infantry.* All were taken between 1861 and 1865 and printed between 1880 and 1889. Credit: Library of Congress, Prints & Photographs Division. From left: LC-DIG-ppmsca-34316; LC-DIG-ppmsca-34296; LC-DIG-ppmsca-34310.

who have no weapons. But the differing positions, postures, and facial expressions also speak to the white supremacy that informed even Union regiments. The white men all appear at ease and in control, standing or lounging comfortably on a chair, while the contrabands are positioned below them. Sitting on the ground are the two youngest; their brows are furrowed, as they gaze in the direction of the photographer.

The racial inequities captured in *Camp Brightwood* come more clearly into focus when juxtaposed with photographs of a similar ilk, yet this connection is obscured by metadata, such as titles and subject headings that render some patterns legible and others not. By itself, *Camp Brightwood* might not immediately convey the racial prejudice that freedmen endured in these camps, but considered collectively, this assemblage of images exposes patterned ways that white soldiers asserted their dominance over the African Americans who tended to them during the war (fig. 17). In many of these group photos, a Black male, generally a boy, is seated on the ground, sometimes holding a pitcher or pan to further mark his role as servant; the white soldiers, comparatively, typically stand erect usually with their guns in hand. Though a notable number of these kinds of group shots exist—several of which are held in the LOC's digital collections—the LOC does not explicitly collate these images through metadata entries that would help make visible this particular generic convention. Intrinsically a rhetorical practice, how visual materials are described, classified, and arranged has a profound effect on how they are accessed, interpreted, and recirculated. While scholars in both critical archive studies and rhetoric have examined how metadata affects archival accessibility, there are mixed thoughts on how best to "resist and transform normative archival description practices without creating newer but still equally damaging or silencing practices," as Rawson phrases it in his discussion of queer archiving ("The Rhetorical Power of Archival Description" 18). Recognizing the value of flexible and evolving metadata practices, however, the LOC adds "[a]pproximately 4,000 new headings, including headings with subdivisions . . . each year," suggestive of the potential to enact changes that disrupt the white supremacist visions of the war that persist in visual collections and are perpetuated through uncritical recirculation practices ("Introduction").

Racialized power imbalances are also readily apparent in the photograph titled *Major Samuel K. Thompson and Unidentified Soldiers of the 39th U.S. Infantry posed with a 10" Rodman Cannon at Fort Massachusetts, Mississippi,* which immediately follows *Dress Parade* and *Camp Brightwood* in the StoryMap.[13] Though the photo was taken after the war sometime between 1868 and 1869,

FIGURE 18. *Major Samuel K. Thompson and Unidentified Soldiers of the 39th U.S. Infantry posed with a 10" Rodman Cannon at Fort Massachusetts, Mississippi,* taken between 1868 and 1869. Featured on the LOC StoryMap. Credit: Library of Congress, Prints & Photographs Division, LC-DIG-ppmsca-39544.

Lindqwister et al. use the image to visually anchor their discussion of the legal changes that allowed Black men to enlist in the military. As they explain, "By the fall of 1862, African Americans were no longer considered property by the Union" (Lindqwister et al.). Though they were often segregated from their white colleagues, as noted in the StoryMap, these regiments were commanded by white Union officers, as alluded in this image. Reinscribing white author-ity in ways generally comparable to the *Camp Brightwood* photo, this image features Major Samuel Thompson, a white lieutenant, positioned near a can-non with several unnamed African American soldiers. The focal point of the photograph, Thompson singularly appears in full view: wearing pants lighter in color, he stands above the Black soldiers who are mostly seated below him. He has one foot perched casually on a cannon ball, and his sword is clearly visible, while, again, Black soldiers appear without weapons. While visuals of racial inequities are important to see, when uncritically recirculated, they can work against representational justice. Although the archive is a highly curated rhetorical site, it is inevitably a "scene of a doubled invention," in the words of Barbara Biesecker ("Of Historicity" 124), where agents consult, interpret, repurpose, and restory artifacts to create new meaning, prompting questions about pictorial rhetorical selection. Why *this* photo if the LOC collection includes others that more squarely attend to the experiences of Black soldiers and their fight for freedom, a main theme of Taylor's book?

The power and authority visually afforded to the white men in the photographs featured in the "At War" section of the StoryMap is bolstered in how these images are described by the LOC, further illustrating how archival description can impede representational justice. As I've argued throughout the chapter, archival description carries both explicit and subtle manifestations of systemic inequities, which inform how these images are interpreted and subsequently put to use. One particular instantiation of racial bias observed in the LOC's description of the photographs of Black soldiers concerns identification. Although there are several images of Black men in uniform depicted on the StoryMap, no Black soldiers are named in *Dress Parade, Camp Bridgewood,* or *Major Samuel K. Thompson.* Even the one photograph of a single Black soldier featured on the StoryMap goes nameless, contrasting the descriptions of white officers.[14] But "[n]ames are important," as Alexis Antracoli and Katy Rawdon assert. "Those who are named are empowered, and those who remain nameless are at best marginalized, and at worst erased. The exclusion of people's names from descriptions of historical records is not merely a barrier to scholarly research. Rather, it is both a symptom and cause of the violence of whiteness in our society" (323). Although the erasure of Black nomenclature is the result of a long legacy of archival exclusion, this omission continues to inform the ways that Black soldiers are slighted even as images documenting their services are repurposed in the StoryMap. While they are more visually represented than Black women, they are not identified or named, a rhetorical move that minimizes their contributions and forecloses the possibility of a greater public legacy.

Though archival scarcity limits how Black men and women are portrayed in commemorations of the Civil War, there is archival excess of visual artifacts that document the experiences of white men. This excess has contributed to the predominantly white narratives of the war that have long circulated, illustrating how "images powerfully invoke memory, and that memory is profoundly informed by visual media, though rhetorical dynamics," in the words of Bradford Vivian and Anne Teresa Demo (6). While their StoryMap complicates conventional narratives of this cataclysmic event, Lindqwister et al. also feature images of several white figures discussed in Taylor's book, including Colonel Thomas Wentworth Higginson and Charles T. Trowbridge. A consequence of archival abundance, the accessibility of both discursive and visual materials allows for fuller and more nuanced retellings of their war experiences. Illustrative of this affordance, a large photograph of Higginson features prominently in the StoryMap's discussion of the 33rd U.S. Colored Troops. As explained on the StoryMap, "Higginson was largely responsible for training the soldiers at the beginning of the war, when the regiment was based at Camp Saxton, located on the Smith Plantation in Port Royal, South Carolina" (Lindqwister et al.). Visually complementing Lindqwister et al.'s discussion of these labors is a wood engraving from *Frank Leslie's Illustrated Newspaper*. In the first panel of this image, Higginson can be seen training the regiment. Though the figures in the image are small and barely decipherable, Higginson sits on a white horse as Black men line up around him. There is also a portrait illustration of Trowbridge, which is scanned from Taylor's book. Looking off into the distance, he is dressed in his Union uniform. While Taylor felt great affection for these men, which she expresses in her book and is subsequently relayed in the StoryMap, they take up visual and textual space in a project devoted to the memory of a Black woman. In stark contrast to archival absence and descriptive practices that impact interpretation and recirculation, the visual presence of Higginson and Trowbridge is suggestive of how archival excess recenters hegemonic perspectives, even in counterstories that expressly attempt to talk back to dominant narratives.

Illustrations as Activism

The scarcity of photographs documenting Black experiences of the Civil War has an impact on contemporary visual memories of the war and representational justice, but Lindqwister et al. model a potential workaround for this pictorial gap. In ways similar to their use of the water-color painting of Tubman, they incorporate wood engravings into the StoryMap to aid their retelling of Taylor's book. Commonly found in nineteenth-century newspapers and magazines, this printmaking method was relatively inexpensive and easy to employ, satiating readers' growing desire for a visual experience. Thousands of these illustrations were published throughout the century and beyond, many of which are now available in the LOC Digital and Physical Prints & Photographs Collection. Drawing from this repository, Lindqwister et al. put several images from *Harper's Weekly* to use in the penultimate section of the StoryMap titled "Postwar Inequality." Following the narrative arc of Taylor's book, this section takes up the challenges that African Americans encountered in the years following the war. Suggestive of another dimension of representational

FIGURE 19. Screenshot of *This Is a White Man's Government* created by Thomas Nast. Originally published in *Harper's Weekly*, 5 Sept. 1868: 568. Featured on the LOC StoryMap. Original image can be found at the Library of Congress, Prints & Photographs Division, LC-DIG-ppmsca-71958.

justice, this approach exemplifies how the visual can inspire social change through the images depicting racial injustice. Lewis speaks to this possibility in her introduction to the special edition of *Aperture,* reminding readers that *Description of a Slave Ship* (1789) impelled the British public to outlaw slavery; in another example, she reminds readers that media coverage of the civil rights protests encouraged people to join the marches in Selma, Alabama (13–14). In analogous ways, the engravings included in the StoryMap present the harsh realities of life for African Americans following the war, depicting emotionally intense and violent scenes. As is the case with Civil War photographs, African American men feature more prominently than Black women in these illustrations. Repurposed in the StoryMap, these engravings work in concert with excerpts from Taylor's text to challenge persistent, progressive memories of emancipation, but this is largely accomplished in broad strokes that gloss over the specific oppressions that African American communities experienced during Reconstruction and beyond. In this way, the particular activist objectives that spurred the original publication of these engravings are often erased or flattened as they migrate from *Harper's* to the LOC's digital collections and then are dispersed outward.

Pointing to the contradiction between the professed values of the United States and the lived experiences of African Americans, Taylor discusses the inequalities that haunted Black communities postwar in the last two chapters of *Reminiscences*. In re-storying Taylor's narrative, Lindqwister et al. rightly note that "[t]he signing of the Emancipation Proclamation and the Union's victory in the Civil War meant progress for racial equality in the United States, but could not alleviate the racial divide still haunting the wounded nation." The quotation excerpted from Taylor's account in this section is particularly illustrative of this point:

> I wonder if our white fellow men realize the true sense or meaning of brotherhood? For two hundred years we had toiled for them; the war of 1861 came and was ended, and we thought our race was forever freed from bondage, and that the two races could live in unity with each other, but when we read almost every day of what is being done to my race by some whites in the South, I sometimes ask, "Was the war in vain? Has it brought freedom, in the full sense of the word, or has it not made our condition more hopeless?" (Taylor quoted in Lindqwister at al.)

"Reconstruction," as Lindqwister at al. explain, "was unpopular in the post-Confederate, post-slavery South. Many white Southerners saw it as an embarrassment to the former Confederacy and took it upon themselves to carry out the legacy of slavery in every way possible." As noted earlier in the StoryMap, several constitutional amendments were ratified following the war in an attempt to nudge racial progress along: "The passing of the thirteen, fourteenth, and fifteenth amendments throughout the 1870s abolished slavery and granted some legal rights to African Americans," specifically the right for Black men to vote (Lindqwister et al.). Countering these advancements, as is noted in the StoryMap, Southern states instituted "'black codes' . . . rules [that] all but forced African Americans into servile and laboring positions . . . and severely restricted their rights as citizens" (Lindqwister et al.). Personalizing this claim, and thus amplifying the emotional impact of the point, they include an excerpt from Taylor's book that describes the difficulties that her husband faced postwar in securing a job: though Edward King "was a boss carpenter . . . the prejudice against is his race . . . [was] still too strong to insure him much work at his trade" (quoted in Lindqwister et al.). Instead, as explained in StoryMap, he took a position as a longshoreman and died in a docking accident in 1866.

To help visualize these social, economic, and political obstacles, Lindqwister et al. repurpose an image from the LOC titled *This Is a White Man's Government* (fig. 19). Engraved by Thomas Nast, a cartoonist known for his illustrations of racial injustices, this illustration was originally published in *Harper's Weekly* in September 1868. A potentially traumatizing scene, this illustration depicts a Black soldier splayed on the ground as three white men stand at atop of him, two of whom are brandishing weapons. The caption at the bottom of the image reads, "'We regard the Reconstruction Acts (so called) of Congress as usurpations, and unconstitutional, revolutionary, and void'—Democratic Platform" (Nast). Linked from the StoryMap, the LOC offers a summary of the engraving in accordance with status quo descriptive practices that "reduce visual images to their visual content and denude them of their original contexts of creation, circulation, and viewing" (Schwartz 157). As described in the LOC finding aid, the white man on the right wears a business suit with a button that says "5 Avenue" and holds a wallet that says "capital for votes." Positioned in the middle is a white man who wears a belt buckle engraved with the letters "CSA," an acronym for Confederate States of America; he wields a knife bearing the words "the Lost Cause." And on the left is a simianesque figure, what the LOC describes as a "stereotyped Irishman," who holds a club that says "a vote." Drawing attention to the background of the image, the LOC summary also notes that "'colored orphan asylum'" and a "'southern school'" are in flames" and "African American children have been lynched near the burning buildings" (Nast). While the LOC description proves potentially useful to those who may not see, recognize, or understand the images featured, the image acquires a new layer of meaning as it is repurposed in the StoryMap. Exemplifying the rhetorical power of contextualization to shape visual interpretation, Lindqwister et al.'s discussion of Southern blowback to Reconstruction, while brief, spotlights the white supremacist laws instituted to control and oppress Black communities. Rendering more visible the ways that African Americans were legally exploited and maltreated in the years following the war, this amalgam of the textual and the visual pushes back against overly simplified but persistent memories that suggest that the Civil War fully liberated people of color.

As employed in the StoryMap, *This Is a White Man's Government* does the vital work of disrupting reductive views of emancipation and Reconstruction, but in the recirculation process, much of the engraving's original context is lost. In moving from *Harper's Weekly* to the LOC Print and Photographs Division, the articles associated with engravings are often excised, prompting questions about the role that contextual specificity plays in descriptions of visual materials. Further illustrating the synergistic relationship between the visual and the textual, this engraving depicts articles featured in *Harper's* that discuss the Democratic Party and its efforts to regain political power and maintain white supremacy. While the LOC finding aid describes the drawing, the articles offer specific historical context, illuminating the ways these visuals facilitated representational justice when originally published. In this case, the articles call out the white men in the image and the various forces that worked to oppress people of color. On the right is Horatio Seymour, the 1868 Democratic nominee for president. The former governor of New York, he represented the northern capitalists, but according to the *Harper's* article "A 'Solemn Key,'" he was also "always an apologist for slavery and a defender of the policy of the slaveholders" (562). Running for presidency under the slogan "This is a white man's country: let white men rule," Seymour constituted a significant threat to Black Americans, as captured in the Nast illustration. Positioned in the center of the engraving is Nathan Bedford Forrest, a Confederate army general and the first Grand Wizard of the Ku Klux Klan. His initials can be seen in the band of his hat, but he also wears a button that says "Fort Pillow," a violent Civil War battle in which over 300 Union soldiers, many of whom were Black, were killed. Referenced in the *Harper's* article "The Stars and Bars at the Democratic Peak," Forrest is sardonically deemed the "hero of the massacre at Fort Pillow," but the piece also comments on his support of the Tennessee "militia bill" developed to obstruct Reconstruction efforts that sought to advance racial parity. Forrest is quoted as saying that his "old troops . . . were already drilled," and he was "*in favor of giving no quarter!*" to the enemy. "Undoubtedly," the author quips, "General Forrest was of the same opinion at Fort Pillow" (562). Although the figure on the left of Nast's engraving has no known distinct identity, his club with the words "A Vote" imprinted upon it correlates with the article titled "Political Terrorism." Describing efforts to control how freemen voted in select Southern states before the Fifteenth Amendment was ratified, this piece explains how Black men were often coerced into voting for "a prescribed ticket" or face losing their jobs and "starvation" (563). Although Nast's illustration conveys a general sense of how Black men were maltreated in the years following the war, "Political Terrorism" provided readers with a more specific account of how voter coercion occurred and to what effect (563).

Selected from the LOC's vast repository of images, *This Is a White Man's Government,* as incorporated into the StoryMap, conveys a general sense of the racial oppression common to the period, but this effect is intensified by the contextual details that the accompanying articles offer. Although an image's

FIGURE 20. *Visit of the Ku-Klux* by Frank Bellew. Published in *Harper's Weekly*, 24 Feb. 1872: 160. Featured on the LOC StoryMap. Credit: Library of Congress, Prints & Photographs Division, LC-DIG-ppmsca-71959.

movement can never be "fully controlled" as Gries observes (*Still Life with Rhetoric* 18), losing and acquiring new meaning as it travels from site to site, descriptions of archival visuals that "explain the context and records systems that produced [them]" ("Description") impact how they are interpreted and deployed. Discussions of provenance and originary circumstances help site users make more informed decisions about how to repurpose visual materials, but such descriptive practices can also help advance representational justice. In outlining in greater detail, the people and policies actively working to oppress communities of color, the *Harper's* articles make clear how *This Is a White Man's Government* subverted social injustices of the moment by critiquing key Democratic politicians and beliefs. Divorced from its context, the image is stripped of this nuance, muddling the ways that it spoke back to racialized oppressions.

In accordance with Taylor's book, the StoryMap also takes up the violence that was inflicted on Black communities in the years following the war. As explained in the project, "[t]he things Taylor saw in the Jim Crow South were horrifying. She wrote frequently of the discrimination she faced, and how such treatment rubbed against her wartime patriotism for America" (Lindqwister et al.). The image titled *Visit of the Ku-Klux* (fig. 20) serves as the backdrop to this discussion, visually portraying the violence that African American communities experienced after the war. Though Taylor does not mention by name the Ku Klux Klan, what the StoryMap defines as "a deadly, racist group that protested Reconstruction and terrorized African Americans" (Lindqwister et al.), she discusses the targeted acts of violence that Black communities experienced postwar. In one scene excerpted in this section of the StoryMap, Taylor talks with a Black train conductor as she traveled South to visit her son: "Each morning you can hear of some negro being lynched," the conductor told her. "We have no rights here" (quoted in Lindqwister et al.). Exemplifying the social injustices and racialized trauma that people of color experienced, the *Visit of the Ku-Klux* serves as a visual proxy for this terrorism.

While the engraving works in tandem with the textual to remind site users of how people of color were intimated and threatened, in ways similar to *This Is a White Man's Government,* the original context in which the image was produced is lost as it travels from *Harper's* to the LOC repository to the StoryMap. Engraved by Frank Bellew, *Visit of the Ku-Klux* was originally published in *Harper's Weekly* in February 1872 to bring greater attention to the power that the Klan wielded during Reconstruction. Exposing how the KKK targeted innocent families, this shocking illustration called for social and political change, a purpose that is made clear in the article also titled "Visit of the Ku-Klux" featured in *Harper's*:

> The artist . . . pictures an outrage of frequent occurrence in some of the most turbulent districts of the Southern States. The scene is the interior of a negro cabin, where the little family—fearing no evil—is gathered after the work of the day is over. Suddenly the door is opened, and a member of the Ku-Klux Klan appears, with a gun in hand, to take the life of the harmless old man who sits at the fire-place, and whose only "crime" is his color. It is to be hoped that under a rigorous administration of the laws that these deeds of violence will soon cease forever. (157)

Such context clarifies the activist intentions behind the image and how it worked to advance representational justice when it was first published. The last line of the article, in particular, is suggestive of the legal efforts that were underway to curtail these terrorist acts. Prior to the publication of Bellew's engraving, the Joint Select Committee had submitted several volumes of reports that documented the violence committed by the KKK in Southern States. The image, with its rare depiction of a Black woman, loosely aligns with the experiences shared by Tilda Walthall in one such testimony. As she explained, white men dressed in "great big gowns, and great big sleeves, wide sleeves" came to her door looking for her husband (*The Condition of Affairs* 407). They shot him and beat him, and he died a day later. These narratives helped bring about the Second Enforcement Act of 1871, also known as the Ku Klux Klan Act. This legislation gave the US President authority to intervene at the state level to address violations of civil rights, which contributed to temporary disbandment of the KKK.

As previously discussed, attending to the context in which an image is produced can bring into greater relief how visual materials advanced representational justice, but description can also be employed to disrupt the perpetuation of marginalization by acknowledging oppressive archival content. Though the *Visit of the Ku-Klux* is a violent image, the LOC takes a neutral approach in describing the engraving. Focusing on the physical dimensions of the image, the illustration, as the summary explains, features "an African American woman cooking over a hearth" with a "man seated alongside" her; "three children [are] nearby, in this home, as a man from Ku Klux Klan stands in the doorway and aims a rifle at them" (*Visit of the Ku-Klux*). In striving for objectivity in its summary of the engraving, the LOC fails to address the potentially traumatizing nature of the image, running the risk of turning this violent image into spectacle. Although such visuals have the potential to advance representational justice through publicly exposing structural acts of racial terrorism, they need to be described with rhetorical care to avoid propagating harm. As a countermeasure, some libraries and archives offer content warnings, calling attention to the harm that these kinds of documents and artifacts can perpetrate. The *Harp-Week* digital archive, for example, includes such a statement, acknowledging that "several of the words, descriptions, and images from *Harper's Weekly* are considered racially offensive by today's standards" ("Toward Racial Equality"). Highlighting how these images continue to inform social constructions of race, gender, and citizenship, such textual interventions attempt to balance the need to preserve the past with present concerns of social and representational justice.

The image titled *(?) Slavery is Dead (?)* (fig. 21) also illustrates the problems with descriptive neutrality and contextual omission. As repurposed in the StoryMap, the engraving helps animate Taylor's condemnation of postwar policies that failed to protect the newly emancipated. Building on their discussion of the racialized inequities that persisted after the war, Lindqwister et al.

FIGURE 21. *(?) Slavery is Dead (?)* by Thomas Nast. Published in *Harper's Weekly,* 12 Jan. 1867: 24. Featured on the LOC StoryMap. Credit: Library of Congress, Prints & Photographs Division, LC-DIG-ppmsca-71960.

share Taylor's incisive critique of the United States in the StoryMap: "They say, 'One flag, one nation, one country indivisible.' Is this true? Can we say this truthfully, when one race is allowed to burn, hang, and inflict the most horrible torture weekly, monthly, on another? No, we cannot sing 'My county 'tis of thee, Sweet land of liberty!' It is hollow mockery" (quoted in Lindqwister et al.). The passage continues to note that "[t]he Southern laws are all on the side of the white, and they do just as they like to the negro, whether in the right or not" (quoted in Lindqwister et al.). Building on the StoryMap's efforts to make visible the lawful acts of racialized violence that persisted after the war, this textual-visual combination further challenges neat narratives about what emancipation meant.

While images are necessarily imbued with new meaning as they are recirculated in different contexts, the hyperlink to the LOC's description of *(?) Slavery is Dead (?)* invites site users to deepen their understanding of the illustration used in the project. Engraved by Nast for *Harper's Weekly* in 1867, this visual is described in the LOC finding aid as "[t]wo illustrations showing . . . [an] enslaved man being sold as punishment for crime, before Emancipation Proclamation; and an African-American man being whipped as punishment for crime in 1866" [*(?) Slavery is Dead (?)*] All description is inevitably rhetorical selective, as Duff and Harris remind us: "[s]omething in the event being represented is always lost. There is always some distortion, even if only through incompleteness. What we choose to stress and what we choose to ignore is always and unavoidably subjective" (275). But the LOC summary of *(?) Slavery is Dead (?)* is notably terse, especially given the complexity of the image, which includes two textboxes located at the bottom of the illustration that offer context about the image. Such truncated descriptions can be the result of limited budgets and resources, but they also reflect a general archival "fixat[ion] on the factual content rather than the functional origins of visual images," to borrow the phrasing of Schwartz (143).

Descriptions of the physical elements of the image that omit context can have significant repercussions for the wide range of users who access the LOC's digital collections. As discussed, this approach can affect how an image is interpreted and repurposed, but such a discursive elision can also affect visual materials' discoverability. Though the LOC shares general publication information, including the date and issue number of the periodical that originally circulated the image, the specific articles in *Harper's* that correspond with the engravings are not mentioned or included in the finding aid, yet the context that they provide can help site users locate relevant images. "Whipping and Selling American Citizens," the textual complement to *(?) Slavery is Dead (?)* was created in response to Reconstruction policies that clashed with long-standing North Carolina state laws that legalized acts of violence against people of color. As the piece explains, then Governor Jonathan Worth protested orders that outlawed the "whipping and selling" of Black men found guilty in the state court (18). After hearing Worth's complaint, President Andrew Johnson overturned this military directive, allowing these brutal punishments to continue. Detailing the barbarity of such practices, personal testimony included in the article explains that during these events "a crowd of nearly five hundred people outside the court-house witness[ed] the public whipping of colored men as fast as they were convicted and sentenced to be whipped by the Court; and to see the victims of the same court sold at auction for a term of years—three years being the usual term" (18). While *(?) Slavery is Dead (?)* clearly acknowledges that sanctioned acts of violence persisted post Emancipation, the article adds critical interpretative context that explains how this was specifically manifested in the years following the war. But as the engraving is absorbed into the LOC's collections, it is cleaved from this textual explanation of events. Stripped of how it exposed and challenged racial inequities, the engraving runs the risk of propagating diluted memories of life postwar, glossing

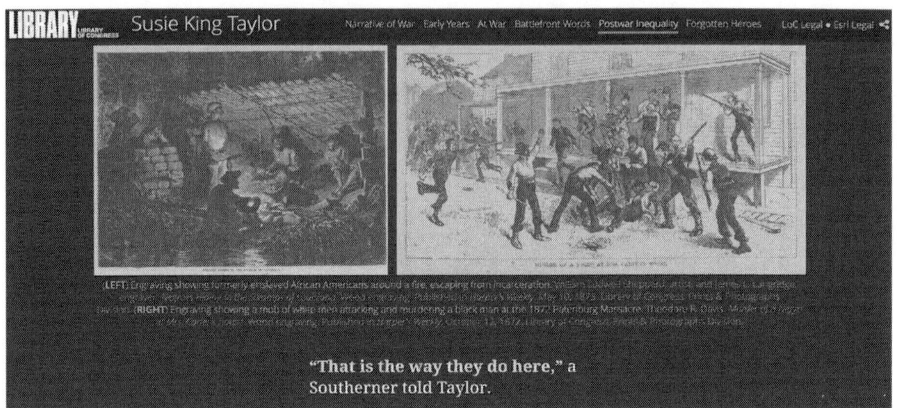

FIGURE 22. Screenshot of a section from "Thoughts on Present Conditions" on the LOC StoryMap. Left: *Negroes Hiding in the Swamps of Louisiana* by James L. Langridge. Published in *Harper's Weekly,* 10 May 1873: 396. Right: *Murder of a Negro at Mrs. Carter's House* by Theodore Davis. Published in *Harper's Weekly* 16, no. 824, 12 Oct. 1872: 796. Originals can be located at the LOC: LC-DIG-ppmsca-71961 and LC-DIG-ppmsca-71962.

over the specific obstacles that made life so challenging for African Americans. But this occlusion also affects accessibility. Because description and the metadata generated about such content shape the search terms associated with a particular object, this exclusion informs how an artifact is made known to site users. Thus, when the descriptive context is constrained, the subject headings and key terms inevitably follow suit. As a result, the realities that Black Americans faced during Reconstruction, such as the violent laws upheld in North Carolina, become more difficult to locate and ultimately weave into the collective memory of Reconstruction.

Concerns with discoverability but also applicability emerge with the image titled *Negroes Hiding in the Swamps of Louisiana* (fig. 22), which is recirculated in the StoryMap to further illustrate the racial plight that African Americans experienced during Reconstruction. Intended to depict the "two completely different worlds" that Taylor inhabited as a Black woman, as described in the StoryMap (Lindqwister et al.), this engraving features a group of "African American men by a campfire under a lean-to," as summarized in the LOC finding aid ("Negros Hiding"). Texturing over the circumstances in which the visual was originally produced, this description buries the context that prompted the creation of the image, which affects how it can be retrieved and repurposed.

Designed by William Ludwell Sheppard and engraved by James L. Langridge, the illustration was concurrently published with an image titled *The Louisiana Murders* in *Harper's* in May 1873. Featuring an injured Black man being dragged away on a sled as a Black woman and small child look on, this engraving is also included in the LOC collection, yet suggestive of the definitive power of authorial agency in re-storying projects, Lindqwister et al. did not incorporate it into their retelling of Taylor's book. While this exclusion misses an opportunity to visually showcase how these violent acts affected Black men and women, the unyoking of these images in the LOC finding aid impacts how they are interpreted by site users and recirculated. Taken together, the images paint a clearer picture of the violence inflicted upon African Americans, which is verified by an accompanying *Harper's* article that is excluded from the LOC's description of the image. Also titled "The Louisiana Murders," the article explains that "[b]etween one hundred and fifty and two hundred colored men had been killed by the whites" in what is now commonly referred to as the Colfax Massacre. In response to a contested gubernatorial election in Louisiana, a group of African American men "intrenched themselves about the court-house at Colfax" and were subsequently attacked by white men who bore guns and a cannon ("The Louisiana Murders"). Describing the scene in graphic detail, the article includes the following passage from the official report of the incident:

> Many [African American men] were shot in the back of the head and neck. One man still lay with his hands clasped in supplication; the face of another was completely flattened by blows from a broken stock of a double-barreled gun, lying on the ground near him; another had been cut across the stomach with a knife after being shot; and almost all had from three to a dozen wounds. Many of them had their brains literally blown out. It is asserted by the colored people that after the flight thirty-four prisoners who were taken before the burning of the court-house were taken to the river-bank two by two, executed, and hurled into the river. We caused to be buried in the ditch near the ruins of the court-house the remains of fifty-four colored men, three of whom were so badly burned as to be unrecognizable. There were inside the court-house the charred bones of one other, and five bodies we gave to their friends for internment elsewhere. We saw also twelve rounded colored men, two of whom will certainly die, and others of whom are very unlikely to recover. We are informed that since the fight parties of armed me have been scouring the country surrounding Colfax, taking the mules and other property of the colored people. (396)

This massacre left African Americans in the community feeling unsafe, impelling them to flee the area. The article reports that "[a] general feeling of insecurity prevails among the colored people of Louisiana, and hundreds are seeking safety in the swamps and forests" (396). While this context brings into greater relief the original purpose of the image, it does not inform the LOC's discussion of the engraving. Impacting the metadata generated about the image, the headings used by the LOC to describe the image are "African Americans-Capture & imprisonment-Louisiana-1870–1880," "Reconstruction (U.S. history, 1865–1877)—Louisiana," and "Lean-tos-Louisiana-1870–1880." Exemplifying how the finding aid informs how an image is located and repurposed, the StoryMap caption for *Negroes Hiding in the Swamps of Louisiana* echoes the first heading, describing the engraving as a depiction of "formerly enslaved African Americans around a fire, escaping from incarceration" (Lindqwister et al.). Because there is no discussion of the Colfax Massacre in the LOC finding aid, there is no discussion of the Colfax Massacre in the StoryMap, burying vestiges of this significant, though underacknowledged, historical event.

Although many of the engravings used in the StoryMap are not adequately contextualized in the LOC's finding aid, there is evidence that suggests the LOC is working to better define and render visible these images and the injustices to which they refer. The illustration titled *Murder of a Negro at Mrs. Carter's House* positioned contiguously to the right of *Negroes Hiding in the Swamps of Louisiana,* depicts the Pattenburg Massacre (fig. 22). Attending to the image's specificity, the LOC summarizes the image as a "[p]rint [that] shows a scene during a riot between Irish American and African American railroad workers employed by the Easton and Amboy Railroad to build the Musconetcong Tunnel, in which Denis Powell, an African American man, is beaten to death by a mob of white men, during the Pattenburg Massacre, Pattenburg, New Jersey" ("Murder of a Negro"). While the South is generally characterized as violent and discriminatory in the StoryMap, this image is indicative of the racism that plagued the North as well. Engraved by Theodore R. Davis, *Murder of a Negro at Mrs. Carter's House* was one of three published in *Harper's* in October 1872 that offered readers a visualization of this violent event that occurred above the Mason-Dixon line. Depicting the fire that emblazoned the African Americans' living quarters and the subsequent murder of Powell, this series of illustrations accompanied the *Harper's* article "The Patenburg [*sic*] Massacre," which shared additional gruesome details of the attack that left one Irishman and four African Americans dead. Though the LOC finding aid does not mention the article or the related images, its discussion of the massacre in its summary of the engraving makes the circumstances surrounding the "Murder of a Negro at Mrs. Carter's House" more discernable. Further illustrating how description informs recirculation practices, the StoryMap describes the engraving as "a mob of white men attacking and murdering a black man at the 1872 Patenburg [*sic*] Massacre" (Lindqwister et al.). A direct result of the LOC's description, this caption helps center specific racialized acts of violence that plagued Reconstruction, disrupting common collective memories that oversimplify the social and political circumstances of African Americans postemancipation.

Toward Intersectional Representational Justice in Depictions of the American Civil War

Closing the StoryMap project, Lindqwister et al. ask, "How do we commemorate heroes like Susie King Taylor?" Set to a backdrop of an engraving that reads "Woman's Work in the Civil War," featuring an image of a white woman unfurling an American flag, they reflect on the erasure of Taylor's story from public memory. Noting that even writers from the North contributed to this neglect by focusing on the efforts of "upper- and middle-class white nurses," they rightly credit Taylor for diversifying narratives of this formative event through the publication of her book. In textually and visually reconstructing Taylor's life via the StoryMap, Lindqwister et al. help make her personal account go public, bringing greater attention to Black women's war experiences. But of import, their retelling also speaks to the limitations of material sources of memory and the challenges of advancing intersectional representational justice, particularly from a historical perspective.

In ways similar to monuments and memorials, images featured in online spaces are threads in the tapestry that construct cultural views of race and gender. And yet, many sites of Civil War memory optically neglect African American women. While Lindqwister et al.'s project textually amplifies memories of Taylor and her service to the Union, images of Black women and their experiences during the war lack visibility in the project. Though Lindqwister et al. ultimately determined the composition of the StoryMap, they were inevitably limited by the constraints of the LOC archive, which includes only minimal visual materials featuring Black women during the Civil War and Reconstruction periods. This representational injustice is indicative of the material ways that multiply marginalized populations are generally excluded from official sources of memory. As Lae'l Hughes-Watkins rightfully notes, "Mainstream archives are steeped in a tradition that makes decisions about the existence, preservation, and availability of archives, documents, and records in our society on the basis of the distribution of wealth and power" (2). Illustrative of the power of the archive, these highly curated repositories contribute to how the past is visualized and thus understood in the present as these images are picked up and recirculated in new contexts.

In the context of the American Civil War, archival images overwhelmingly reflect a decidedly white, male perspective, participating in a visual rhetorical tradition that has notably contributed to how this foundational event has historically been remembered. Recognizing the need to work toward greater representational justice, many collections have attempted to diversify their collections of underrepresented populations. As a corrective to its homogenous collection of visual materials, the LOC recently acquired many of the photographs of Black women that were repurposed in the StoryMap. The *carte de visite* of Tubman, for example, was purchased by the LOC in 2018, and the images of the women taken at the Smith plantation were procured in 2015 and 2016. But my study of the StoryMap also illustrates how the textual and the optical work in tandem to inform how visual materials in archival collections are located, understood, and repurposed. Because conventional practices often fail to adequately contextualize archival images and make them discoverable, attending to how the visual artifacts are described in the archive can also work toward greater representational justice.

In the context of the American Civil War, archival records and images overwhelmingly reflect a decidedly white, male perspective, but countering that master narrative, Taylor reminds us that other ways of seeing this foundational historical event are possible, but they require different ways of looking and listening. But thinking more capaciously about representational justice, Lindqwister et al. model other ways of optically representing the past by incorporating illustrations of women of color from the LOC into their project. Repurposing the watercolor of Tubman and the engraving from *Harper's Weekly* into the StoryMap, Lindqwister et al. address the dearth of photographs depicting Black women and the war. Such a strategy opens up new possibilities for enacting representational justice, particularly concerning periods that extend beyond the recent past. As these images move outward and are adopted in new sites of memory, they disrupt white-centered visions of the war, expanding conceptions of citizenship and narratives of emancipation.

Conclusion

Creating New Memories

[T]he Civil War is still going on. It's still to be fought and regrettably it can still be lost.

—Barbara Fields, quoted in Ken Burns's *The Civil War*

Rhetoric, after all, is how ideologies are carried, how hegemonies are maintained. Rhetoric, then, would be the means by which hegemonies could be countered.

—Victor Villanueva, *Bootstraps*

As is readily observed, Civil War monuments and memorials are overwhelmingly cast in the image of white men, reflecting and reinforcing dominant structures of power and the taxonomies of identity created to support their maintenance. Though these sites of memory tend to have considerable longevity, they are subject to change: weather and other natural factors, graffiti, recontextualization efforts, and removal alter how these sites appear and are understood. Broadly instructive of all sites of memory, these markers are dynamic and ever evolving, much like the recollections that they evoke. As Kendall Phillips affirms, "Despite our best efforts . . . memories refuse to remain stable and immutable. Their appearance, often unbidden, within our cultural experience is like a mirage: vivid and poignant but impermanent and fluid. No matter their importance or revered place in our collective lives, we cannot grasp them fully nor fix them permanently" ("Introduction" 9). Ever malleable, memory, as an epideictic enterprise, carries with it both the promise and threat of social and cultural change. As recollections shift, so, too, do ways of thinking, knowing, and being. Because memories and the myriad rhetorical sites that give rise to them are the building blocks of culture and community, what we remember *matters*.

A powerful cultural symbol, the Civil War is intricately tied to how we define the nation and answer its most pressing questions of intersectional parity and citizenship. But as exemplified by the extant physical sites, Lost Cause and reconciliationist visions have long dominated common memories of the war. Reflecting and reproducing white masculinist ideologies, these ways of remembering continue to inform common visions of this nation-defining event. Though there has been a notable push to diversify what we remember, particularly on the web, even recollections of women and people of color are still often written in a white ink that fails to account fully for the documented role that slavery played in their lives and in the conflict more generally. To illustrate this phenomena, I presented several case studies that examine the biographical retellings of Civil War women on the web, a powerful source of public memory that is widely accessible to people all over the globe. Concentrating on women who are frequently broached in the context of the war, I focused my analyses on Rose O'Neal Greenhow, Belle Boyd, Harriet Tubman, Sarah Emma Edmonds, Loreta Janeta Velazquez, and Susie King Taylor. Exemplifying how the unusual continues "to win our wonder," these six women performed extraordinary labors as nurses, soldiers, and spies, making them popular additions to the vast array of digital sites that shape public memory of the war. Though their gender transgressions are worthy of note, their published personal narratives reveal the various ways that slavery and racial hierarchies informed their lives. Yet as their stories are retold and remediated into biographies that circulate on the web, matters of gender take priority over as their discussions of race and slavery.

Echoing Lost Cause visions, common retellings of Greenhow and Boyd tend to emphasize their extraordinary experiences as spies, minimizing or omitting entirely their proslavery positions, as I argued in chapter 1. Such a reframing depicts Greenhow and Boyd as Civil War heroes, neutralizing the intentions driving these devoted Confederate women while generally distancing slavery from Southern secession. Reflective of reconciliationist priorities, retellings of Tubman historically focused on her work with the Underground Railroad, often failing to acknowledge the considerable role she played in executing the Combahee River Raid, her many pension requests, and the racialized acts of discrimination that she experienced, as I asserted in chapter 2. Texturing these traditional retellings, the biographical accounts offer new ways of remembering Tubman and the war, illustrating the site's potential for quickly responding to changing values. Demonstrating how even participatory sites of memory reflect the priorities of dominant white, cishet, patriarchal culture, chapter 3 illustrates how an ostensibly democratic source like Wikipedia can fail to address documented racial inequities. Analyzing the entries of Edmonds and Velazquez, two women who dressed as men during the war, I demonstrate how these retellings have increasingly come to focus on the veracity of their claims while ignoring their discussions of race and slavery, reflecting the concerns of the editors—often white, male, and from the West. Finally, the Library of Congress StoryMap of Taylor invites reflection on visual ways of remembering, particularly as it concerns representational justice, as I addressed in chapter 4. Fleeing slavery at the start of the Civil War, Taylor was committed to liberation efforts, working as a nurse, cook, laundress, and teacher for the 33rd United States Colored Troops, experiences which she documents in her self-published book. While the StoryMap does the necessary work of sharing the challenges that Taylor faced as a Black woman, there is a notable discrepancy between its alphabetic retellings and visual depictions of these events, revealing an archival scarcity that fails to adequately document how enslaved men and women contributed to their liberation.

Altering the tone and tenor of the memories they evoke and, subsequently, the sociocultural values they reinforce, these narrative configurations are imbued with various shades of whiteness that contribute to oversimplified visions of women and the war and, more generally, the role that slavery and race played in the conflict. To be clear: the observations born from this study are not motivated by a *nunc pro tunc* instinct to judge these Civil War women according to contemporary standards of social justice, although their white supremacist beliefs are truly abhorrent. But because the battle over Civil War memories continues to be fought today, shaping how we see ourselves as a nation, it is necessary to make clear the stakes of that conflict. In the words of Reverend Fred Shuttlesworth, "If you don't tell it like it was, it can never be as it ought to be" (quoted in Blight, "If You Don't" 33).

While retellings such as those examined in the case studies in this book begin the important work of diversifying these homogenous visions of the past, because many circulate shallow, distorted, and otherwise imbalanced views, the interventions they make ultimately replicate the whiteness that begot them. Making clear the ways in which these retellings conceal the realities of slavery brings us a step closer to acknowledging the legacy of this institution and its considerable impact. As the core texts studied verify, slavery was frequently broached in women's personal narratives of the war, suggestive of how it was a central concern for those on both sides of the Mason-Dixon line. Though it is rarely addressed in common retellings, Confederate women supported and benefited from slavery. But even white women from the North questioned racial equality. Although many supported abolition, they still often subscribed to racialized social hierarchies that positioned the white race as superior. While there are notable efforts to acknowledge Black women's service to the Union, limited by sources of memory, these sites of memory are still few and far between. Such framings, too, often perpetuate a vision of the past that makes slavery a concern only for people of color. But even in these retellings, representations of slavery are often minimized, and white supremacist beliefs go unacknowledged. In omitting the "tough stuff" of history (Horton and Horton xiii), these sanitized narratives perpetuate common perspectives that continue to downplay slavery's lasting effects. "Simply put," as Ira Berlin explains, "American history cannot be understood without slavery. Slavery shaped America's economy, politics, culture, and fundamental principles. For most of the nation's history, American society was one of slaveholders and slaves" (2). Yet popular digital accounts of notable Civil War women fail to tangle with this legacy, a carryover from memories past.

Though the biographies that I discuss in this book focus specifically on Civil War women, how historical women's stories are retold in online spaces generally warrants broader consideration. Although these narratives do the important work of diversifying dominant narratives of the past, offering much-needed perspective, they exemplify the problems of an "add and stir" approach to representation. Merely inserting women, particularly those deemed "exceptional," into the commemorative landscape without attending to the power dynamics that first contributed to the initial erasure invites problematic replication of those systems, as early feminists teach us. As Virginia Woolf famously observes, "we think back through our mothers if we are women" (76), but acknowledging the "potentia[l] dange[r]" of this "quest," Christine Mason Sutherland observes that there is a "tendency simply to ignore . . . inconvenient beliefs, or worse still, to misunderstand" these women and thus reproduce shallow narratives that engender troubling memories (14, 16).

Making New Memories

Because feminist rhetorical practices, particularly those inspired by theories of intersectionality, can be applied as an analytic and put to use as praxis, I want to close this project by exploring how retellings can shift public memory and thus alter, even ever so slightly, status quo ways of thinking, being, and doing. As I contemplate this particular endeavor, I do so with caution: I am reminded of Ta-Nehisi Coates's observation that "many lifetimes went into the creation of the problem of white supremacy" and thus "solutions . . . [will] likely require the work of generations" (152). But we must nudge liberation along as we can. While memory bears traces of earlier incarnations, it is ever shifting, though intervention is often needed to propel these changes. With its ease of use, virtually unlimited storage, general accessibility, and cultural significance, the World Wide Web carries great commemorative potential. But, of import, while sites can be readily updated, they often leave no traces of alterations made, thereby erasing fragments of the past. But attending to the moment in which websites are accessed, consumed, and in many cases, recirculated, digital sites contribute extensively to contemporary public memories, "transform[ing] the content and appearance of cultural memory writ large," as Bradford Vivian and Anne Teresa Demo phrase it (2). While these sites reflect the concerns of dominant social groups, they also have the potential to recalibrate collective acts of remembrance and shift the distribution of power. Feminist rhetorical practices can guide such transformations to help alter digital sources through centering marginalized subjects and complicating oversimplified recollections of the past that minimize challenging aspects of the past. These kinds of interventions are needed now more than ever as we more fully enter the age of generative artificial intelligence technologies and the influence of digital biographies and the memories they propagate are intensified. Because these large language models are trained on content from the internet, what is recorded about women like Greenhow, Boyd, Tubman, Edmonds, Velazquez, and Taylor on general websites will help determine what computer programs like ChatGPT will generate. The resultant composites shape how these women are remembered, but because memory both reflects and constructs ideologies of race and gender, they also exemplify how seeming innocuous websites can inform sociocultural norms.

As stories of these Civil War women are retold and remediated, their narratives carry with them traces of historical memories that have occluded the role that slavery played in the conflict in favor of white reunion. While these residual memories continue to haunt common reconstructions of Civil War women, they also are suggestive of the power of the digital to counter persistent, though problematic, memories. While the internet is vast and fractured, digital sites of memory are easier to amend than stone and steel fixtures and potentially have a larger, more diverse audience. Because "we are responsible for our own recall," as David Blight reminds us, we can help shape the content we absorb in digital spaces that gives rise to how we remember women and the war and the attendant ideologies that they inspire ("If You Don't" 22).

In the years that I spent working on this project, I have witnessed individuals, organizations, and institutions correct fallacious or otherwise problematic material. Amending the inaccuracy regarding the death of Greenhow's mother, the American Battlefield Trust (ABT), for example, modified its account of the Confederate spy. If sites like the ABT were more aware of Greenhow's support of slavery, might they also revise their retelling to account for this highly relevant historical fact? To be clear, I am not suggesting a *damnatio memoriae* approach that erases women such as Greenhow from the historical record. We need to hear her story, but retellings of her life should render visible what she was fighting for. Vocalizing problematic narratives in online forums can help move the needle of memory, as new perspectives challenge and change the paradigmatic views of the past that can inspire discursive and material revision. As official versions of memory clash with vernacular accounts, new stories are born that reflect but also shape community values. In this way, feminist rhetorical interventions are more than shallow alterations or commemorative posturing. Attending to the dual function of race and gender in mechanisms of public memory helps expose and correct distorted recollections, working at the molecular level to inspire greater equity.

In addition to correcting information and revising narratives of the past, official and vernacular sources of memory have taken an additive approach to account for new information, findings, and viewpoints. As discussed, Black women have traditionally been excluded from public memories of the war, but suggestive of the internet's capaciousness, the web can accommodate the discovery of additional Black women's war stories and potentially share them with a large audience. Notable exceptions, Tubman and Taylor are now regularly discussed in the context of the war, but even as they are folded into recollections of this highly influential event, digital retellings often peddle simplified narratives of their war experiences. But as demonstrated by the National Park Service (NPS), these prevailing memories can be layered with additional text to shift collective acts of remembrance. Through linking a new article that focuses explicitly on her Civil War exploits, the NPS textures its base biography of Tubman, adding a new layer of information for site users to consume. In this way, the NPS's handling of its Tubman pages demonstrates how online platforms can nuance memories through the use of hyperlinks, adding significant depth to a given subject. Illustrative of just one of the affordances of digital platforms, hyperlinking new materials to existing pages can be a meaningful and efficient way to tell better stories.

Further illustrative of expansive digital possibilities, the Library of Congress StoryMap of Taylor exemplifies how institutions can amplify memories of underrepresented groups through repurposing digital artifacts into new compositions. While this particular iteration also illustrates the limitations of the archive, specifically as it concerns Black women and the Civil War, it more generally calls attention to how digital sources can augment memory through appropriating materials and remixing them into new compositions. Such an assemblage, as the StoryMap illustrates, magnifies the exposure of the subject, demonstrating how the web can enhance public memory through the rhetorical acts of digital collage and circulation.

But the web also invites the public to participate in commemorative acts in ways not previously conceived. As Ekaterina Haskins elucidates, "No longer a privilege of state and cultural institutions, the recording of events and experiences for posterity—and sharing them with intimates and strangers—has become a pastime of regular people. The emergence of the Internet as a medium of both private remembrance and public commemoration calls for a reconsideration of traditional distinctions between memory . . . and popular forms of memory that are often ephemeral and localized" (*Popular Memories* 44). While Haskins explores how such memory practices are operationalized in the context of the September 11 Digital Archive, a repository that collects artifacts and personal stories related to the event from the general public, collaboratively built sites such as Wikipedia also help shape general recollections of the millions of pages it hosts. Though I demonstrate how Wikipedia perpetuates overly simplified visions of the war through its depictions of Edmonds and Velazquez, the "history" function of the site makes clear how everyday users can influence public memory by calling into question flawed narratives. In this way, this interface can help counter problematic memories. Recollections are always changing, as are the pages of Wikipedia. As more editors with intersectional priorities help shape the content and bring to the fore intersectional erasures and misremembrances, they help propagate a more equitable vision of the past that informs the present and future.

For all too long, memories of the Civil War have been haunted by androcentricity and whiteness. While some progress has been made in diversifying these memories, women's Civil War stories continue to minimize or outright ignore slavery, particularly in digital spaces, a critical apparatus of public memory. Because the war is a major historical event, attending to how women are remembered in this context subtly shifts the ideological fabric that helps define a given community. As suggested by the case studies discussed herein, white supremacist ways of remembering continue to haunt reminiscences of women and the war. But advocating for more inclusive and nuanced commemorations while exposing and dismantling asymmetrical power relations in digital spaces can encourage new narratives and new memories that better answer Reverend Shuttlesworth's pressing call to make things how they "ought to be" (quoted in Blight, "If You Don't" 33).

Acknowledgments

In writing this book, I devoted considerable time and attention to thinking about memory, how it circulates, what makes it stick, and what loosens its hold. As I sit with my own memories of this project and those who have supported me along the way, I am overwhelmed by the considerable love and support that I have received over the many years that this journey took. Many people have left their imprint on this book, both directly and implicitly. I am grateful for them all.

This book would not be possible without Aurora Bell, an amazingly understanding and patient editor. Thank you for believing in this project from the very beginning; your confidence helped me to see this endeavor through to the end. I also want to extend my appreciation to the two anonymous reviews of my manuscript. Your keen insights pushed me to deepen my explication of the theories, ideas, and examples offered herein.

Cristy Beemer offered me some of the earliest feedback on this project, which would influence my understanding and approach to women's Civil War stories for years to come. Cristy has continued to be a source of knowledge, advice, and support. I appreciate her continued willingness to help me navigate the waters of academia.

I also want to extend a special note of thanks to Gesa Kirsch. A smart and devoted scholar, Gesa opened her mind, heart, and home when she invited me to participate in a writing group that met regularly at her house in Boston. When she moved to California, we took the writing group online, incorporating new members over the years. These meetings contributed to my growth as a scholar and introduced me to new ways of approaching rhetorical theories and research. Gesa is the kind of teacher-scholar that I aspire to be. She has, no doubt, been a force in the field of rhetoric and composition, but it is her generosity, inclusiveness, and care that truly distinguish her.

I also want to thank the colleagues I have met during my time at Washington State University (WSU) who have supported me in various ways: Vanessa

Cozza, Nishant Shahani, Johanna Phelps, Bibhushana Poudyal, Melissa Nicolas, Jon Hegglund, Donna Potts, Julie Staggers, Ashley Boyd, Nora Kuster, and Jennifer Lodine-Chafey. A particularly heartfelt thank you to Wendy Olson who has been in my corner since I arrived at WSU. I have had the good fortune, too, of working with some very smart and talented graduate and undergraduate students who have listened to me talk about this project for way too long: Brigette Hinnant, Sherwin Kawahakui Ranchez Sales, Sumaiya Sarker Sharmin, and Justine Trinh. It has been a joy to work with them and watch them launch their own scholarly endeavors. And a special note of gratitude to Kathryn Manis: Being her co-dissertation advisor was a privilege, but being her writing partner is even better. I am so very thankful that our paths crossed in this lifetime.

At WSU, I was also fortunate enough to receive the Buchanan Summer Research Fellowship and the Buchanan Distinguished Scholar in English Fellowship, both of which were used to fund research related to this project. The Center for the Arts and Humanities at WSU also financially supported my research endeavors with a stipend that helped fund my attendance to the National Endowment for the Humanities Summer Institute "Civil War Archives: A New Social and Cultural History of the Civil War" facilitated by Jim Downs. This formative intellectual experience helped me refine my thinking about this book in significant ways. I am very grateful to have participated in this institute.

Outside of academia, I have walked through life with some of the most thoughtful, kind, patient, and fun friends and family members: Somer Bauer, Patty and Bob Lasich, Stephen and Jennifer Dewey, Seth and Kay Miller, Kris Fink, Samm Erickson, Andy Zboralski, Erin Maronick, Melissa (Mitch) Brown, Margaret Bray, Mary Weisensee, Chris Cushman and Carrie Sutton, Suzie and Alan Rom, Madie Kenny, Sheila Canty, Minnie Zemp, Molly Scrutton, Erin McGibbon, and Deena Walker. They graciously have all given me time and space to work, celebrated my successes, and picked me up during setbacks and moments of frustration. A special note of love and gratitude goes out to my mother-in-law, Elizabeth (Buffy) Dewey, who passed away before this book was published. She was a true force in all the best ways. I think of her often.

No one else fielded my frantic texts and calls about this project like Trish Portanova and Erin Costello Wecker, two dear friends I met at the University of New Hampshire. Both have been generous with their time, minds, and hearts, allowing me to talk through ideas openly and without judgment. Trish provided savvy advice and many words of encouragement at all hours of the

FIGURE 23. A cardboard sign that Genevieve and Elizabeth made for me while I worked on the book. When the manuscript was accepted for publication, they emended the sign in acknowledgment of its completion. Courtesy Genevieve Dewey.

day and night. I always learn so much from her. Erin's honest and thoughtful feedback helped me put the pieces of my argument together, but it was her love, support, and good humor that made the endeavor manageable. Mankato forever.

My brother Ryan Wilde and sister-in-law Kelley Wilde have also patiently stood by me throughout the long and winding road of writing this book. The youngest in our family, I can't remember a time when I didn't look up to Ryan, who has consistently been a kind and encouraging presence in my life. An inspiring leader, he continues to serve as an example of how to treat people with respect and collectively work toward challenging goals. I am equally grateful for Kelley, my trusted sister, friend, and running partner, who has long listened to me talk about this book and other life happenings with care and goodwill. I am very fortunate to have them in my life.

This journey would not have been possible without the love and encouragement of my parents, Robert and Genevieve Wilde. Since I was a little girl, they fostered my curiosity and love of learning. Their investment in my education and their own examples of hard work have directly contributed to my success, and their wisdom helped me to appreciate the experience in all of its challenges and glories.

My children Genevieve and Elizabeth both lived with me and this project from the earliest moments of their existence. To see this endeavor through took a considerable amount of time and energy, which often meant that I worked in the evenings and on weekends. I thank them for their patience and understanding and for cheering me on along the way. It is my greatest hope that they, too, will have the opportunity to live out their wildest dreams.

While all the people named herein helped me in some way push this book into the world, no one else held my hand along the way like my husband, Graham Dewey. Without him, this book simply would not be. He shouldered many extra responsibilities so that I could have a "room of my own" to write, but he also saw me through the emotional ups and downs of this undertaking. Graham: you go above and beyond for me and our family. Thank you will never adequately covey my gratitude for you and all that you do and have done. I love you forever. And that fricassee is coming right up.

Notes

Introduction

1. See Edward S. Casey's chapter "Public Memory in Place and Time" for an overview of individual memory, social memory, collective memory, and public memory. Matthew Houdek and Kendall Phillips also touch upon some of the different iterations of memory in their overview of public memory.

2. While most Civil War monuments commemorate the efforts of white men, there are notable exceptions. As Caroline Janney explains, the United Confederate Veterans organization "launched a campaign to place a monument to Confederate women on the grounds of every southern state capitol. The goal was only partially realized. Only seven states built such monuments between 1912 and 1926—in part because of women's objections in favor of a commemoration they deemed more appropriate, such as retirement homes, colleges, or scholarship funds" (370). Janney continues to note that, in the twentieth century, some statues were erected for Union women, but they "were almost exclusively memorials to nurses" (370).

3. As explained in the report, Monument Lab defines monument as "a statement of power and presence in public" (4); their team specifically researched "conventional" monuments: "statues or monoliths constructed with stone or metal, installed or maintained in a public space with the authority of a government agency or institution" (5).

4. Variations of this passage are often attributed to Elizabeth Cady Stanton, as she wrote something very similar in her 1898 autobiography *Eighty Years and More*: "The story of the War will never be fully written if the achievements of women are left untold. They do not figure in the official reports; they are not gazetted for gallant deeds; the names of thousands are unknown beyond the neighborhood where they lived, or the hospitals where they loved to labor; yet there is no feature in our War more creditable to us as a nation, none from it positive newness so well worthy of record" (235).

5. Through her exploration of Hester Ann Rogers's spiritual narrative, Burton illustrates how women's "core texts" were altered through discursive and paratextual features that modified Rogers's ethos as well as the text's original meaning. Several scholars have expanded Burton's work in notable ways, studying the ways that women overlay subsequent editions of their own texts (Bordelon), how accretions (both self-authored and not) can reveal the agency asserted by non-normative bodies (Stuckey), and how material considerations impact archival research (Gaillet; Clary-Lemon,

"Archival Research Processes") and our understanding of museum sites (Clary-Lemon, "Museums as Material").

Chapter 1: Selective Memories

1. The Trent Affair, which involved the North intercepting a British ship carrying two Confederate diplomats, almost resulted in a war between the Union and Great Britain in 1861. A long-term issue with a British shipyard that was building warships and blockade-runners for the Confederacy was also a source of tension between the English and the Union.

2. Boyd asserted in her missive to Lincoln that unless he agreed to release her husband from Union prison, she would publish her book, which was highly critical of the Union.

3. Although the Somerset v. Stewart case of 1772 is commonly cited as the beginning of legislative efforts that effectively ended slavery, the Slavery Abolition Act of 1833 prohibited the practice in most of England's colonies.

4. This particular passage is included in a letter that Greenhow wrote to Seward, which is incorporated into her narrative.

5. When the Association for the Preservation of Civil War Sites merged with the Civil War Trust, its name was first changed to the Civil War Preservation Trust and then to the American Battlefield Trust ("Three Decades in the Trenches").

6. Eliza O'Neale, Greenhow's mother, died on 18 February 1850, at the age of 55 (Blackman 145).

7. The circumstances of Greenhow's father's death are taken up in a handful of web pages, though often in problematic ways. In "The Wild Rose of Washington," an article featured in the *New York Times* "Disunion" series, Cate Lineberry asserts that O'Neal had been murdered by one of the men he enslaved. In a move that can be read as an attempt to evoke sympathy for the Confederate spy, Lineberry writes that "Wild Rose" was "familiar with tragedy . . . her father had been murdered by one of his slaves when Greenhow was still a girl." Because of this, continues Lineberry, "She and her siblings were separated and sent to live with relatives." The sequencing of these events is suggestive of a causal relationship that implicitly blames the enslaved man for O'Neal's unfortunate circumstances.

Chapter 2: Layers of the Past

1. Though James Chase Sanchez and Kristen R. Moore specifically discuss the Confederate Defenders monument in Charleston, South Carolina in their article, their discussion of reinscription is applicable here.

2. Benjamin Drew's *A North-Side View of Slavery* is a notably written exception to this established oral tradition. In this collection of slave narratives, Drew included a section on Tubman. Though it mentions her by name, it does not describe her efforts

with the Underground Railroad: "I grew up like a neglected weed,—ignorant of liberty, having no experience of it. Then I was not happy or contented: every time I saw a white man I was afraid of being carried away. I had two sisters carried away in a chain-gang,— one of them left two children. We were always uneasy. Now I've been free, I know what a dreadful condition slavery is. I have seen hundreds of escaped slaves, but I never saw one who was willing to go back and be a slave. I have no opportunity to see my friends in my native land. We would rather stay in our native land, if we could be as free there as we are here. I think slavery is the next thing to hell. If a person would send another into bondage, he would, it appears to me, be bad enough to send him into hell, if he could" (30).

3. These include Benjamin Drew's *A North-Side View of Slavery: The Refugee, or The Narrative of Fugitive Slaves in Canada* (1856); Franklin B. Sanborn's "Harriet Tubman" article, which I discuss at length in this chapter, was featured in the *Commonwealth* (1863); and Ednah Cheney published "Moses" (1865) in the *Freedman's Records*.

4. Both Sernett (113) and Clinton (*Harriet Tubman* 181) address the letters Bradford wrote on behalf of Tubman's parents.

5. Illustrative of the intersectional oppressions she faced, the pension Tubman drew was legally attributed to the death of her husband, Nelson Davis, who was a Union soldier (Blight, *Race and Reunion* 393). Then, in 1898, after powerful friends intervened on her behalf, she was awarded a veteran's pension for her own contributions to the Federalist forces.

6. The full passage of the event reads as follows: "I was carrying *two pigs* for a poor sick woman, who had a child to carry, and the order 'double quick was given, and I started to run, stepped on my dress, it being rather long, and fell and tore it almost off. . . . I made up my mind then I would never wear a long dress on another expedition of the kind, but would have a *bloomer* as soon as I could get it" (*Scenes* 86, emphasis in original).

7. For other discrepancies, see Larson 267–69; Sernett 125–30.

8. According to the National Monument Audit, Tubman is the second most memorialized women in the United States after Joan of Arc (Monument Lab).

9. The National Park Service defines a National Historical Park as "historic parks that extend beyond single properties of buildings" ("Designations").

10. In addition to the two national historical parks commemorating Tubman, the Maggie L. Walker National Historic Site was established in Richmond, Virginia, in 1978, celebrating Maggie L. Walker, the first woman to become president of a bank.

11. Bordered in red, the unaltered photo of Tubman displays more of her dress, the spacious but blank background behind her, the patterned carpet on which she sits in the chair, and the penciled name "Harriet Tubman" that is inscribed in cursive toward the bottom of the image.

Chapter 3: Questionable Memories

1. Edmonds's book was first published in 1864 as *Unsexed: The Thrilling Adventures, Experiences and Escapes of a Woman, As Nurse, Spy and Scout, in Hospitals, Camps and Battle-fields* by the Philadelphia Publishing Company. All other versions of Edmonds's account are published under the title *Nurse and Spy in the Union Army.*

2. Of note, Wikipedia users primarily hail from the Global North, with over 25 percent of its traffic coming from the United States, followed by Japan at 6.38 percent, the United Kingdom at 5.81 percent, Germany at 5.81 percent, and Russia at 4.86 percent; the remaining 52.25 percent is split among other countries ("Wikipedia").

3. A letter to Edmonds from her publisher, A. M. Hurlbert, comments that "We as publishers gave the Sanitary Commission and other causes hundreds of dollars from the profits of the book; also gave you, I think, two $500 bonds $1000 which you used among the sick and wounded at Harper's Ferry." Leonard also adds that Edmonds donated $2,000 of her earnings from the memoir to the Christian Commission (*All the Daring* 183).

4. Cataloging these occurrences, "Fraud in Authorship" identifies the specific passages that Edmonds lifted from the Hackett text, many of which are battlefield scenes. While this particular criticism does have merit, the review takes its censure a step further: "In its exaggerations and falsehoods," conclude the reviewers, the book "honors neither [the sick nor wounded Union soldiers]" ("Fraud in Authorship" 18–19).

5. Although it is anachronistic to label Edmonds and Velazquez "transgender," a neologism that was first coined in the mid-1960s (Rawson and Williams), as G. G. Bolich maintains, "We need a flexibility of mind sufficient to seek relevant links to the past without insisting that past ideas and experiences are identical to our own" (16). Calling into question what it means to be "biologically born, self-identified, or historically identified women" (Rawson, "Queering" 40), some sites speculate that Edmonds's identity as Thompson is suggestive of her transgender identity. Lauren Rene Hotchkiss, for example, includes Edmonds in her article "TGF Re-Run: Trans America, Part 4: Fightin' Femmes," while the entry for *Outhistory* examines how she "crisscrossed Confederate and gender lines" ("Sarah E. Edmonds"). These sites align with other historical accounts that have incorporated both Edmonds and Velazquez into transgender histories. Leslie Feinberg's groundbreaking *Transgender Warriors* (1996) is a personal journey through a history of various people, including Edmonds, who deviated from expected gender expression. As Feinberg explains, she was driven to pursue this project because, as ze explains "I couldn't find *myself* in history. No one like me seemed to have ever existed" (11). G. G. Bolich's three-volumes of *Transgender History and Geography: Crossdressing in Context* (2007) offers an extensive review of people across cultures throughout history that defy binary gender categorization, including both Edmonds and Velazquez in this work. And Susan Stryker's *Transgender History* (2008) reviews "one hundred years" of transgender history, which incorporates Velazquez into her discussion.

6. Kady Brownell, who served the Union with her husband Robert, and Dr. Mary Edwards Walker, who was a surgeon for the Union Army, are also believed to be inductees.

7. As Robbins conveys in his journal, Edmonds eventually shared her true identity with him. Their relationship became strained, however, when Edmonds developed feelings for Robbins, who was then committed to another woman. When Edmonds later turned her attention to Assistant Adjutant General James Reid, Robbins seemingly grew jealous. Shortly thereafter, in April 1863, Edmonds left her post, claiming to be ill with malaria, but Fladeland speculates that she "deserted from the army not because she was sick and afraid to go to the hospital," but rather because she was in love with . . . Reid and "did not want to be separated from him" (361).

8. In this footnote, Fishel turns to Allan Pinkerton's list of Civil War agents as evidence of Edmonds's fabrication, noting that Edmonds's name is missing from the roster. He also points out discrepancies between the "diary of the fellow soldier with whom Emma Edmonds had an extended romance" (presumably Robbins) and her book as evidence of Edmonds's imposture (624–25).

9. Though I have chosen to redact it in my analysis, the word "ni****r" appears several times in its entirety in Edmonds's *Nurse and Spy in the Union Army.*

10. Hatuey is known as Cuba's First National Hero, although he was from Hispaniola. Having fled Hispaniola, he attempted to help the Cuban Taíno resist the Spanish.

11. In her "Address to the American Congress on 'Cuba,'" delivered in 1877, Velazquez requests that the United States support Cuba in its fight against colonial Spain for independence. She asks her "noble countrymen . . . [to] speak out, and act, if need be" against the "barbaric Spain" (2).

12. Davis questions the veracity of Velazquez's story of Venezuela (107–9).

Chapter 4: Visual Memories

1. Three years after the Emancipation Memorial was erected in Washington, DC in 1876, a replica was installed in Boston, Massachusetts in 1879. But following the murder of George Floyd, Tory Bullock, an artist from Dorchester, started a petition that called for the statue's removal. Commenting on the statue, Bullock explains that "[t]his man will never stand. He will always be on his knees" (quoted in R. Young). After gathering more than 12,000 signatures in less than a month, the Boston Art Commission voted unanimously to remove the statue (Wintersmith). On 29 December 2020, the city of Boston removed the Emancipation Memorial.

2. As Maurice O. Wallace and Shawn Michelle Smith note in *Pictures and Progress,* Douglass delivered several lectures on images, including "The Age of Pictures," "Lectures on Pictures," "Pictures and Progress," and "Life Pictures," all of which discussed "photography's social and epistemological potential" (5).

3. Lindqwister, Chittenden, and Messenheimer's StoryMap won the C. Herbert Finch Online Publication Award in 2020.

4. Lindqwister completed the project on Taylor in 2019, when she held the Prints & Photographs Division Stanford in Government Liljenquist Fellowship at the LOC; she was then an undergraduate student at Stanford University pursuing a degree in history.

5. The StoryMap of Lindqwister et al.'s StoryMap won the C. Herbert Finch Online Publication Award in 2020.

6. Of import, some Black women such as Sojourner Truth, Elizabeth Keckley, and Mattie J. Jackson did publish autobiographical accounts that describe their Civil War experiences. And journalists and political writers, including Sattira Douglas, Mary Ann Shad Cary, and Sarah Parker Redmond, collectively produced a body of work that advanced the emancipatory vision of the war. But calling attention to the intersectional discrepancies that haunt such discursive records, Frances Smith Foster observes that while "[w]e can only speculate about the numbers of African American women who wrote for publication . . . the number of extant texts suggest there were more African American men and more Anglo-American women published than there were African American women" (9).

7. Taylor's *Reminiscences* was republished in 1968 by Arno Press, in 1988 and 1999 by Markus Wiener Press, and in 2006 by the University of Georgia Press. For some of the earlier publications featuring Taylor, see Cythnia Dannett's *Profiles of Negro Womanhood 1619–1900, Vol.1* (1964); Simeon Booker and Harold Laymont James's *Susie King Taylor, Civil War Nurse* (1969); Eve Merriam's *Growing Up Female in America: Ten Lives* (1971); Ruth Bogin and Bert J. Loewenberg's *Black Women in Nineteenth-Century American Life: Their Words, Their Thoughts, Their Feelings* (1976); Cheryl G. Hoople's *As I Saw It: Women Who Lived the American Adventure* (1978); and Renate Simson's *The Unsung Past: Afro-American Women Writers of 19th Century* (1979).

8. Official archives have historically referred to materials attributed to a single source that are organized according to principles of provenance, original order, collective control, and permanence. In contrast, "collection" often refers to the aggregation of materials that are "assembled by a person, organization, or repository from a variety of sources" ("Collection"). While the LOC's Digital and Physical Prints & Photographs Collection would be classified as the latter, I refer to this repository in the general sense of "archives," to mean "records created or received by a person, family, or organization and preserved because of their continuing value" ("Archives").

9. On the StoryMap website, a "sidecar" is described as a feature that allows composers to layer alphabetic text, images, videos, audio clips, and hyperlinks; they are located on the side of the StoryMap (Wilber).

10. In a review of her book published in the *Boston Sunday Post*, Chickering is identified as the photographer of Taylor's photograph ("Mrs. Susie King Taylor").

11. The camp was named in honor of General Rufus Saxton, who organized a large reading of the Emancipation Proclamation in 1863 for the people of color who inhabited the area, including Taylor and the 33rd US Colored Troops.

12. The stereoscope card is a type of photograph that features two nearly identical photographs that appear three-dimensional when viewed through a stereoscope.

13. The sidecar text accompanying this photograph notes that it's possible that these soldiers featured in the image are part of an integrated group that Thompson oversaw postwar (Lindqwister et al.). While Thompson served as lieutenant in the 54th US Colored Infantry during the war, this unit was reorganized in April 1869 into the 25th Infantry Regiment. As one of the four "buffalo soldier" regiments created after the war, Thompson's group helped patrol the South during the first years of Reconstruction.

14. As summarized in the LOC catalog, this photo captures an "[u]nidentified African American soldier in Union uniform with an Austrian Lorenz rifle-musket and Remington revolver in front of painted backdrop showing weapons and American flag at Benton Barracks, Saint Louis, Missouri" ("Unidentified African American").

Works Cited

"About this Collection: Brady-Handy." Library of Congress. https://www.loc.gov/. Accessed 14 Jul. 2021.

"About Us." National Park Service. 9 Jun. 2021. https://www.nps.gov/aboutus/index.htm.

Adams, Heather Brook. "Goodbye, 'Post-Pill Paradise': Texturing Feminist Public Memories of Women's Reproductive and Rhetorical Agency." *Quarterly Journal of Speech* 104, no. 4 (2019): 390–417.

"African-American Soldiers During the Civil War." Library of Congress. https://www.loc.gov/. Accessed 18 May 2025.

Ahmed, Sara. "A Phenomenology of Whiteness." *Feminist Theory* 2, no. 1 (2007): 149–68.

Alemán, Jesse. "Introduction: Authenticity, Autobiography, and Identity: *The Woman in Battle* as a Civil War Narrative." In *The Woman in Battle*, by Loreta Janeta Velazquez. Rpt. ed. University of Wisconsin Press, 2003.

American Historical Association. "AHA Statement on Confederate Monuments." Aug. 2017, https://www.historians.org/news-and-advocacy/.

Anderson, Benedict. Imagined Communities: Reflections on the Origin and Spread of Nationalism. 1983. Verso, 2016.

Anderson, Daniel, and Jentery Sayers. "The Metaphor and Materiality of Layers." In *Rhetoric and the Digital Humanities,* edited by Jim Ridolfo and Bill Hart-Davidson. University of Chicago Press, 2014, pp. 80–95.

Antracoli, Alexis, and Katy Rawdon. "What's In a Name? Archives for Black Lives in Philadelphia and the Impact of Names and Name Authority in Archival Description." In *Ethical Questions In Name Authority and Control,* edited by Jane Sandberg, Library Juice Press, 2019, pp. 307–36.

"ArcGIS StoryMaps." ArcGIS StoryMaps. https://storymaps.arcgis.com/. Accessed 13 Sept. 2021.

Balch, Oliver. "Making the Edit: Why We Need More Women in Wikipedia." *The Guardian,* 28 Nov. 2019. https://www.theguardian.com/.

Ballou, Maturin Murray. *The Female Pirate Captain.* E.D. Long & Co., Bookseller, 1844.

Barthes, Roland. *Camera Lucida: Reflections on Photography.* Hill and Wang, 1982.

Berger, John. *Ways of Seeing.* Penguin, 1990.

Berlin, Ira. "Coming to Terms with Slavery in Twenty-First-Century America." In *Slavery and Public History: The Tough Stuff of American Memory*, edited by James Oliver Horton and Lois E. Horton, 1–18. Norton, 2006.

Betts, Anna. "Harriet Tubman Webpage Targeted Amid Trump-led Anti-DEI Efforts." *The Guardian*. 7 Apr. 2025. https://www.theguardian.com/us-news/2025/apr/07/park -service-harriet-tubman-underground-railroad

Biesecker, Barbara. "Coming to Terms with Recent Attempts to Write Women into the History of Rhetoric." *Philosophy and Rhetoric* 25 (1992): 140–61.

Biesecker, Barbara. "Of Historicity, Rhetoric: The Archive as Scene of Invention." *Rhetoric & Public Affairs* 9, no.1 (2006):124–31.

Blackman, Ann. *Wild Rose: The True Story of a Civil War Spy.* Random House, 2006.

Blight, Daniel C. *The Image of Whiteness: Contemporary Photography and Racialization.* SPBH Editions, 2019.

Blight, David W. "If You Don't Tell It Like It Was, It Can Never Be as It Ought to Be." In *Slavery and Public History: The Tough Stuff of American Memory*, edited by James Oliver Horton and Lois E. Horton, 19–34. Norton, 2006.

Blight, David W. *Race and Reunion: The Civil War in American Memory.* Harvard University Press, 2001.

Bodnar, John. *Remaking America: Public Memory, Commemoration, and Patriotism in the Twentieth Century.* Princeton University Press, 1992.

Bolich, G. G. *Transgender History and Geography: Crossdressing in Context.* Vol. 3. Psyche Press, 2007.

Bolter, Jay David. *Writing Space: Computers, Hypertext, and the Remediation of Print.* 2nd ed. Lawrence Erlbaum Associates, 2001.

Bolter, Jay David and Richard Grusin. *Remediation: Understanding New Media.* MIT Press, 2000.

Bordelon, Suzanne. "Embodied *Ethos* and Rhetorical Accretion: Genevieve Stebbins and the *Delsarte System of Expression*." *Rhetoric Society Quarterly* 46, no. 2 (2016): 105–30.

Boyd, Belle. *Belle Boyd in Camp and Prison.* 1865. Edited by Sharon Kennedy-Noelle. Louisiana State University Press, 2006.

Boyd, Belle. "Letter to Abraham Lincoln." 24 Jan. 1865. The Abraham Lincoln Papers, Library of Congress. https://www.loc.gov/item/mal4022200. Accessed 3 Oct. 2017.

Bradford, Sarah Hopkins. *Harriet, The Moses of Her People.* 1886. George R. Lockwood & Son, 1897.

Bradford, Sarah Hopkins. *Scenes in the Life of Harriet Tubman.* W. J. Moses, Printer, 1869.

Burke, Kenneth. *Language as Symbolic Action.* University of California Press, 1966.

Burns, Ken, Geoffrey C. Ward, Ric Burns, David G. McCullough, Colleen Dewhurst, Laurence Fishburne, Morgan Freeman, Jeremy Irons, Derek Jacobi, Jason Robards, Sam Waterston, Hoyt Axton, and Bruce Shaw. *The Civil War.* PBS Home Video, 2004.

Burton (Collins), Vicki Tolar. "The Speaker Respoken: Material Rhetoric as Feminist Methodology." *College English* 61, no. 5 (1999): 545–73.

Butler, Judith. Gender Trouble: Feminism and the Subversion of Identity. Taylor and Francis, 2011.

Calhoun, John C. "The 'Positive Good' of Slavery." 6 Feb. 1837.

Campbell, Jacqueline Glass. "The Cultural Politics of Memory: Confederate Women and General William T. Sherman." In *The Civil War in Popular Culture: Memory and Meaning*, edited by Lawrence A. Kreiser Jr. and Randall W. Allred, 101–16. University Press of Kentucky, 2014.

Casey, Edward S. "Public Memory in Place and Time." In *Framing Public Memory*, edited by Kendall Phillips, 17–44. University of Alabama Press, 2004.

Cheney, Ednah Dow. "Moses." *Freedmen's Record*, vol. 1. March 1865, 34–38.

Chernock, Arianne. "Gender and the Politics of Exceptionalism in the Writing of British Women's History." In *Making Women's Histories: Beyond National Perspectives*, edited by Pamela S. Nadell and Kate Haulman, 115–36. New York University Press, 2013.

Christen, Kimberly. "Relationships not Records: Digital Heritage and the Ethics of Sharing Indigenous Knowledge Online." In *Routledge Companion to Media Studies and Digital Humanities*, edited by Jentery Sayers, 403–12. Routledge, 2018.

Cicero, Marcus Tullius. *Cicero: On the Ideal Orator*. Translated by James M. May and Jakob Wisse. Oxford University Press, 2001.

Clary-Lemon, Jennifer. "Archival Research Processes: A Case for Material Methods." *Rhetoric Review* 33, no. 4 (2014): 381–402.

Clary-Lemon, Jennifer. "Museums as Material: Experiential Landscapes and the Canadian Museum of Human Rights." *Enculturation* 20 (2015). Accessed 16 Jul. 2017.

Clinton, Catherine. *Harriet Tubman: The Road to Freedom*. Back Bay Books, 2004.

Clinton, Catherine. "Introduction: Let Us Not Forget That Terrible War." In *Reminiscences of My Life in Camp*, by Susie King Taylor. University of Georgia Press, 2006.

Clinton, Catherine. "'Noble Women as Well.'" In *Ken Burns's* The Civil War*: Historians Respond*, edited by Robert Brent Toplin, 61–80. Oxford University Press, 1997.

Clinton, Catherine. "Susie King Taylor: '*I Gave My Services Willingly*.'" In *Georgia Women: Their Lives and Times*, edited by Ann Short Chirhart and Betty Wood, 130–46. University of Georgia Press, 2009.

Coates, Ta-Nehisi. *We Were Eight Years in Power*. One World Publishing, 2017.

Collins, Patricia Hill, and Sirma Bilge. *Intersectionality*. Polity Press, 2016.

Combahee River Collective. "Combahee River Collective: A Black Feminist Statement." 1977. In *This Bridge Called my Back: Writings by Radical Women of Color*, 4th ed, edited by Gloria Anzaldúa and Cherrie Moraga, 210–18. State University of New York Press, 2015.

The Condition of Affairs in the Late Insurrectionary States, Georgia, vol. 1. 42 Cong, Joint Select Committee. Government Printing Office, 1872.

Connors, Robert. "Dreams and Play: Historical Method and Methodology." In *Methods and Methodology in Composition Research*, edited by Gesa Kirsch and Patricia Sullivan, 15–36. Southern Illinois University Press, 1992.

Cook, Robert. *Civil War Memories: Contesting the Past in the United States Since 1865.* Johns Hopkins University Press, 2017.

Coser, Lewis A. "Introduction: Maurice Halbwachs 1877–1945." In *On Collective Memory,* by Maurice Halbwachs. Translated by Lewis A. Coser, 1–36. University of Chicago Press, 1992.

Cox, Karen L. *Dixie's Daughters: The United Daughter of the Confederacy and the Preservation of Confederate Culture.* 2nd ed. University Press of Florida, 2019.

Davis, William C. *Inventing Loreta Velasquez: Confederate Soldier Impersonator, Media Celebrity, and Con Artist.* Southern Illinois University Press, 2016.

DeMarco, Michael. "Boyd, Belle (1844–1900)." *Encyclopedia Virginia: Virginia Humanities.* 12 Feb. 2021. https://encyclopediavirginia.org/.

"Designations." National Park Service, 2 Apr. 2015. https://www.nps.gov/goga/planyourvisit/designations.htm.

Dickinson, Greg, Carole Blair, and Brian Ott. "Introduction: Rhetoric/Memory/Place." In *Places of Public Memory: The Rhetoric of Museums and Memorials,* edited by Greg Dickinson, Carole Blair, and Brian Ott, 1–54. University of Alabama Press, 2010.

Douglass, Frederick. "Lecture on Pictures." In *Picturing Fredrick Douglass: An Illustrated Biography of the Nineteenth Century's Most Photographed American,* edited by John Stauffer, Zoe Trodd, and Celeste-Marie Bernier, 126–41. Liveright Publishing, 2015.

Dowie, Ménie Muriel, ed. *Women's Adventures.* T. F. Unwin Press, 1893.

Downs, Jim. *Sick From Freedom: African-American Illness and Suffering During the Civil War and Reconstruction.* Oxford University Press, 2012.

"Dress Parade of First South Carolina, (U.S.C.T), Beaufort, S.C." Library of Congress. https://www.loc.gov/item/2013649032/.

Drew, Benjamin. A North-Side View of Slavery. The Refugee: or the Narratives of Fugitive Slaves in Canada. Related by Themselves, with an Account of the History and Condition of the Colored Population of Upper Canada. John P. Jewett and Company, 1856.

Du Bois, W. E. B. *Black Reconstruction in America 1860–1880.* 1935. Simon & Schuster, 1998.

Dubriwny, Tasha, and Kristan Poirot. "Gender and Public Memory." *Southern Communication Journal* 82, no. 4 (2017): 199–202.

Duff, Wendy, and Verne Harris. "Stories and Names: Archival Description as Narrating Records and Constructing Meanings." *Archival Science* 2, no. 3 (2002): 263–85.

Early, Jubal. Letter to William H. Slemons. 22 May 1878. Museum of the Confederacy. Richmond, Virginia.

Edmonds, Sarah Emma. *Memoirs of a Soldier, Nurse, and Spy: A Woman's Adventures in the Union Army.* 1864. Edited by Elizabeth D. Leonard. Northern Illinois University Press, 1999.

Edmonds, S. Emma E. *Unsexed: Or, The Female Soldier: The Thrilling Adventures, Experiences and Escapes of a Woman, As Nurse, Spy and Scout, In Hospitals, Camps and Battle-Fields.* Philadelphia Publishing Co, 1864.

Enoch, Jessica. "Releasing Hold: Feminist Historiography without the Tradition." In *Theorizing Histories of Rhetoric,* edited by Michelle Ballif, 58–73. Southern Illinois University Press, 2013.

Enoch, Jessica, and Jean Bessette. "Meaningful Engagements: Feminist Historiography and the Digital Humanities." *College Composition and Communication* 64, no. 4 (2013): 634–60.

Enoch, Jessica, Katie Bramlett, and Elizabeth A. Novara. "Decoding (a Woman's) Diaries: The Transcribe-A-Thon as an Undergraduate Public Memory Project." *College Composition and Communication* 81, no. 5 (2019): 407–31.

Enoch, Jessica, Danielle Griffin, and Karen Nelson. "Circulating Feminist Rhetorics: An Introduction." In *Feminist Circulations: Rhetorical Explorations Across Time and Space,* edited by Jessica Enoch, Danielle Griffin, and Karen Nelson. Parlor Press, 2021, pp. 3–17.

Erll, Astrid, and Ann Rigney. "Introduction: Cultural Memory and Its Dynamics." In *Mediation, Remediation, and Cultural Memory,* edited by Astrid Erll and Ann Rigney, 1–14. Walter de Gruyter Press, 2009.

Fahs, Alice. "The Feminized Civil War: Gender, Northern Popular Literature, and the Memory of the War, 1861–1900." *The Journal of American History* (1999): 1461–94.

Fahs, Alice. *The Imagined Civil War: Popular Literature of the North and South 1861–1865.* University of North Carolina Press, 2001.

Faust, Drew Gilpin. *Mothers of Invention: Women of the Slaveowning South in the American Civil War.* University of North Carolina Press, 1996.

Feimster, Crystal N. "General Benjamin Butler & The Threat of Sexual Violence During the American Civil War." *Daedalus* (2009): 126–34.

Feinberg, Leslie. *Transgender Warriors: Making History from Joan of Arc to Dennis Rodman.* Beacon Press, 1996.

"The Female Volunteer of Company F." Burton Historical Collection Manuscripts Collection, Detroit Public Library Special Collections, Detroit. https://detroitpubliclibrary.org/research/burton-historical-collection

Fields-Black, Edda L. *Combee: Harriet Tubman, the Combahee River Raids, and Black Freedom during the Civil War.* Oxford University Press, 2024.

Finnegan, Cara. "What Is This a Picture Of? Some Thoughts on Images and Archives." *Rhetoric & Public Affairs* 9, no. 1 (2006): 116–23.

Fishel, Edwin. *The Secret War for the Union: The Untold Story of Military Intelligence in the Civil War.* Houghton Mifflin, 1996.

Fladeland, Betty. "New Light on Sarah Emma Edmonds, Alias Franklin Thompson." *Michigan History* 27 (1963): 357–62.

Foreman, Amanda. *A World on Fire: Britain's Crucial Role in the American Civil War.* Random House, 2010.

Foster, Frances Smith. *Written By Herself: Literary Production by African American Women, 1746–1892.* Indiana University Press, 1993.

"Fraud in Authorship." *Boston Review*. Edited by W. M. Barrows, J. C. Bodwell, E. P. Marvin, and J. T. Tucker, 11–18. Vol. VI. Boston: The Proprietors, 1866. Accessed 15 Jun. 2013.

Frick, Rachel L., and Merrilee Proffitt. *Reimagine Descriptive Workflows: A Community-informed Agenda for Reparative and Inclusive Descriptive Practice.* OCLC Research, 2022. https://doi.org/10.25333/wd4b-bs51. Accessed 28 Dec. 2022.

Gaillet, Lyneé Lewis. "Archival Survival: Navigating Historical Research." In *Working in the Archives: Practical Research Methods for Rhetoric and Composition,* edited by Alexis E. Ramsey, Wendy B. Sharer, Barbara L'Eplattenier, and Lisa S. Mastrangelo, 28–39. Southern Illinois University Press, 2010.

Gallagher, Gary W. *Causes Won, Lost, and Forgotten: How Hollywood and Popular Art Shape What We Know about the Civil War.* University of North Carolina Press, 2008.

García-Gavilanes, Ruth, Anders Mollgaard, Milena Tsvetkova, and Taha Yasseri. "The Memory Remains: Understanding Collective Memory in the Digital Age." *Science Advances,* 5 Apr. 2017. https://www.ncbi.nlm.nih.gov/.

Garde-Hansen, Joanne, Andrew Hoskins, and Anna Reading. "Introduction." In *Save As . . . Digital Memories,* edited by Joanne Garde-Hansen, Andrew Hoskins, and Anna Reading, 1–21. Palgrave/Macmillan, 2009.

Gates, Henry Louis, Jr. "Frederick Douglass's Camera Obscura." *Vision & Justice: Aperture 223* (2016): 27–29.

Gates, Henry Louis, Jr. *Stony the Road: Reconstruction, White Supremacy, and the Rise of Jim Crow.* Penguin, 2019.

"General Information." Library of Congress. https://www.loc.gov/about/general-information/. Accessed 30 Jul. 2021.

Glymph, Thavolia. *The Women's Fight: The Civil War's Battles for Home, Freedom, and Nation.* University of North Carolina Press, 2019.

Greenhow, Rose. *My Imprisonment and the First Year of Abolition Rule at Washington.* London, Spottiswoode, 1863. Createspace, 2010.

Greer, Jane, and Laurie Grobman. "Complicating Conversations: Public Memory Production and Composition & Rhetoric." In *Pedagogies of Public Memory: Teaching Writing and Rhetoric at Museums, and Memorials,* edited by Jane Greer and Laurie Grobman, 1–31. Routledge, 2016.

Gries, Laurie E. "Iconographic Tracking: A Digital Research Method for Visual Rhetoric and Circulations Studies." *Computers and Composition* 30 (2013): 332–48.

Gries, Laurie E. *Still Life With Rhetoric: A New Materialist Approach for Visual Rhetoric.* Utah State University Press, 2015.

Griffin, Cindy, and Karma Chávez. "Introduction: Standing at the Intersections of Feminisms, Intersectionality, and Communication Studies." In *Standing in the Intersection: Feminist Voices, Feminist Practices in Communication Studies,* edited by Karma Chávez and Cindy Griffin, 1–31. State University of New York Press, 2011.

Groh, Mary Lou. "Maria 'Belle' Boyd." American Battlefield Trust. https://www.battle fields.org/learn/biographies/maria-belle-boyd. Accessed 8 Jun. 2021.

Grosfoguel, Ramon. "What is Racism?" *Journal of World-Systems Research* 22, no.1 (2016): 9–15.

Hadar, Mary. "Behind the Bitter War to Preserve the Civil War Battlefields." *Washington Post,* 21 Jul. 2017. https://www.washingtonpost.com/.

Halbwachs, Maurice. *On Collective Memory.* Edited by Lewis A. Coser. University of Chicago Press, 1992.

Hansberry, Lorraine. *Lorraine Hansberry Speaks Out: Art and the Black Revolution.* Caedmon, 1972.

"Harriet Tubman." National Park Service. https://www.nps.gov/hart/index.htm. Accessed 20 Sept. 2021.

Harrison, Kimberly. *The Rhetoric of Rebel Women: Civil War Diaries and Confederate Persuasion.* Southern Illinois University Press, 2013.

Haskins, Ekaterina. "Between Archive and Participation: Public Memory in a Digital Age." *Rhetoric Society Quarterly* 37, no. 4 (2007): 401–22.

Haskins, Ekaterina. *Popular Memories: Commemoration, Participatory Culture, and Democratic Citizenship.* University of South Carolina Press, 2015.

Hess, Aaron. "In Digital Remembrance: Vernacular Memory and the Rhetorical Construction of Web Memorials." *Media, Culture, & Society* 29, no. 5 (2007): 812–30.

Hirsch, Marianne, and Valerie Smith. "Feminism and Cultural Memory: An Introduction." *Signs: Journal of Women in Culture and Society* 12, no. 1 (2002): 1–19.

"History of Wikipedia." *Wikipedia,* Wikimedia Foundation, 7 Aug. 2021, https://en .wikipedia.org/.

Holterhoff, Kate. "From Disclaimer to Critique: Race and the Digital Image Archivist." *Digital Humanities Quarterly* 11, no. 3 (2017): http://www.digitalhumanities.org/. Accessed 13 Oct. 2021.

hooks, bell. *Black Looks: Race and Representation.* Routledge, 1992.

Horton, Oliver and Lois E. Horton. "Introduction." In *Slavery and Public History: The Tough Stuff of American Memory,* edited by James Oliver Horton and Lois E. Horton, vii–xiv. Norton, 2006.

Houdek, Matthew, and Kendall Phillips. "Public Memory." *Oxford Research Encyclopedias,* Jan. 2017, https://www.oxfordreference.com/.

Hughes-Watkins, Lae'l. "Moving Toward a Reparative Archive: A Roadmap for a Holistic Approach to Disrupting Homogenous Histories in Academic Repositories and Creating Inclusive Spaces for Marginalized Voices." *Journal of Contemporary Archival Studies* 5, art. 6 (2018): 1–17.

Humez, Jean M. *Harriet Tubman: The Life and the Life Stories.* University of Wisconsin Press, 2003.

Hynes, Samuel. "Personal Narratives and Commemoration." In *War and Remembrance in* the Twentieth Century, edited by Jay Winter and Emmanuel Sivan, 205–20. Cambridge University Press, 2000.

Janney, Caroline. *Remembering the Civil War: Reunion and the Limits of Reconstruction.* University of North Carolina Press, 2013.

Jensen, Annika. "Beneath the Mulberry Tree: Sarah Edmonds and Women in Memory." *Gettysburg Compiler: On the Front Lines of History.* 2012.

Johnson, Nathan R. *Architects of Memory: Information and Rhetoric in a Networked Archival Age.* University of Alabama Press, 2020.

Jones, J. William. "Book Notices." *Southern Historical Society Papers* 2, no. 4 (October 1876): 208.

Kennedy-Noelle, Sharon. "Introduction." In *Belle Boyd in Camp and Prison,* by Belle Boyd, 1–45. Louisiana State University Press, 1998.

Laffrado, Laura. *Uncommon Women: Gender and Representation in Nineteenth-Century US Women's Writing.* The Ohio State University Press, 2009.

Larson, Kate Clifford. *Bound for the Promised Land: Harriet Tubman: Portrait of an American Hero.* One World, 2004.

Le Bon, Gustave. *The Crowd: A Study of the Popular Mind.* T. Fisher Unwin, 1895.

Leonard, Elizabeth. *All the Daring of the Soldier: Women of the Civil War Armies.* Norton, 1999.

Leonard, Elizabeth. "Introduction." *Memoirs of a Soldier, Nurse, and Spy: A Woman's Adventures in the Union Army,* 1864, edited by Elizabeth D. Leonard, xiii–xxxvi. Northern Illinois University Press, 1999.

Lerner, Gerda. "Placing Women in History: Definitions and Challenges." *Feminist Studies* 3, no. 1–2 (1975): 5–14.

Levi, Amalia S. "Intersectionality in Digital Archives: The Case Study of the Barbados Synagogue Restoration Projection Collection." In *Intersectionality in Digital Humanities,* edited by Barbara Bordalejo and Roopika Risam, 127–98. Arc Humanities Press, 2019.

Levin, Kevin M. *Searching for Black Confederate Soldiers: The Civil War's Most Persistent Myth.* University of North Carolina Press, 2019.

Lewis, Sarah Elizabeth. "Vision & Justice: Guest Editor's Note." *Vision & Justice: Aperture* 223. 26 Apr. 2016.

Lih, Andrew. *The Wikipedia Revolution: How a Bunch of Nobodies Created the World's Greatest Encyclopedia.* Hyperion, 2009.

Lindberg, Melissa. "Susie King Taylor: The Courage of an African American Nurse and Teacher." *Picture This: Library of Congress Prints & Photos Blog.* 6 May 2020. https://blogs.loc.gov/.

Lindqwister, Elizabeth, Karen Chittenden, and Micah Messenheimer. "Susie King Taylor: An African American Nurse and Teacher in the Civil War." 2019. https://www.loc.gov/.

Lineberry, Cate. "The Wild Rose of Washington." Opinion Pages: Disunion Series, *New York Times,* 22 Aug. 2011. opinionator.blogs.nytimes.com/2011/08/22/the-wild-rose-of -washington.

Linger, Theo. "Harriet Tubman and the 54th Massachusetts." National Park Service. 8 Jan. 2023 https://www.nps.gov/articles/harriet-tubman-and-the-54th-massachusetts .htm.

Linger, Theo. "Personal Interview." 13 Jul. 2021.

Lipsitz, George. "The Possessive Investment in Whiteness: Racialized Social Democracy and the 'White' Problem in American Studies." *American Quarterly* 47, no. 3 (1995): 369–87.

Livermore, Mary. *My Story of the War: The Civil War Memoirs of the Famous Nurse, Relief Organizer, and Suffragette.* 1887. De Capo Press, 1995.

Longinus. *On the Sublime.* Translated by W. H. Fyfe; revised by Donald Russell. Loeb Classical Library, Harvard University Press, 1995.

"Loreta Janeta Velázquez." *Wikipedia.* 11 Aug. 2021. https://en.wikipedia.org/.

Lott, Eric. *Love & Theft: Blackface Minstrelsy & the American Working Class.* Oxford University Press, 1993.

MacNeil, Heather. "Metadata Strategies and Archival Description: Comparing Apples to Oranges." *Archivaria* 39 (1995): 22–32.

Magness, Phil. "What the Data Say about Civil War Monuments." *The Daily Economy.* 23 Jun. 2020. https://thedailyeconomy.org/.

"Major Samuel K. Thompson and Unidentified Soldiers of the 39th U.S. Infantry Posed with a 10" Rodman Cannon at Fort Massachusetts, Mississippi." Ambrotype/Tintype Filing Series, Liljenquist Family Collection. Library of Congress. https://www.loc.gov /item/2015647716/. Accessed 13 Sept. 2021.

Manning, Chandra. *What This Cruel War Was Over: Soldiers, Slavery, and the Civil War.* Vintage, 2008.

Mattingly, Carol. "Woman's Temple, Women's Fountains: The Erasure of Public Memory." *American Studies* 49, nos. 3–4 (2008): 133–56.

May, Vivian. "Under-Theorized and Under-Taught: Re-examining Harriet Tubman's Place in Women's Studies." *Meridians* 12, no. 2 (2014): 28–49.

McCurry, Stephanie. *Women's War: Fighting and Surviving the American Civil War,* Harvard University Press, 2019.

McDowell, Zachary J., and Matthew A. Vetter. *Wikipedia and the Representation of Reality.* Routledge, 2022.

McIntosh, Peggy. "Interactive Phases of Curricular Re-Vision: A Feminist Perspective." Center for Research on Women, Working Papers Series No. 124, 1983.

Menking, Amanda, and Ingrid Erickson. "The Heart Work of Wikipedia: Gendered, Emotional Labor in the World's Largest Online Encyclopedia." *Proceedings of the 33rd Annual ACM Conference on Human Factors in Computing Systems,* 2015, 207–10.

Mills, Cynthia. "Introduction." *Monuments and Memorials to the Lose Cause: Women, Art, and the Landscapes of Southern History*, edited by Cynthia Mills and Pamela H. Simpson, xviii–xxxiv. University of Tennessee Press, 2003.

Monument Lab. *National Monument Audit*. 2021. https://monumentlab.com/audit.

Moore, Frank. *The Rebellion Record, A Diary of American Events and Documents*. D. Van Nostrand, 1864.

Moore, Frank. *Women of the War; Their Heroism and Self-Sacrifice*. S. S. Scranton & Co., 1866.

Morgan, Wendy. "Heterotropes: Learning the Rhetoric of Hyperlinks." *Education, Communication & Information* 2, no. 2/3 (2002): 215–33.

"Mrs. Susie King Taylor, Boston's Colored Woman Author—She was Once a Slave." *Boston Sunday Post*, 4 Jan. 1903. *Newspaper Archive*. Accessed 2014.

Myatt, Alice Johnston. "From Erasure to Restoration: Rosalind Franklin and the Discovery of the DNA Structure." In *Remembering Women Differently: Refiguring Rhetorical Work*, edited by Lyneé Lewis Gaillet and Helen Gaillet Bailey, 49–68. University of South Carolina Press, 2019.

Nakayama, Thomas K., and Robert L. Krizek. "Whiteness: A Strategic Rhetoric." *Quarterly Journal of Speech* 81 (1995): 291–309.

National Park Service. "Hispanics and the Civil War: From Battlefield to Homefront." U.S. Department of the Interior. 2011. https://permanent.fdlp.gov/gpo23709/Hispanics-in-Civil-War-8x8-booklet-lowres.pdf.

Noble, Safiya. *Algorithms of Oppression: How Search Engines Reinforce Racism*. New York University Press, 2018.

Nora, Pierre. "Between Memory and History: *Les Lieux de Memoire*." *Representation* 26, (1989): 7–24.

"NPS.gov: Our Flagship Web Presence." National Park Service, 19 Jan. 2021. https://www.nps.gov/subjects/digital/nps-website.htm.

Omi, Michael, and Howard Winant. *Racial Formation in the United States*, 3rd ed. Routledge, 2015.

Ore, Ersula J. *Lynching: Violence, Rhetoric, and American Identity*. University of Mississippi Press, 2019.

"Organic Act of 1916." National Park Service. https://www.nps.gov/grba/learn/management/organic-act-of-1916.htm. Accessed 13 Aug. 2021.

"Our Work: About the American Battlefield Trust." American Battlefield Trust. https://www.battlefields.org/our-work. Accessed 8 Jul. 2021.

Parnell, Sean. "Digital Content Refresh." Department of Defense. 26 Feb. 2025. https://media.defense.gov/2025/Feb/27/2003652943/-1/-1/1/DIGITAL-CONTENT-REFRESH.PDF. Accessed 25 May 2025.

"The Patenburg [*sic*] Massacre." *Harper's Weekly*, 19 Oct. 1872, p. 798.

Pentzold, Christian. "Fixing the Floating Gap: The Online Encyclopedia Wikipedia as a Global Memory Place." *Memory Studies* 2, no. 2 (2009): 255–72.

Phillips, Kendall. "The Failure of Memory: Reflections on Rhetoric and Public Remembrance." *Western Journal of Communication* 74, no. 2 (2010): 208–23.

Phillips, Kendall. "Introduction." In *Framing Public Memory*, edited by Kendall Phillips, 1–14. University of Alabama Press, 2004.

Phillips, Steve. *How We Win the Civil War.* The New Press, 2022.

"Political Terrorism." *Harper's Weekly*, 5 Sept. 1868, p. 563.

Pollard, Edward Alb. *The Lost Cause: A New Southern History of the War of the Confederates.* E.B. Treat & Co., 1867.

"A Printer in Luck." *Hartford Courant* (Hartford, CT), 1 Apr. 1865: 2. *Newspapers.com.* Accessed 1 Jun. 2017.

Quijano, Anibal. "Coloniality of Power and Eurocentrism in Latin America." *International Sociology* 15, no. 2 (2000): 215–32.

Quintilian, Marcus Fabius. *Institutes of Oratory: or, Education of an Orator.* Translated by John Selby Watson, edited by Lee Honeycutt and John Selby Watson. CreateSpace, 2015.

Rawson, K. J. "Queering Feminist Rhetorical Canonization." In *Feminist Rhetorical Methods and Methodologies,* edited by Eileen Schell and K. J. Rawson, 39–52. University of Pittsburgh Press, 2010. https://doi.org/10.2307/J.CTT5VKFF8.7.

Rawson, K. J. "The Rhetorical Power of Archival Description: Classifying Images of Gender Transgression." *Rhetoric Society Quarterly* 48, no. 4 (2017): 1–25.

Rawson, K. J., and Cristan Williams. "Transgender*: The Rhetorical Landscape of a Term." *Present Tense: A Journal of Rhetoric in Society* 3, no. 2 (2014). Accessed 10 Jul. 2015.

Reyes, Mitchell G. "Introduction: Public Memory, Race, and Ethnicity." In *Public Memory, Race, and Ethnicity,* edited by Mitchell G. Reyes, 1–14. Cambridge Scholars Publishing, 2010.

Rhetorica ad Herennium. Translated by Harry Caplan. Loeb Classical Library, Harvard University Press, 1954.

Rich, Adrienne. "Notes on a Politics of Location." *Blood, Bread, and Poetry: Selected Prose 1979–1985,* Norton, 1986, 210–31.

Rich, Adrienne. "What Does a Woman Need to Know?" *Blood, Bread, and Poetry: Selected Prose 1979–1985,* Norton, 1986, 1–10.

Robbins, Jerome John. Civil War Journal, 20 May 1861–6 Aug. 1865. Jerome John Robbins Papers. Michigan Historical Collections, Bentley Historical Library, University of Michigan, Ann Arbor.

Rosenheim, Jeff L. *Photography and the American Civil War.* Metropolitan Museum of Art, 2013.

Rosenzweig, Roy. "Can History Be Open Source? *Wikipedia* and the Future of the Past." *Journal of American History* 93, no. 1 (June 2006): 117–46.

"Rose O'Neal Greenhow." American Battlefield Trust. https://www.battlefields.org/. Accessed 20 Jun. 2021.

"Rose O'Neal Greenhow." Britannica. https://www.britannica.com/. Accessed 20 Sept. 2020.

Ross, Ishbel. *Rebel Rose: The Life of Rose O'Neal Greenhow, Confederate Spy.* Mockingbird Press, 1954.

Royster, Jacqueline Jones. "Disciplinary Landscaping, or Contemporary Challenges in the History of Rhetoric." *Philosophy & Rhetoric 36,* no. 2 (2003): 148–66.

Royster, Jacqueline Jones, and Gesa Kirsch. *Feminist Rhetorical Practices: New Horizons for Rhetoric, Composition, and Literacy Studies.* Southern Illinois University Press, 2012.

Sanborn, Franklin B. "Harriet Tubman." *Commonwealth,* 17 Jul. 1863.

Sanchez, James Chase, and Kristen Moore. "Reappropriating Public Memory: Racism, Resistance and Erasure of the Confederate Defenders of Charleston Monument." *Present Tense: A Journal of Rhetoric in Society* 5, no. 2 (2015). www.presenttensejournal.org/volume-5/.

"Sarah E. Edmonds." *Outhistory: It's about Time!* https://outhistory.org/exhibits/show/aspectsofqueerexistence. Accessed 9 Aug. 2020.

"Sarah the Soldier." *Daily Evening News* (Maysville, KY). Vol. 3, No. 100. *Daily Evening Bulletin.* (Maysville, KY), 24 Mar. 1884. *Chronicling America: Historic American Newspapers.* Library of Congress. Accessed 1 Jun. 2017.

Schwartz, Joan M., and Terry Cook. "Archives, Records, and Power: The Making of Modern Memory." *Archival Science* 2 (2002): 1–19.

Schwartz, Joan. "Coming to Terms with Photographs: Descriptive Standards, Linguistic 'Othering,' and the Margins of Archivy." *Archivaria* 54 (2002): 142–71.

Sernett, Milton C. *Harriet Tubman: Myth, Memory, and History.* Duke University Press, 2007.

"Silver Nitrite." *National Museum of Civil War Medicine.* "Artifacts Revealed Season 2." https://www.civilwarmed.org. Accessed 2 Jul. 2020.

Shackel, Paul A. Memory in Black and White: Race, Commemoration, and the Post-Bellum Landscape. AltaMira Press, 2003.

Smith, Sidonie, and Julia Watson, eds. *Before They Could Vote: American Women's Autobiographical Writing, 1819–1919.* University of Wisconsin Press, 2006.

Society of American Archivists. "Visual Materials." https://dictionary.archivists.org/entry/visual-materials.html. Accessed May 18 2025.

"A 'Solemn Key.'" *Harper's Weekly,* 5 Sept. 1868, p. 562.

Sorensen, Kristin. *Media, Memory, and Human Rights in Chile.* Palgrave, 2009.

Southern Poverty Law Center. "SPLC Reports Over 160 Confederate Symbols Removed in 2020." https://www.splcenter.org/. Accessed 10 Oct. 2021.

Stanton, Elizabeth Cady. *Eighty Years and More: Reminiscences, 1815–1897.* New York: T. Fisher Unwin, 1898.

"The Stars and Bars at the Democratic Peak." *Harper's Weekly,* 5 Sept. 1868, p. 562.

Steele, Catherine Knight. *Digital Black Feminism*. New York University Press, 2021.

"Story Maps." Geography & Map Reading Room. 30 Sept. 2021. Library of Congress. https://www.loc.gov/rr/geogmap/storymaps.html.

Stryker, Susan. *Transgender History*. Seal Press, 2008.

Stuckey, Zosha. "Staring Back: The Rhetorical Fitness and Self-fashioning of Ann E. Leak and Lavinia Warrant, 19th Century Side Show Performers." *Enculturation: A Journal of Rhetoric, Writing, and Culture,* 23 Nov. 2010. http://enculturation.net/staring-back.

Sturken, Marita. "Memory, Consumerism, and Media: Reflections on the Emergence of the Field." *Memory Studies* 1, no. 1 (2008): 73–78.

Sturken, Marita. *Tangled Memories: The Vietnam War, the AIDS Epidemic, and the Politics of Remembering*. University of California Press, 1997.

Sutherland, Christine Mason. "Women in the History of Rhetoric: The Past and the Future." In *The Changing Tradition: Women in the History of Rhetoric,* edited by Christine Mason Sutherland and Rebecca Sutcliffe, 9–31. University of Calgary Press, 1999.

Tagg, John. *The Burden of Representation: Essays on Photographies and Histories*. University of Minneapolis Press, 1993.

Tai, Jessica. "Cultural Humility as a Framework for Anti-Oppressive Archival Description." *Radical Empathy in Archival Practice,* special issue of *Journal of Critical Library and Information Studies* 3, no. 2 (2021): 1–23.

Taylor, Amy Murrell. *Embattled Freedom: Journeys through the Civil War's Slave Refugee Camps*. University of North Carolina Press, 2020.

Taylor, Susie King. *Reminiscences of My Life in Camp*. University of Georgia Press, 2006.

"Ten Facts: Civil War Battlefield Monuments, Markers, and Tablets." American Battlefield Trust. https://www.battlefields.org/. Accessed 18 May 2025.

Thompson, Jerry. "Introduction." In *Tejanos in Gray: Civil War Letters of Captains Joseph Rafael de la Garrza and Manuel Yturri,* edited by Jerry Thompson and translated by José Roberto Juárez. Texas A&M University Press, 2011.

"Three Decades in the Trenches of Battlefield Preservation: A National Movement to Protect America's Hallowed Ground." American Battlefield Trust. https://www.battlefields.org/. Accessed 9 Jul. 2021.

Toplin, Robert Brent. "Introduction." In *Ken Burns's The Civil War: Historians Respond,* edited by Robert Brent Toplin, xvi–xxvi. Oxford University Press, 1997.

"Toward Racial Equality: *Harper's Weekly* Reports on Black America, 1857–1874." HarpWeek. https://blackhistory.harpweek.com/1Introduction/IntroLevelOne.htm. Accessed 18 Nov. 2021.

Trouillot, Michel-Rolph. *Silencing the Past: Power and the Production of History*. Beacon Press, 1995.

Tsui, Bonnie. She Went to the Field: Women Soldiers of the Civil War. TwoDot, 2006.

Ulrich, Laurel Thatcher. "Vertunous Women Found: New England Ministerial Literature, 1668–1735." *American Quarterly* 28, no. 1 (1976): 20–40.

"Unidentified African American Soldier in Union Uniform with a Austrian Lorenz Rifle-Musket and Remington Revolver in Front of Painted Backdrop Showing Weapons and American Flag at Benton Barracks, Saint, Louis, Missouri." Photo, Print, Drawing. Library of Congress. https://www.loc.gov/item/2010647218/. Accessed 18 Aug. 2021.

VanderHaagen, Sara C. *Children's Biographies of African American Women: Rhetoric, Public Memory, and Agency.* University of South Carolina Press, 2018.

Van der Velden, Maja. "Decentering Design: Wikipedia and Indigenous Knowledge." *International Journal of Human-Computer Interaction,* 29, no. 4 (2013): 308–16.

VanHaitsma, Pamela, and Cassandra Book. "Digital Curation as Collaborative Archival Method in Feminist Rhetoric." *Peitho* 21, no. 2 (2019). https://cfshrc.org/. Accessed 20 Sept. 2020.

"Various National Parks Bill." Discover U.S. Government Information. 11 May 2011, https://www.govinfo.gov/.

Velazquez, Loreta Janeta. "Address to the American Congress on 'Cuba.'" 1878. New York Public Library.

Velazquez, Loreta Janeta. Letter to Jubal Early. May 18, 1878. Museum of the Confederacy. Richmond, VA.

Velazquez, Loreta Janeta. Letter to Reverend J. William Jones. 27 Oct. 1876. Museum of the Confederacy, Richmond, VA.

Velazquez, Loreta Janeta. Letter to Reverend J. William Jones. 12 Nov. 1876. Museum of the Confederacy, Richmond, VA.

Velazquez, Loreta Janeta. *The Woman in Battle: The Civil War Narrative of Loreta Velazquez, Cuban Woman & Confederate Soldier.* Edited by Jesse Alemán, University of Wisconsin Press, 2003.

Villanueva, Victor, Jr. *Bootstraps: From an Academic of Color.* National Council of Teachers of English, 1993.

Vivian, Bradford, and Anne Teresa Demo. "Introduction." In *Rhetoric, Remembrance, and Visual Form: Sight Memory,* edited by Bradford Vivian and Anne Teresa Demo, 1–12. Routledge, 2021.

Wagner, Claudia, Eduardo Graells-Garrido, David Garcia, and Filippo Menczer. "Women Through the Glass Ceiling: Gender Assymetries in Wikipedia." *EPJ Data Science* 5, no. 5, 2016, pp. 1–24.

Walker, Jeffery. *Rhetoric and Poetics in Antiquity.* Oxford University Press, 2000.

Wallace, Maurice O., and Shawn Michelle Smith. *Pictures and Progress: Early Photography and the Making of African American Identity.* Duke University Press, 2012.

Warren, Robert Penn. *The Legacy of the Civil War.* 1961. Bison Books, 1998.

"Welcome to Wikipedia." *Wikipedia,* Wikimedia Foundation, 11 Sept. 2021. https://en.wikipedia.org/.

"Whipping and Selling American Citizens." *Harper's Weekly,* 12 Jan, 1867, p. 18.

White, Jonathan W., and Scott Sandage. "What Frederick Douglass Had to Say About

Monuments." *Smithsonian Magazine,* 30 Jun. 2020. https://www.smithsonianmag .com/.

White, Rosie. *Violent Femmes: Women as Spies in Popular Culture.* Routledge, 2007.

"Wikipedia." Wikipedia. 18 May 2025. https://en.wikipedia.org/wiki/Wikipedia. Accessed 18 May 2025.

"Wikipedia: About." *Wikipedia,* Wikimedia Foundation, 10 Sept. 2021. https://en .wikipedia.org/.

"Wikipedia: Core Content Policies." *Wikipedia,* Wikimedia Foundation, 18 Jun. 2021. https://en.wikipedia.org/.

"Wikipedia Editors Study: Results from the Editor Survey, April 2011." Wikimedia Foundation. https://upload.wikimedia.org/.

"Wikipedia: Five Pillars." *Wikipedia,* Wikimedia Foundation, 5 May 2025.

"Wikipedia: Purpose." *Wikipedia,* Wikimedia Foundation, 7 Aug. 2021.

"Wikipedia: Systemic Bias." *Wikipedia,* Wikimedia Foundation, 28 Aug. 2021. https://en .wikipedia.org/.

"Wikipedia: Wikipedians." *Wikipedia,* Wikimedia Foundation, 8 Sept. 2021. https://en .wikipedia.org/.

Wilber, Hannah. "Add a Sidecar to Your Story." Ersi StoryMaps. https://arcg.is/bebWr. Accessed 8 Oct. 2021.

Wilde, Patricia. By Her Available Means: The Sensational Rhetoric of Women's Civil War Memoirs. 2015. University of New Hampshire, PhD dissertation.

Wilde, Patricia. "(Re)telling the Times: The Tangled Memories of Confederate Spies Rose O'Neal Greenhow and Belle Boyd." *Rhetoric Review* 38, no. 3 (2019): 297–310.

Willis, Deborah. *The Black Civil War Soldier: A Visual History of Conflict and Citizenship.* New York University Press, 2021.

Winter, Jay. *Remembering War: The Great War between Memory and History in the 20th Century.* Yale University Press, 2008.

Wintersmith, Saraya. "Boston Will Remove Park Square Statue of Lincoln Freeing Slaves." *GBH News,* 30 Jun. 2020. https://www.wgbh.org/news/.

Woolf, Virginia. *A Room of One's Own.* 1929. Mariner, 1989.

Young, Elizabeth. *Disarming the Nation: Women's Writing and the American Civil War.* University of Chicago Press, 1999.

Young, Robin. "Boston Artist Doesn't See Freedom in Lincoln Statue Featuring Enslaved Man, Calls for Removal." *WBUR,* 29 Jun. 2021, https://www.wbur.org/.

Zack, Aaron. "The 54th Massachusetts and the Second Battle of Fort Wagner." National Park Service, 7 Jan. 2023, https://www.nps.gov/. Accessed 18 May 2025.

Zelizer, Barbie. "Reading the Past Against the Grain: The Shape of Memory Studies." *Critical Studies in Media Communication* 12 (1995): 214–39.

Zelizer, Barbie. "The Voice of the Visual in Memory." In *Framing Public Memory,* edited by Kendall R. Phillips, 157–86. University of Alabama Press, 2004.

Zeller, Bob. *Fighting the Second Civil War: A History of Battlefield Preservation and the Emergence of the Civil War Trust.* Civil War Trust, 2017.
Zinn, Howard. "Secrecy, Archives, and the Public Interest." *The Midwestern Archivist* 2, no. 2 (1977): 14–26.

Index